TOMBSTONE

TOMBSTONE

An Iliad of the Southwest

W A L T E R   N O B L E   B U R N S

PUBLISHED IN COOPERATION WITH THE
UNIVERSITY OF NEW MEXICO CENTER FOR THE AMERICAN WEST
UNIVERSITY OF NEW MEXICO PRESS
ALBUQUERQUE

15 14 13 12 11 10   3 4 5 6 7 8

ISBN-13: 978-0-8263-2154-1

Library of Congress Cataloging-in-Publication Data

Burns, Walter Noble.
Tombstone : an Iliad of the Southwest / by Walter Noble
Burns : foreword by Casey Tefertiller.
     p. cm.—(Historians of the frontier and American West)
"Published in cooperation with the University of New
Mexico Center for the American West."
ISBN 0-8263-2154-2 (alk. paper)
1. Tombstone (Ariz.)—History—19th century.
2. Frontier and pioneer life—Arizona—Tombstone.
3. Outlaws—Arizona—Tombstone—History—19th
    century.
4. Tombstone (Ariz.) Biography.
I. University of New Mexico. Center for the American
    West.
II. Title.
III. Series.
F819.T6B936 1999
979.1'53—dc21   99-36552
                                          CIP

TO MY WIFE

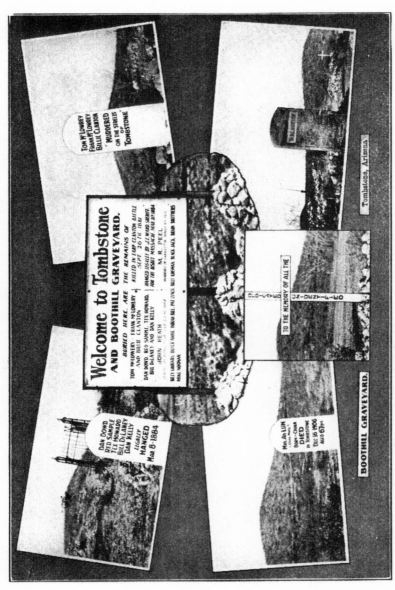

The headstones of Boot Hill Cemetery, Tombstone. There are 259 more graves unmarked.

PUBLISHER'S NOTE

Tombstone may be only a town, but it is a town hallowed with ghosts and memories such as few American towns possess. Frontier history was made in the colonization of the West; a colorful and romantic history, unique and unparalleled in the text books. And nowhere did color and romance mingle more riotously than in Tombstone, where today relics and monuments of a past that will never lose its fascination are to be found in quantity. The lure which Tombstone exerts on travelers is tangibly evident. Main traffic arteries, carrying countless visitors, converge on this little town of 1200 souls, set in the midst of desert splendor. The Old Spanish Trail, now a part of U.S. 80, (the "Broadway of America") winds past the Oriental, where Buckskin Frank once tended bar. Southern Pacific trains stop not far from the now embalmed Bird Cage theater, and Greyhound busses pass close to the spot where Johnny Behind-the-Deuce almost made the acquaintance of his Maker. One of Tombstone's attractions in the past was the nearby border of Mexico and the many pleasant oases of wetness to be found but an hour's ride south. But today the long mahogany bar in the Crystal Palace has taken on a new lustre and tourists need no longer dread the parched air of the desert. To really get close to those thrilling frontier days the traveler must go to Tombstone, heart of the old Southwest, where history was written with six-shooters.

SOURCES

Bound volumes of old files of the Tombstone *Epitaph,* Tombstone *Nugget,* and Tucson *Star* fill certain shelves in the rooms of the Arizona Pioneers Historical Society in Tucson. In these old newspapers, yellow with age, is to be found, if you take the time to dig it out—and it may take you weeks on end—a full history of Tombstone. The stories were news in their day and are as vivid now as when the ink on the type was still wet. These files constitute a full and authentic record of Tombstone, and they are the source of most of the tales told in this book. The bibliography of Tombstone is meagre. McClintock, in his *History of Arizona,* has sketched the town's development, and Frederick Bechdolt, as a literary pioneer in the romantic field, has done some brilliant work in *When the West Was Young;* but nothing has been written or ever will be written of early days in southeastern Arizona of such intimate interest as the day-by-day history set forth in these old files.

My account of the origin of the Earp-Clanton feud and the street battle in which it culminated is based on testimony from the witness stand. At his trial after the fight in which Tom and Frank McLowery and Billy Clanton were killed, Wyatt Earp read a long and carefully prepared paper which gave in detail the Earp side of the vendetta, and Ike Clanton gave the Clanton side. The Tombstone *Epitaph* published this testimony in full and that of many other eyewitnesses to the battle from stenographic notes. From these authentic records I have presented both sides of the case. For my version of the assassination of Morgan Earp and the subsequent killing of Frank

Stilwell and Florentino Cruz, or Indian Charlie, I have depended on the evidence brought out at the coroner's inquests.

My Schieffelin chapter is based on the manuscript written by Schieffelin himself and now in the archives of the Arizona Pioneers Historical Society; my stories of Billy Breakenridge among the Curly Bill outlaws are based on the reminiscences of the adventurer himself, now Col. William P. Breakenridge of Tucson; my chronicles of John Slaughter are based on the recollections of Mrs. John Slaughter of Douglas, on the clippings treasured in her scrapbook and on the manuscript memoirs of the famous sheriff written by Mrs. W.E. Hankin of Bisbee, a lifelong friend of the Slaughter family.

My research into the printed records of Tombstone's past has been supplemented by interviews with pioneers, and for information on many subjects dealt with in the book I am under obligations to William Lutley, C.L. Cummings, Porter McDonald, Mr. and Mrs. J.H. Macia, James Marr, A.H. Gardner, and Frank Vaughan of Tombstone; Jeff Milton of Fairbank; Leonard Redfield of Benson; United States Marshal George A. Mauk, and State Historian George H. Kelly of Phoenix; Edward Vail, Mrs. George F. Kitt, George R. Roskruge, L.D. Walters, and Melvin Jones of Tucson; Ross Sloan of Skeleton Cañon; James C. Hancock and Rube Hadden of Paradise; Henry Smith, Mrs. B.F. Smith, and Bill Sanders of Turkey Creek Cañon; and half a hundred other old-timers who knew Tombstone in its roaring days.

Walter Noble Burns
Chicago, Illinois.

CONTENTS

FOREWORD

BY CASEY TEFERTILLER

By the time Walter Noble Burns tracked down Wyatt Earp, Burns had already emerged as one of America's legend-makers. In his flashy, novelistic style, he built the tales of gangsters and gunfighters, telling of Billy the Kid in a book that had already found a hungry audience. In the summer of 1926, he set out upon a new quest, to find the story of one of America's surviving folk heroes.

Wyatt Earp burst into national fame in the spring of 1882, when he led his vendetta against the Arizona outlaws who killed one of his brothers, badly wounded another, and threatened the safety of the residents of Cochise County. From that adventure, he would become perhaps the most controversial figure in the West, the subject of continuing debates as to his righteousness or villainy. Some of his old townsmen would hail him as hero and protector, while others would call him a murderer and thief. Earp again drew national attention in 1896 when he made the poor choice to accept the position of referee for the prize fight between Tom Sharkey and Bob Fitzsimmons in San Francisco. Earp awarded the decision to a badly beaten Sharkey, ruling that he had been fouled in the eighth round. This set off a national scandal that erupted into the headlines of sporting pages across the country, with constant claims that Earp had "fixed" the fight so that Sharkey would be the winner. Newspapers derided Earp and questioned his character and motives. Some papers retold the old Arizona stories and, this time, had Earp emerging as a villain and coward. The once-proud Earp grew quiet, stung by the taunts of the press.

"The falsehoods that were printed in some of the newspapers about him and the unjust accusations against him hurt Wyatt more deeply than anything that ever happened to him during my life with him, with the exception of his mother's death and that of his father and brother, Warren," Josephine Earp, Wyatt's third wife, later told her biographers. "He was not a man to show emotion by tears, but I knew him so well that I could read the extent of his mental pain. . . . It had left Wyatt weary and despirited, sick with longing to get away again to unsettled country and to be wrapped in its quiet and obscurity."

The Earps would spend nearly three decades trying to wrap themselves in quiet obscurity, but the old stories would never go away. Newspapers and magazines kept reviving the tale of Tombstone, alternatingly portraying Earp as a gunfighting hero or a murdering criminal mastermind. Through most of this, Earp remained stalwart in his silence. A 1924 interview in a San Francisco paper reported that it was "like pulling teeth" to get any personal information from him. He had been burned by the press, and he did not want to let it happen again.

In his silence, Earp remained a proud man, but the false stories kept building around him. In 1919, the *Saturday Evening Post* published an article by Frederick Bechdolt confusing the whole situation, and, three years later, the *Los Angeles Times* ran a story describing Earp as the worst of criminals and stating that he was dead, although he was very much alive and living in Los Angeles at the time. Earp came to realize that the only way to resurrect and rehabilitate his legacy would be through getting his story to the public. Earp contacted silent-film star William S. Hart and suggested Hart make a movie of his life. Hart supported the idea but wanted Earp first to have a book done on which he could base the movie. Earp's close friend, John Flood, volunteered for the task.

The problem was that Flood wrote so poorly that his manuscript read more like a bad B-movie western than a biography.

Flood spent more than two years attempting to piece together the Earp story and nearly had it completed when legend-maker Walter Noble Burns showed up on the doorstep of the cheap Los Angeles bungalow the Earps rented.

"Poor fellow, he burst in upon Mrs. Earp and myself just a few hours after our arrival at our new address, all smiles; he thought he had reached the end of his rainbow," Earp wrote to Hart in September of 1926. "It made me feel badly to have to explode his dream: he had made the trip west from Chicago especially to get my story, and then I had to break him the news. But he was mighty fine about it, and determined too. Instead of going back empty handed, he caught the train to Tombstone, and has been gathering together material for a story of Doc Holliday. He is deserving, and I know it will be good."

Hart did not have such a high opinion of Burns, telling Earp that much of the material in Burns's book, *The Saga of Billy the Kid*, had been pirated from a story written by Charlie Siringo years earlier. According to Hart, Burns even stole some of the language.

Burns went off to Tombstone and took a room at the Rose Tree Inn. He set about checking newspaper files and interviewing the surviving old timers who could tell him the stories from years past. He may have started by trying to tell the story of Doc Holliday, but what he discovered in that remote Arizona mining town was a story far too remarkable to ignore—a story that Burns would help build and will forever echo through the American consciousness. Outlawry in Tombstone had driven Cochise County into chaos and forced Wyatt Earp to become a maverick lawman who overstepped the law to enforce justice and preserve the public safety. It was a story too good to ignore, and Wyatt Earp stood out as the central character.

Burns kept writing Earp for information, and, finally, on March 15, 1927, Earp sat down to respond. Josephine may have actually written the letter, with Wyatt telling the story as they sat near a campfire at their mining claim near Vidal, California. Wyatt's response, an eleven-page outline of the events in Tombstone, tells his side of the story—a major contribution to our historical understanding.

Through all this, publishers kept rejecting Flood's horrendous manuscript, telling him honestly of his limited skill and making clear the story needed a different writer. On March 28, 1927, Flood sat down to write to Burns and invited him to take over the project, but, by this time, Burns had his own story, without the restrictions of co-authorship, biographical subjects, and shared royalties. Burns's publisher, Doubleday, Page & Company, responded by telling Earp that the book would be published and was highly complimentary to him. But Earp had been impugned in print too often, and he responded that it was "my firm stand that no story of myself shall be written or published without my sanction or consent, and that, in this instance, I am unwilling to give."

Permission granted or not, Doubleday and Burns forged ahead and later that year the book appeared. *Tombstone: An Iliad of the Southwest* was a triumph of blood and thunder, a tale of action so well-written as to mesmerize an American audience looking for heroes. Through his research, Burns developed a sense of those involved in the story. His descriptions ring out from the pages to mold forever the characters. He called Chochise County's inept first sheriff, John Behan, "a twenty-two calibre man in a forty-five calibre town. Tombstone thirsted for strong waters; John Behan had only sarsparilla and lemon pop on tap." Burns compared Wyatt Earp to a lion in both movement and appearance, with "hair as yellow as a lion's mane." Burns christened Earp, "The Lion of Tombstone," a moniker that would stick through the passing decades. His portrayal of outlaw John Ringo created a figure of great mystique.

The book made a big splash and was serialized in newspapers across the United States. It is a delight to read and a masterpiece of the Wild West action genre. The problem is that it cannot be considered history. Burns used the techniques of a novelist—invented dialogue, dramatizations, leaps of research—and created a book in which he gives a wonderful *sense* of the history, including deep legitimate research and some of the words of those who lived the story, but Burns was not bounded by the limits of his empirical research in telling the story.

For later generations trying to find the truth on Wyatt Earp and Tombstone, this book is a source of intense frustration because there are so many wonderful quotations and stories that cannot be verified through other sources. Burns's notes at the University of Arizona Special Collections yield a little light, but too little.

Tombstone enjoyed four years in publication before it drew competition from another Earp book, Stuart N. Lake's *Wyatt Earp: Frontier Marshal*. Shortly after the publication of Burns's *Tombstone*, Lake began a series of perhaps half-a-dozen meetings with Earp and an intense correspondence. This was to be Earp's authorized biography—the story told the way he desired, the truth as he saw it. However, Earp died in January of 1929, and Lake took great artistic license in dramatizing much of the story. Lake presented Earp almost as a white knight on horseback, an image that would carry into the 1950s when ABC ran the series, *The Life and Legend of Wyatt Earp*, starring Hugh O'Brian.

As the fifties ended, a new breed of researchers stepped forward to rediscover the old stories of villainy that surrounded Earp. However, the debunkers also were not above stretching the truth to make their points. Frank Waters's *The Earp Brothers of Tombstone* is purportedly based on a series of interviews with Allie Earp, Virgil's wife, but Waters took far too many liberties. In the 1960 book Waters uses Allie Earp's quotes to make it seem Wyatt masterminded stage robberies and a criminal syndicate. However, the first draft of Waters's manuscript, written in the 1940s, quotes Allie telling only a few rich family stories and shows that she actually liked and admired Wyatt. This falsification of material would continue for generations as numerous writers stepped well beyond their research to tell *their* Earp story. Fabrications have been more plentiful than facts for generations of Earp writers.

Wyatt Earp has never been able to ride off quietly into the sunset to be forgotten with most of the one-time legends. His story is too transcendent and a lesson for future generations: When the courts cannot control outlawry, extreme measures must be taken to protect the citizenry. A new generation rediscovered Wyatt Earp in the early 1990s through the movies *Tombstone* and *Wyatt Earp*. Kevin Jarre, scriptwriter for *Tombstone*, leaned heavily on Burns for his Earp tale, extracting some of his best lines from the book and others from the newspaper accounts of the time. Perhaps the most noted line in the movie is Doc Holliday's saying to John Ringo, "I'm your huckleberry, Ringo, that's just my game." That bit comes directly from the pen of Walter Noble Burns.

Burns's *Tombstone* may not be a model of historical authenticity, but it is a masterpiece of legend making. The legend of Wyatt Earp thrives to this day. Perhaps the greatest surprise we are learning is that the truth of Earp's life is even more fascinating than the legend.

Casey Tefertiller
San Francisco, California
February 1999

WYATT EARP LETTER
TO WALTER NOBLE BURNS[1]

Vidal, March 15th 1927

Dear Mr Burns:

Your letter came several days ago, having been forwarded to me from Oakland here to Vidal. I was out to my mining property and only returned here yesterday. I was glad to get your letter, and to know you are getting along so fine with the Doc Holiday story. I will give you what information you ask as near as I can. I would much rather not have my name mentioned to freely. I am getting tired of it all, as there have been so many lies written about me in so many magazines in the last few years that it makes a man feel like fighting. I know you mean to do the right thing by me, but I would ask of you please to say as little as possible about me and I am more then sorry Mr. Burns, that I was not in the position to give you my life story. Have as yet done nothing with it. And I may have it all rewritten.

No doubt you were filled up with lots of things which never happened about me while you were in Tombstone. Naturally I have my enemies as well as friends. I may take a run into

---

1   The letter is from the Walter Noble Burns Papers, Special Collections, University Arizona Library, Tucson, Arizona. The transcription retains Wyatt Earp's idiosyncratic spelling, grammar, and syntax. Paragraph breaks ease reading, and bracketed insertions clarify Earp's meaning.

Arizona while I am in this part of the country. Yes, I met Mr. Brekenridge two years ago. I can't undersand why they dont let me alone. I can <u>truthfully</u> say that I have never had any trouble with a living being as an officer and then I was very careful <u>always</u> that I was in the right and I can't understand why they don't let me alone and I think it time to put a stop to it all. Now here for your story and I will give you facts as near right as I know. And I think you are getting the right thing. You know your self, that every and each man you talk to, all have a different tale to tell.

Holiday was a friend of Lenards, having known him in Las Vegas New Mexico, where Lenard was established in the jewelry business, and was considered at that time a respectable citizen. And from Las Vegas he came to Tombstone and with Harry Head, Jim Crane, Bill Crane, also Bill King and himself, all went batching in a house ten miles north from town, which was known as the Wells. And all three remained there for several months. Holiday would make them a visit now and then, knowing Lenard so well, which many people knew how friendly they were. Holiday went to the livery stable on this day, hired a saddle horse which he did quite often to visit Lenard at the Wells. The horse came from Dunbar stable, and not Tribletts, as Tribletts did not have any stable in Tombstone. Holiday remained there until 4 P.M. Old Man Fuller was hauling water into Tombstone at that time and leaving the Wells with a load of water. Holiday tied his horse behind the wagon and rode into town with Fuller, and which many people knew. After Holiday ate his dinner, he went to playing faro, and he was still playing when the word came to Tombstone from Bob Paul to me that there had been a hold up, and the coach was stopped and held up. And lots of Doc enemies started the report that he was one of them, because he was known to be friendly with Lenard. There were 4 men in that hold up, who were Billy Lenard, Harry Head, Jim Crane, and Billy King. They were the four men who attacked the coach. King was arrested the second day out, and we turned him over to Sheriff Behan. He took King to Tombstone. King then made his escape and was never again heard from. Lenard and Head were both killed by the Hesletts brothers. Crane was killed by the Mexicans while in possession of a bunch of stolen cattle.

Texas Jacks real name was John Vermilion, was a carpenter by trade. Died in Chicago. McMasters was prospecting around Tombstone Came from very nice people in Denver Colorado. I heard he went to the Philippines and I have never heard from him again. Jack Johnson was from Missouri, was a book keeper and very well educated. He died in Salt Lake City twenty five years ago.

Curly Bill was killed at Iron Springs where the whetsone mountains and Mustang come together, and about thirty five miles a little west of north from Tombstone, and about half way from Tombstone to Tucson. It was Luke Short who killed Storms. Jack Vermilion, Jack Johnson[,] McMasters, Holiday were my depties.

Virgil Earp died in Goldfield Nevada, buried in Portland Oregon. James died in Los Angeles, twenty eighth day of Jan [19]26, and buried in San Bernardino, Cal.

Doc and I were the only ones in Tucson at the time Frank Stillwell was killed. Others remained in Bensen. The men who murdered my brother were Curly Bill, Ringo, Stillwell, Hank Swilling, and the Mexican Florentine. I was told by their lawyer that I must be careful that they were going to assassinate us all. I don't care to tell who the lawyer was who told me, as he was good friend of mine, and at the same time was handling the other side.

The Behan posse was not very anxious to find us, as Hooker told them where they could find us. Hooker a fine man was also our friend. Pete Spence was a stage robber and at the time my brother Morgan was killed, was out on bonds. I am satisfied that Spence had nothing to do with the assassination of Morgan, although he was a against us. In Behans party were Ike and Finn Clanton, John Ringo, Pete Spence, Hank Snelling, and two of the Tyle brothers, and besides those who I have mentioned were several others who names I have since forgotten. And all of them were outlaws of the worst kind, and a very tough bunch of men. Hooker did just as you said he did. Put Behan at a table by himself. After Behan told him that those men not his associates only in that one occasion to hunt the Earps. A nice bunch of men for a sheriff to have for a posse. Hooker did [not] hesitate in telling them that the whole bunch of them were cattle and horse theifs, and that they have every one of them stolen cattle and horses from him.

Doc was not in the Benson stage hold up, and he never did such a thing as hold ups in his life. He was his own worst enemy, comes from a very respectful family in the south, gratuated as a dentist. Slaughter did not know everything.

I am telling you right, and I hope my information which you asked for will be of some help to you. But I am going to ask you please to pardon this very poorly written letter. I am afraid you will find it very <u>hard</u> to make out. I am just down from my camp, and it is hot as H and I wanted to get this away to you as soon as possible, so I did not wait to send it to Los Angeles to have it typed. But hope you will be able to read it. I am sending it by express so as to make sure you will get it, as the mails are very irregular here, so everything must be well sealed. I will be glad to read your book when it is completed, and lots of good luck to you. Remember us kindly to your wife, and best wishes for your self.

Always Sincerely Yours,
Wyatt S. Earp

P.S. I will remain here until April 18th, should you write me here. Kindly seal letter with wax. A letter will always reach me at my Oakland address.

TOMBSTONE

CHAPTER I

GERONIMO and his warriors were out of their
stronghold in the Dragoons. Through all the
southeastern part of Arizona from the San
Simon to the Huachucas and from the Gila to the
Mexican line, the Apache bands were relentlessly harry-
ing the thinly settled land with a warfare of ambuscade
and assassination. Through desert mesquite and cactus, the invisible savages slipped with the noiseless
swiftness of running water; like poisonous reptiles they
wriggled upon their bellies to points of murderous van-
tage; as still as cougars and as patient, they lurked beside the trails or watched a cabin door. The sudden
cough of a rifle through the golden peace of the sunshine gave the first intimation of their ghostly near-
ness. A wagon train was ambushed in some pass in the
hills; a miner in some lonely gulch was murdered from
a cholla thicket; a settler with his wife and children
was massacred on his homestead claim. Back to their
mountain fastnesses from their slinking, silent war
trails, the red butchers bore their spoils—a side of bacon,
a sack of flour, a bag of beans, a little tobacco, a pair of
overalls, a calico wrapper, a baby's rattle. Then the
riotous feasting, the pæans of drumming tom-toms, the

wild, impassioned dance of triumph. This was the
Apache way in war. No battles, only murder. If the
soldiers pressed hard upon their traces, the savages,
on their tough, swift ponies, vanished as by magic
through secret mountain paths to safety in old Mexico.

Into this wilderness land of ambushed death, Ed
Schieffelin, unknown as yet to fame or fortune, came
as a civilian scout in 1877, with a flying column recruited
in the Hualapai country on the borders of the Grand
Cañon and under the command of Al Sieber, celebrated
in Apache campaigns as one of the greatest government
scouts of the Southwest. The troopers made their headquarters at Camp Huachuca, a newly established army
post at the north end of the Huachuca range, and
scoured the country round about for Indians.

Eastward across the San Pedro Valley from the post,
a group of high hills cut the skyline. Unlovely hills,
treeless, their brown slopes a dreary monotony of huge
rocks and boulders among which cactus and grease-
wood made hard shift to live. A sheer desert tumultu-
ously uplifted and set on edge. There was a look of
frank poverty about them. One sweep of the eye took
them in. No dark, mysterious gorges, no hidden pockets,
no shadowy valleys invited curious investigation. Spaniards of Coronado's time coming up from Mexico on
their quest for the Seven Cities of Cibola had passed
them by with only an incurious glance. Scouts had
threaded through them, troops of cavalry had circled
them, Mexican smugglers had camped in their lower
draws. But no one had suspected that their drab paup-
er's mantle was only a masquerade hiding one of the
continent's richest treasures. They were hills of silver,
veined through and through with ore of fabulous rich-

ness, filled to the cactus roots and ready to burst with precious metal. One rip of their sides with a miner's pick and the hoarded wealth would have come gushing forth in resplendent flood. But their hour had not yet struck. The man with the pick had not yet arrived.

On one of their scouting expeditions from Camp Huachuca, Al Sieber and his men rode through the northern reaches of these hills. Schieffelin's eye caught the gleam of deep mineral stains on a stone. He dismounted and examined the piece of float intently. Silver! Schieffelin looked up in astonishment at the piled-up ugliness of the range. For one skeptical moment, the squalid ridges seemed a sky-high lie. He shook his head. It was impossible. And yet . . . He dropped the chunk of rock in his coat pocket and rode on after his comrades. He said nothing. But his secret thrilled him like wine. He would be a scout no longer. When the Apache hunt was over, he would turn prospector again and hit the trail for the end of the rainbow.

On his return to Camp Huachuca, Schieffelin rode off alone on his mule to seek his fortune. For a while, he made his headquarters with George Woolfolk, who had just taken up land on Barbacomari Creek, sleeping at Woolfolk's place at night and going out every day into the hills. He found the spot where he had picked up the float, but he was unable to trace the rock to its source. Falling in with William Griffith and a partner who had come from Tucson to do assessment work on the old Brunckow mine, he was induced to stand guard for them against the danger of Indian attack while they completed their job in the shaft.

The old Brunckow house, a long three-room adobe,

stood in a little bowl of a valley a mile east of the San
Pedro River. Its history even then was long and romantic. It was built in 1858 by Frederick Brunckow, a
native of Berlin, graduate of the University of West-
phalia, scholar and scientist who, exiled from Germany
because of his activities in the revolution of 1848, had
drifted out into these solitudes. Brunckow had begun
to dig a mine near the house, and it had reached the
depth of a grave when an Indian arrow toppled him over
into it dead.

Science on that primitive frontier connoted a sort of
magic, and a story spread that the German wizard,
by occult divination, had located a vast treasure deep
in the earth. So a long succession of adventurers came
and dug in the shaft, but death was all any man-jack
of them ever found. Two in addition to Brunckow were
killed by Apaches, and claim-jumping fights over the
worthless hole in the ground brought the toll of dead
men, it is said, up to seventeen. But the myth of treasure deeper down still lives, and year after year assessment work is done to hold the claim. Nowadays, the
old house and mine are said to be haunted. Travellers
along the old Charleston road, it is declared, hear cries
and groans at night or see shadowy forms stalking in
the moonlight.

Here at the old Brunckow mine, Al Sieber riding up
with a party of scouts found Schieffelin sitting on a pile
of rock on guard with his rifle across his lap.

"What're you doin', Ed?" asked Sieber.

"Prospecting, mostly," Schieffelin drawled.

"Whar?"

"Over yonder." Schieffelin waved his hand eastward
toward the hills.

"Them hills?" scoffed Sieber. "Thar ain't nothin' thar."

"I've picked up some mighty nice-looking stones."

"All you'll ever find in them hills 'll be your tombstone," warned the scout. "Geronimo'll git you ef you don't watch out, and leave your bones fer the buzzards to pick."

"I'll take a chance," Schieffelin replied.

His life against a million dollars. That was his chance.

A wide, shallow dry wash leading up from the San Pedro Valley, its sloping sides green with gramma grass and flowering weeds. Ocotillos whose tall, curving, graceful wands springing from a central root were like green jets from a fairy fountain. Chollas armed with needle-sharp spines as thick as bristles on a wild boar, brandishing weirdly deformed arms like truculent devils. Green and yellow mescal plants that shot thirty feet in air skyrocket stalks that exploded in starry white blooms. Schieffelin on his mule, rifle across his saddlebow, travelling through the wash at a walk, looking for stones.

From the yellow, shadowy ramparts of the Dragoons nine miles across the mesquite mesa, a tall slender column of smoke, shimmering darkly in the sun, rose straight into the sky. It broke from its base and drawing slowly upward into space melted from view. A quick, ball-like puff of smoke shot upward like a bursting bomb. Again a slim spiral shorter than the first. Another explosive puff. Another. Once more a brief pillar. Dash. . . . Dot. . . . Dash. . . . Two dots. . . . Dash. Up there somewhere on the mountain wall a half-naked Apache, manipulating a deerskin over a brush fire, was telegraphing a code message to some war party in the valley. A queer little smile twisted the corner of Schieffelin's mouth. What was that fellow saying? Humph! He tightened a bit his grip on his rifle and went on looking for stones. Find his tombstone? Well, maybe.

He turned a corner of the wash. His mule halted abruptly, ears pricked, forelegs stiffly braced. What was that that gleamed so snowy white among the clumps of bear grass? An outcropping of white rock, perhaps. Or the mouldering skull of some long-dead, crow-bait pony. But no. Schieffelin dismounted. A step forward and there before him lay a human skeleton. Just beyond it another. The sparse grass had laid green tendrils across the glistening shanks. Weeds had shot up between the ribs. A prickly pear was crawling greenly across a disarticulated spinal column. The disjointed bones, bleached to ghastly whiteness by the suns and rains of years, were only slightly out of place here and there, and the two dead men seemed to have lain undisturbed since the moment of sudden tragedy that had overwhelmed them.

The skeletons lay at full length, breast downward, head to head, with the finger bones of the long outreaching arms almost touching. Between them stood a pile of silver ore perhaps a foot high, the dissevered arm bones almost enclosing it in a glimmering, broken circle. One skull lay turned on its side; the other was firmly imbedded upon its base in the earth, but the dark, hollow eye-sockets of both were trained, as if with conscious intensity, on the little heap of stones that suggested some idol's shrine before which these ghastly spectres bowed to the ground in unending worship. High above them, on a single stem, a yucca lifted a great cluster of drooping lily-white blossoms that swayed gently in the breeze like a swung censer.

The story of the tragedy that had left these bones to bleach on the desert was as clear as if the skeletons themselves suddenly had sat upright and unfolded every vivid detail. Picture two prospectors beside their camp fire. Rugged men they are, bearded, clear-eyed, ruddy with health. Luck has been with them. They have located a rich ledge of silver during their day's wanderings. They pour their specimens of ore on the ground. In the red glow of the firelight they gloat over their treasure. Wonderful ore. What will it run? Twenty thousand to the ton? These questions can wait. The assay in Tucson will tell. They pick up the stones, scrutinize them, weigh them in their palms. They are like misers threading fingers joyously through gold. They laugh exultant laughter. But it is growing late. They roll themselves in their blankets and go to sleep under the stars to dream of riches.

But out in the darkness, a devil's ring has closed around them. While they are slumbering peacefully, fierce eyes keep them all night under baleful surveillance. Apache gods forbid a night attack; the night is sacred to ancestral ghosts. Rosy dawn is a choice time for murder. When morning breaks in rose and gold over the Dragoons, the two men tumble out of bed. For a happy moment they stand facing each other above their pile of ore. They stretch out comradely hands. "Put her there, pardner." Their fortune's made. Good-bye to desert hardships. They have struck it rich at last. . . . Apache rifles spit fire. Snaky wisps of blue powder smoke wriggle off across the mesquite. . . .

Schieffelin climbed down off his mule, and stepping

gingerly among the bones, examined the pieces of ore one by one. Quick certainty flashed upon him like sunlight. This ore had come from the same source as the float he had found while scouting with Sieber. He was near the treasure for which he had hunted so long. Possibly this spot of dreams was now within the sweep of his vision. But where? He replaced the rocks as he had found them in the half-formed circle between the skeleton arms and rode away, leaving the dead at their eternal salaam before the tiny altar on which they had poured the oblation of their life blood.

At sunset, Schieffelin, several miles farther up the wash, prepared to camp. He picketed his mule in good grass in a secluded hollow and threw down his blankets on top of a hill a mile away. This was good strategy; a man will lie silent at night in Indian country but a mule may burst into song at any moment. The conical hill on which he made camp extended out into the wash in promontory wise and was thickly strewn with broken, gigantic fragments of rock. Just east of it was a fine spring in a clump of cottonwoods.

It was twilight when Schieffelin started for the spring to fill his canteen. As he turned a point of rock, he saw on the brow of the hill scarcely twenty yards from him an Apache warrior standing in fine, bold silhouette against the golden pallor of the sky, every detail delicately outlined—the dingy white turban, the single eagle's feather in the hair, the necklace of bear's claws, loincloth, high boot-moccasins. A rifle rested in the crook of the Indian's arm; beneath his cupped palm, he was peering into the shadows beginning to veil the mesa. A noble picture, but appealing to Schieffelin more poignantly as a noble target. He dropped abruptly behind a rock and drew a careful bead.

As he was about to pull the trigger, a second savage, emerging noiselessly from behind the hilltop, seemed to float up against the sky like a manikin manipulated against a lighted screen by strings. Well! A third mysteriously materialized. The tragic situation was achieving a certain comic relief. Two more Indians rose ghostlike against the sky from the nether shadows. Five! It began to look as if Sieber's prophecy might come true, after all. A tombstone for the cornered prospector loomed just then as a not improbable tailpiece for his adventure. Schieffelin lowered his rifle. This thing was being overdone. He had had enough. Threading his way among the towering rocks, bent on stealthy flight in the gathering dusk, he espied from the verge of the crest twenty more Indians down by the spring.

But they were mounting their ponies. Schieffelin realized with a surge of relief that they were making ready to go away. The five that had floated up against the sky floated down again. Digging their heels into their ponies' sides, the band got under way. Hoo-hoo-hoo-ah-hoo! Their chanted grunting came to Schieffelin's ears in jolting rhythms as they rode off in the thickening darkness. But there was still danger. They were heading in the direction of Schieffelin's mule. Would that fool beast have sense enough to stick to cropping grass or, under sudden lyric urge, would it intone a hymn to the evening star? An aria at this crisis would be fatal. Or would those desert bloodhounds pick up Schieffelin's own trail in the wash and come back to lift his hair? Hoo-hoo-hoo-ah-hoo! The muffled cadence was growing rainter. With straining eyes, Schieffelin watched the huddle of jostling forms dwindle in the distance. It faded into a formless blur, winked out at last in blank darkness. They were gone. Still from far off the rhythmic whisper throbbed through the night. Hoo-hoo-hoo-ah-hoo!

Sweet music to Schieffelin's ears after a night of sleepless vigilance was the hee-haw of his mule uplifted in joyous salute to the morning. When the sun again shone serenely over the familiar landscape, exorcising the lurking terrors of darkness, he felt the happy elation of one who has awakened in the nick of time to escape the hobgoblins of a nightmare. Three miles beyond him rose the hills that had so long intrigued and baffled him. He had had his first glimpse of them in April; this was the middle of August. Before him the wash led upward to the sunlit heights. Once more astride his mule, he set off on the day's adventures.

Float was plentiful. The fragments scattered along the sides of the wash were like markers left to guide him. He entered the vestibule of the hills; the wash divided. Which branch should he take? One possibly led to poverty; the other to wealth. While he paused in momentary quandary, a cottontail rabbit darted from a covert, scurried across the wash from the left, and disappeared up the right-hand gulch, leaving a trail of tiny footprints in the sand. It seemed an augury. Schieffelin staked his mule in the brush and on foot followed the cottontail. Destiny at the crossroads was determined by a trifle.

He worked up the draw to its head far back in the range. The barren hills swept down in flowing curves that flattened into tables and dipped into hollows and saddles and were cut deeply by innumerable ravines. Far up toward the summit, he spied an irregular ledge of grayish rock marbled with black and reddish-yellow splotches; he estimated its length at fifty feet and its width at six or eight inches. There were other ledges in plain view striping the hills. But this ledge stretching its undulant length along the dark slant of mountain stirred him like a battle flag. Toward it, as if drawn by a magnet, he laid his course, never swerving or turning aside as, labouring upward, he stumbled across arroyos and crashed through thickets of cat-claw and pear.

Breathless, wet with sweat, his heart pounding, he stood before the ledge at last. He sank his prospector's pick into the rock; it came crumbling down in a heap of brittle lumps. In a hand that trembled as with an ague, he picked up a fragment; he examined it with feverish eyes. It was streaked and veined and stained with silver. His brain reeled with the richness of it.

No one was there to see the climax of this one-man drama staged on the bleak hillside. No one but Schieffelin knew the thrill and romance of it. He was alone with his mountain, alone with his dreams come true, alone with his achievement, alone in the glory of it. For this he had wandered in poverty for years through mountains and deserts, starved, suffered, braved death. Here was the goal of his life, his ultimate destination. This desolate spot was the end of the rainbow.

He fished from his pants pocket a silver twenty-five-cent piece and pressed it against a slab of ore. In the soft, rich, metal content of the rock, the coin left an imprint so clearly defined that in it Schieffelin was able to decipher the national motto. Beneath his feet was a hill crammed as full of silver as was ever pirate treasure chest with doubloons and pieces-of-eight, but this quarter of a dollar was all the money he had in the world. With it, later on, he bought a plug of tobacco in Globe.

As Schieffelin leaned on his pick and in a brief moment of reverie gazed over the San Pedro Valley shimmering under a blazing sun, Al Sieber's warning at the old Brunckow house came back to him: "All you'll ever find in them hills 'll be your tombstone." It flashed upon him now that, as a prophet, old Sieber was a great Indian fighter. Schieffelin grinned at the merry conceit. Instead of a tombstone, he had discovered a silver mine —a million-dollar silver mine, perhaps. But if those Indians had caught him last night . . . After all, he had missed a tombstone—or death, at least—only by an inch or two. Tombstone. Not such a bad name for his mine considering his close squeak and Sieber's fool prediction. Well, what was the matter with that name, anyway? Why not? The mine might be his tombstone some day—or his monument. So he made his decision. His mine was the Tombstone . . . now . . . for all time. That was settled on the spot. The name was coloured with a little irony, a little cynicism, a little drama, a little romance, a little fun, a little seriousness. Unconsciously, with an unuttered word, Schieffelin had christened not only the mine but the hills, a whole silver field, and an unborn town whose story was to develop into one of the most picturesque and dramatic chronicles of the Southwest.

Schieffelin filled a bag with specimens from the ledge for assay, built a small monument of stones to mark his claim, and trudging down the hill, mounted his mule. Settling into the saddle, he gave the beast a kick in the ribs with his boot heel. "Giddap," he said.

A stranger had ridden out of the desert into Signal and startled the raw mining town up in the Bill Williams River country of northwestern Arizona with his ineffable sartorial chaos. As the tall, lean, broad-shouldered newcomer stalked past the unpainted shanty saloons and gambling places of the main street, the citizens loitering on the plank sidewalks, themselves roughly clad and familiar with the uncouth dress of frontier riffraff, turned to stare in amazement at the ruinous figure. His corduroy clothes, shiny and threadbare, a thorn-torn hole showing here and there, were patched like a crazy-quilt with deerskin, flour sacking, and rags of saddle blanket. His ancient slouch hat was so thickly pieced with rabbit skin that little of the original felt remained visible. His pants were stuffed into rusty boots run down at heel and his coat flapped open to reveal a flaming expanse of red flannel shirt. His face was half-hidden by a heavy curly brown beard and a mass of dark, tangled, unkempt hair fell upon his shoulders.

But, oddly enough, no one laughed at this weird figure that would have frightened crows from a cornfield; no sly, snickering comment accompanied the sidelong glances. There was something in the bearing of the stranger that touched his rags with a certain nobility; the unmistakable quality of spiritual vision lighted his serious deep gray eyes, and through the bronze of his weather-beaten face shone the purpose and fine courage of a vivid personality. The face of this rugged man was that of a poet who dreamed splendid dreams but had never learned to sing. This was Ed Schieffelin, if you please, discoverer of the Tombstone mines and potential millionaire, "thirty years old, looking forty."

The late afternoon whistle blew at the McCracken mine. The miners coming off shift swarmed into town. To one striding along with swinging dinner pail, Schieffelin stuck out a grimy paw.

"Hello, Al. Haven't seen you for four years."

"Don't believe I know you."

"Hardly blame you. I look like the devil, but I happen to be your brother."

Beside a stove fire in Al Schieffelin's cabin that night, Ed Schieffelin poured out the tale of his wanderings. From the Tombstone hills he had ridden to Tucson, living on game he shot on the way, and on August 25, 1877, while the Mexicans of the little adobe town were celebrating the fiesta of San Juan's Day, he had filed upon his claim and inscribed its name as the Tombstone in the official records. Thence to Globe in search of Brother Al to help him work or finance his new mine, only to learn that Brother Al long ago had gone to Signal. His last twenty-five cents spent for tobacco, Schieffelin had worked for fourteen days on the windlass at the Champion mine and, having purchased provisions with his earnings and got his mule newly shod, had struck out for Signal, three hundred miles westward across deserts and mountains. At the end of his journey, he found Brother Al's interest in the fancied bonanza only lukewarm. Brother Al's long experience as a miner was littered with collapsed bonanzas. But Ed Schieffelin had brought along his ore specimens. He spread them on the table in the shine of the tallow dip. Here was his proof. Practical Brother Al examined them calmly and shook his head.

"Poor," he said. "Nothing to get excited about."

But Schieffelin's enthusiasm was not to be easily squelched. He wanted a more authoritative opinion. Next day Brother Al brought in the foreman of the McCracken plant.

"Mostly lead," the foreman declared.

Still unconvinced, Schieffelin showed his specimens to twenty or thirty other mining men who might reasonably be assumed to have expert knowledge. All pronounced the ore of little value. The verdict seemed unanimous.

"Better forget your bonanza and go to work," suggested Brother Al.

Schieffelin, in a fit of disillusion, stepped to the cabin door and hurled his specimens one by one as far as he could throw them out on the hill. He was on the point of throwing away a whole splendid future in one mad impulse, but restrained himself in time and saved three pieces of ore. Gloomy and disgusted, he went to work in the McCracken mine and wielded a pick and shovel for four weeks.

The miners at Signal sometimes referred to Richard Gird, who recently had arrived to assume the position of mining and mechanical engineer and assayer at the properties, as "the famous Mr. Gird." He had had an extensive mining experience, and his reputation as an expert had preceded him. A dour, hard-featured, hard-headed, competent man was the famous Mr. Gird, without a drop of romance in his practical soul, his shrewd gray eyes looking upon adventure only as an opportunity to make money, but with a gambler's cold nerve in his willingness to take risks in a game for big stakes.

The early dusk of a winter afternoon was darkening the windows of Gird's office. A draft of cold air as the door opened accompanied a sound of boots scraping on the floor. Working at his desk by lamplight, Gird looked up. Before him stood a bearded young giant, evidently painfully embarrassed. Well? Schieffelin laid his three remaining specimens on the desk. Everybody had said they were no good, but he wanted to know for sure; then he could sleep better of nights. Would Mr. Gird take a look at them? And did he think them worth assaying? Gird picked up the pieces and turned them over in his hands. A sudden gleam kindled in his eyes and as suddenly died out. Well, yes, he would assay them. Fine. He could send word of the result by Brother Al who was on night shift and could call at the office any afternoon after work was over. Ed himself was working days.

Ed Schieffelin was sleeping soundly in his bunk a few nights later when Brother Al came bustling and stamping into the cabin and shook him vigorously by the shoulder.

"Get up, Ed," said Brother Al quite out of breath. "Mr. Gird wants to see you right away in his office. Come on now. Hurry up."

"I've assayed your ore," said Gird when the two brothers arrived at the office. "One piece runs $2,000 to the ton, another $600, and the third only $40. You can't always estimate the richness of a lode by two or three samples of rock. But I'm convinced you've made a strike. Where is your claim?

"Over on the San Pedro."

"That's not very definite."

No, it wasn't very definite. But that's all the information Gird got just then. Ed Schieffelin had a certain shrewdness himself. He knew how to keep a bonanza secret. He hadn't even told Brother Al.

"How much money have you?"

"Not much. All I've got's a mule."

"I'm willing to throw in with you," Gird went on. "If you'll let me in on this, I'll buy a second mule to make a span, outfit a travelling rig, and furnish a grubstake, you and Al and myself to be equal partners in the venture and everything we find to be split three ways."

"That suits me," shot back Schieffelin. "We're partners from now on."

The business partnership entered into this night in the little office at Signal and ratified by a handshake all round never was put in writing. Though it lasted for years and involved the handling of millions of dollars, it rested wholly on honour and was held inviolate by the three men to the end.

"What about your position here at the mines?" asked Schieffelin.

"To hell with my position!" snapped Gird.

The question of the time for starting came up. Gird thought they had better wait until the warm weather of spring had opened the trails.

"No." Schieffelin banged his fist on the table. "We'll start now."

The famous Mr. Gird was slightly taken aback by this imperious vehemence. No immediate rush seemed necessary. He had certain affairs to be arranged, certain business matters that——

"Right now," thundered Schieffelin. "Or never."

So preparations for an immediate departure were

made. Gird resigned; the company, in an effort to hold
him, offered him the general superintendency of the
mines, but he refused it. Gird bought a second-hand
blue spring wagon and loaded it with provisions, cooking equipment, and firearms, including in the cargo his
assay outfit and a surveyor's transit and level. He also
purchased a mule which, paired with Schieffelin's, made
the team. As the three men were ready to pull out,
the noon whistle at the mines blew for dinner. Gird
and Brother Al wanted to take time to eat. Ed Schieffelin refused to wait for food or anything else. Then
prudent Brother Al changed his mind at the last moment and decided he wouldn't go; he was dubious about
leaving a good job at $4 a day. Without a word either of
anger or persuasion, Ed Schieffelin whipped up his
mules and left Brother Al standing lonely and wistful
behind. So Ed Schieffelin and Gird, in the first week of
February, 1878, started for the San Pedro. Brother Al
joined them on horseback at their first night's camp at
Dripping Spring; the lure of bonanza had changed his
mind again.

Past Martinez, Hassayampa, Wickenburg into Salt
River Valley, their route led them, across Salt River at
Hayden's Ferry, on through Tempe to Maricopa, where
they struck the old Overland stage trail, and so to Tucson. They were entering the Apache country now. The
old stage station at Pantano bore the bullet scars of a
recent attack. They doused their camp fire at night,
spread their blankets at a distance from their wagon
and mules, and at daybreak climbed to a hilltop to
search the country with field glasses for any sign of red
marauders. Beyond the old Ohnersorgen stage station
where they crossed the San Pedro, they found the fresh

graves of two men murdered by Indians. Up the east bank of the San Pedro through the new Mormon settlement of St. David, on past the present site of Fairbank, they came at last to the old Brunckow house in sight of the Tombstone hills. Here they made permanent camp, and Gird built a crude assay furnace in the corner fireplace with old adobe bricks and a sheet of iron.

Out at once they hurried with picks and shovels to the Tombstone ledge. Gird the expert soon determined that, though the ore was rich, the pocket was shallow and would quickly be exhausted. This was a blow to Gird and Brother Al. Deep gloom settled upon them that night at the Brunckow house. Gird regretted his resignation at Signal; Brother Al mourned over his lost $4 a day. Gird talked of going on into Mexico; Brother Al wondered plaintively if there wasn't a mine somewhere around there where he could find a job. But Ed Schieffelin remained cheerfully confident. The silver was here in these hills—he knew it. These two disconsolate ones might do as they pleased; he would stay.

Followed meagre, disappointing weeks. The silver hills, it appeared, were not to be taken by quick assault but must be besieged. The three partners settled down into systematic routine, with Ed Schieffelin as prospector, Gird as assayer, Brother Al as cook. No longer was Ed Schieffelin in doubt as to the value of his finds; every evening he brought in ore, and Gird determined its richness in his furnace.

Brother Al, riding out one morning after deer, encountered Ed in the hills, elated over a piece of float.

"Here, Al, look at this," said Ed in a glow of excitement. "This is the best-looking piece of ore I've found yet."

But Brother Al was not to be bothered. "I'm looking for a deer," he said, and rode on.

Ed Schieffelin was building a monument when Brother Al rode back with a fat buck slung across his saddle.

"I've struck it rich this time," Ed called out joyously.

"You're a lucky cuss," Brother Al flung back indifferently over his shoulder as he moved off toward camp dreaming of venison steaks for supper.

So the Lucky Cuss mine got its name. The ore samples Gird assayed that night ran $15,000 to the ton.

No more gloom or despondency now. Gird was full of enthusiasm. Brother Al showed a flash of optimism. Bonanza dreams were on the verge of fulfilment. Off to Tucson, Gird and Brother Al hurried to stock up on provisions for a long stay, dropping there incidentally a hint of the richness of the new treasure field. A few days after their return, Hank Williams and John Oliver were exploring the Tombstone hills. While Gird and Brother Al were building a cabin on the Lucky Cuss claim, Ed Schieffelin discovered the Tough Nut lode, rich in horn silver.

Ed Schieffelin laid off prospecting for three days to help move camp from the Brunckow house to the Lucky Cuss cabin, forever afterward blaming these lost three days for his failure to discover the Grand Central mine. Two mules belonging to Williams and Oliver, who were camped over a hill from the Lucky Cuss, broke loose at night and wandered off on a hunt for water. Searching for the animals next morning, Williams spied the gleam of metal in the trail left by the dragging halter chains, and lost no time in staking a claim. Gird contended this claim infringed upon a prior claim of the three partners. After a wrangle, Williams and Oliver agreed to divide the location; the part they retained, they named the Grand Central; the part that fell to the share of Gird and the Schieffelins was christened, because of the quarrel, the Contention. These two mines, discovered through vagrant mules, turned out to be the richest ever found in the district.

The period of discovery was drawing to a close; the time of consolidation and development was at hand. News of the strike spread abroad; crowds of adventurers took the trail for the hills; the town of Tombstone evolved overnight, as if out of thin air, to become one of the greatest silver camps of the West. Mining machinery was freighted in, stamp mills for reducing ore sprang up, bullion began to flood out across the desert to world markets.

Gird and the Schieffelins jumped at the first chance to sell the Contention for $10,000; the purchasers took millions from it. The three partners sold a half interest in the Lucky Cuss, but the other half, retained for years, poured a steady stream of money into their coffers. The two Schieffelins sold their two thirds of the Tough Nut group for a million dollars; Gird sold his one third later for an equal sum. Gird long remained in the country building his fortune to greater proportions; the Schieffelins took their departure. The two brothers had come into the hills almost penniless; they went out millionaires.

Flushed with achievement, rich, famous, still young, Ed Schieffelin turned to civilization to prospect for new adventures. Civilization to him was little more than a name; he had glimpsed its peaks only from far off; he might find misery there or strike it rich in happiness; he would see what it held for him. He went to New York and lived there for a time; passed on to Chicago, Washington, other cities; travelled extensively; met many distinguished people. Everywhere this picturesque young plutocrat with his background of romance was lionized.

But fortune and adulations made no change in him; he remained always the same simple-hearted, kindly, sympathetic soul, helping poor relations and old friends generously, responding to every appeal for charity, his hand forever in his pockets. For a summer, he flitted to the Yukon in a steamer built at his own expense, on an unsuccessful hunt for gold. On his return, he married Mrs. Mary E. Brown and built a mansion for his bride in Alameda on San Francisco Bay. He purchased a residence in Los Angeles later, and, with his wife, father, and Brother Al to share its comforts, relaxed into tranquil domesticity, Brother Al dying here in 1885.

But civilization had failed to drug his memories of old wilderness days. He was a wilderness man, bred to its solitudes, trained to its primitive conditions. Born in a coal-mining region in Pennsylvania, he had gone as an infant with his parents to a gold-mining region in Oregon. His earliest recollections were of washing sands for gold with a milk pan in a creek that meandered past the family log cabin. At twelve he had run away to join the gold rush to Salmon River; an old family friend had captured him and led him home by the ear. He had started out on his own as a prospector and miner at seventeen. For years there was hardly a mining stampede in the Western country in which he had not shared, hardly a boom camp in Oregon, California, Nevada, Idaho, Utah, Colorado in which he had not tried his luck. Deserts and mountains had been home to him; on their lonely trails he had found happiness.

For twenty years since he had stood in thrilling triumph beside his new-found riches in the Tombstone hills, he had heard the still small insistent voice of the wilderness calling him back. He had assayed civilization and found only disillusion. The pleasures of wealth were not in its possession, but in the adventure of finding it. Society, with its pride, pretense, jealousies, and vainglory, was for others. Sweeter far to him were camp-fire bacon and coffee in a desert than the luxuries of cities. One lonely purple mountain was worth all the world's Broadways. So the rich man laid off his fine raiment, put on his old corduroys and his old red flannel shirt, buckled on his old canteen, and, with his old pick on his shoulder, went home to the wilderness.

Night had fallen in the Oregon forest. Schieffelin sat alone in his cabin in the ruddy glow of the firelight shining through the chinks of the stove. A pot of beans was boiling and bubbling with a cozy, cheerful murmur, sending up a cloud of savoury steam. A pan of biscuits was baking in the oven. . . . A sudden blinding effulgence filled the cabin. Out of the heavens, through the night, a long beam of splendour was slanting down to him, like a wide, gleaming pathway. Far up along its dazzling reaches he saw with a quick glow of happiness the loom of the Tombstone hills; there were the Lucky Cuss, the Contention, the Tough Nut, all his old mines as plain as day. Beyond, against a radiant suffusion of silver light, towered a great gateway flashing as with opals and sapphire and gold, and from its wide-flung portals were streaming glorious winged figures with snowy, shimmering garments; they were coming toward him, their arms outstretched as in welcome. He started from his chair, his rapt eyes filled with the wonder of the vision, his face transfigured and glorified. With his old corduroy pants stuffed in his boots, his old red flannel shirt open at the throat, its sleeves rolled to the elbows, he stumbled forward to climb the resplendent pathway leading to the skies.

A traveller along the lonely trail that passed the cabin found Schieffelin next morning. He lay face downward at full length on the floor. A tramp hound he had befriended crouched and whimpered at his feet. The stove was cold; the pot of beans had boiled down to a charred mass; the bread in the oven was burned black.

Schieffelin's body was taken to Tombstone. His funeral was the largest in the camp's history. Stores were closed and dwellings deserted on this May day in 1897, and everybody followed the dead man to his last resting place on the rock-strewn eminence beside the dry wash where he had had his adventure with the Indians and from which he had gone up to discover the riches of the hills of silver. The body was dressed in Schieffelin's red flannel shirt and prospector's clothes and, in accordance with his last wishes expressed in his will, with his pick and shovel and canteen lying beside him in the coffin. To mark his last claim, they erected over his grave, in the likeness of a prospector's monu-ent, a tall, massive, tower-like structure of rough stones visible for miles across the rolling mesquite mesa.

But town, mines, and hills are all likewise his monu-ments. The very name of Tombstone, with all it implies

of history, drama, romance, and achievement, is itself
an intangible but enduring monument to the pioneer
who, with steadfast faith and courage, followed his
dream into the deserts. Schieffelin rests in the glamour
of it. He sleeps forever in the shadow of a name.

CHAPTER II

RED LIGHTS AND ALTAR CANDLES

TOMBSTONE was unique among the frontier towns that have achieved lurid distinction in the history of the American West. It had, according to its legend, its man for breakfast every morning, but it was touched with the refinements of old and ordered communities. It had its desperadoes, but it had also its hard-working citizens who established homes and built prosperity. It was isolated in an Arizona desert, but civilization was just over the horizon.

A mining town in the heart of a cattle country, it had the picturesqueness of a boom silver camp and the colour of a trail-end, cowboy capital. It was a town of lawlessness and law, saloons and schools, gambling halls and churches, lurid melodrama and business routine, red lights and altar candles. It was Hangtown of the gold-rush days of 'Forty-nine. It was San Francisco of the Stranglers. It was Virginia City, Alder Gulch, Poker Flat, and Deadwood. It was the Hays City and Abilene of Wild Bill Hickok, the San Antonio of Ben Thompson and King Fisher, the Dodge City of Bat Masterson. It was all the hectic, mad romance of the old Western border, but in a stage setting of modern comforts and conveniences.

Bad men, cattle thieves, stage robbers, and gamblers brushed elbows with wealthy mine owners, merchants, and men of the professions. Six-shooters flamed in the shadow of churches. Desperadoes died in the streets in swirls of gunpowder smoke while pastors expounded the gospel to devout congregations. Sunday schools were next door to bagnios. Gospel hymns were sung to an accompaniment of spinning roulette wheels and the clatter of faro chips. College-bred women nibbled wafers at pink teas while the underworld whirled in drunken orgies in roaring dance halls. Courts sat in session while stage drivers threw out their treasure boxes to road agents at the edge of town. *Pinafore* sung by town amateurs drew patronage from the bacchanalian allurements of the Bird Cage Opera House. Tombstone was Bret Harte brought up to date.

News of Schieffelin's discovery flew far and fast, and from the four corners of the West came the stampede of fortune hunters. From the ends of railroad steel at Deming on the east and Yuma on the west, they poured into the Arizona valleys. Gila River trails were white with their canvas-topped caravans. Their mule teams, ox teams, and pack trains crawled under burning suns across the Santa Cruz deserts, streamed in endless procession through gaps in the Eastern mountain wall, and came into the promised land of the San Pedro through Dragoon Gap, Texas Cañon, and Mustang Pass. Villages in New Mexico and southern California were almost emptied, northern mining camps were deserted, and industries in many Western cities felt the drain of the exodus. Many died in the rush: froze in the mountain snows, famished in the flaming deserts, fell by the way from hardships and accidents. Apaches, watching from their mountains, swooped down upon the stragglers, leaving dead bodies beside the trails among the blackened ruins of burned wagons. Buzzards and coyotes had fat pickings on the Mogollon plateau, and skeletons bleached along the lonely sands of the Camino del Diablo.

Tombstone, magic city of the desert, was born in April, 1879. Where the Hills of Silver stretch out a lion's paw into the mesa to the east, the town blossomed flowerlike as a cluster of white tents. No faint presage of the future glimmered in this shabby genesis. But beyond the desert's rim, the tidal wave of destiny was curling to its crest. Evolution became the swift process of a dream, and the town, in swirling metamorphoses, rushed to full development. A twinkling camp fire on the mountain grew into a splendour of lights; a miner's canvas shelter changed into streets and homes and market-places. A year was compressed into a minute; a century was packed into an hour. Daybreak surged to blazing noon; while the dawn was still red, the clock struck twelve. A city suddenly stormed into being out of a clear sky.

Tombstone soon covered the lion's paw down to the claws in the mesquite. Allen was the main street, paralleled by Tough Nut and Fremont, also business thoroughfares. Allen was a street of stately width. From the O. K. corral at one end to the Bird Cage Opera House at the other, it was solidly built up with one-story business houses of frame, brick, and adobe, above which two or three two-story structures towered like sky-scrapers. The sidewalks were sheltered from the sun by projecting roofs—wooden awnings—supported by posts at the curb. These long arcades swarmed with people— mine labourers, cowboys, capitalists, Mexicans, children out of school, flashy women of the half-world, dainty young ladies out for a promenade or a tour of the shops, whose windows were gay with bonnets, lingerie, and fashionable gowns.

The broad street roared with traffic. Wagon trains loaded with lumber were coming in from the sawmills in the Chiricahuas and Huachucas. Rustlers were arriving from the San Pedro or the San Simon. Sheriff's posses were clattering out on the trail of stage robbers. Stages were departing, shotgun messengers on the box beside the driver, for Benson, Bisbee, Fort Huachuca, Tucson, Lordsburg, and mining towns across the Mexican border; stages robbed so frequently that the stamp mills cast the silver bullion in two-hundred-pound bars which road agents found difficulty in carrying off on horseback. Heavy wagons loaded with ore and drawn by sixteen mules, two abreast along a trace chain half a block long, were constantly rumbling through town from the mines on the hill to the mills at Charleston and Contention. The skill with which the skinners brought these teams around a corner was a form of art; these drivers, it was said, could flick a fly from a mule's ear at twenty paces with their long whips. One sees the ruts of these ponderous wains to-day, cut three and four inches deep in solid limestone in the old trails.

Night was distinguished from day in Tombstone only by darkness and stars. Saloons and gambling houses were never closed. Day and night, the long bars were crowded. Night and day, the gambling tables girdling the saloon walls were surrounded by tense throngs. Gamblers dealt or sat lookout with their sombreros on and their six-shooters buckled around them. Monte tables were stacked with gold and silver money. Faro was played in feverish silence. The little ivory ball in the roulette wheels and the dice in the chuck-a-luck boxes rattled noisily. When a player dropped out at the tables of stud poker and draw poker, another was waiting to take his chair. Play at noon was as heavy as at midnight. A thousand dollars won or lost at a sitting was nothing to cause excitement; a loser to-day was a winner to-morrow. Professional gamblers lived in clover and were known at a glance by their immaculate clothes, their silk shirts, and their headlight diamonds.

The saloons were not the boozing kens of old frontier tradition. Such places as the Crystal Palace, Oriental, and Alhambra were resplendent with oil paintings, mirrors, brass and mahogany, three bartenders—sometimes five—always on duty. Few rough fellows thumped on the bar and roared out orders for raw whisky; Tombstone displayed connoisseurship in mixed drinks. The spruce, white-aproned chaps behind the bars were adepts in concocting cocktails, mashes, sours, cobblers, flips, and sangarees. The bungler who fumbled a silver fizz or a pousse café or was so crass as to crush the sprig of mint in a julep was shipped back to San Francisco or Chicago, where libationary art was less exquisite.

Adjoining the business district was the populous region of red lights, its streets lined with cribs, palatial establishments, saloons of the rougher sort, and dance halls where, to the music of Mexican orchestras, men and women revelled all night in wild saturnalia. In the small hours, the sirens of the resorts drove in cabs and barouches to the Crystal Palace, Oriental, or Alhambra, swarmed in with gusts of tipsy laughter—pompous old mesdames, reckless young beauties in paint and finery, low-cut gowns, and satin slippers—and drank with the men at the bars or bucked the games until morning.

Nightly the Bird Cage Opera House offered "stupendous attractions," and nightly the famous old honky-tonk was packed to the doors. There was a bar at the front and a horseshoe of curtained upper boxes around the walls. Seated on wooden benches, the audience guzzled whisky and beer and peered through a fog of tobacco smoke at vaudeville performers cutting their capers in the glare of kerosene-lamp footlights. Beautiful painted ladies in scanty costumes sang touching ballads of home and mother on the stage and then hurried to the boxes where, by their voluptuous charms and soft graces, they swelled the receipts of the downstairs bar and received a rake-off on every bottle of beer they induced their admirers to buy. When the performance ended, the benches were moved against the walls to clear the floor, and the crowd reeled in drunken dances until the sun peeped over the Dragoons.

Billy Hutchinson was proprietor of the Bird Cage, succeeded in later years by Joe Bignon. From a yellow, tattered old programme, one gains an idea of the character of entertainment the Bird Cage had to offer.

"First Appearance of Mr. Tommy Rosa, King of Comedians and Laugh Makers," announces the ancient show bill in impressive capitals. "Mr. Walter Phœnix, America's Premier Song and Dance Artist. The Campbell Sisters, Serio-Comic Stars and Sketch Artists. Professor King in His Wonderful Suspension Wire Act. Mr. James Holly and Miss Lola Cory, America's Own Specialty Stars. In Addition to Our Own Great Company. Our Petite Star Miss Annie Duncan, the Tombstone Nightingale. Mr. Harry K. Morton, Comedian and End Man, in His Great Specialty, the Dublin Dancing Man. Our Serio-Comic Queen, Miss Lottie

Hutchinson, in Her Selections of the Latest Gems. Mr. Neal Price, Author and Vocalist, in His Original Budget of Songs of the Day." A comforting footnote adds, "No Advance in Prices. General Admission Twenty-five Cents. Boxes According to Location."

The mouldering old playbill, which seems ready to crumble at a touch, gives one a twinge of sadness, and one wonders mournfully what may have become of all these kings and queens and nightingales of other days who sang and kicked up their heels so merrily in the old Bird Cage. Where now are America's Own Specialty Stars? Who can recall a single bar of the Songs of the Day that the gifted Author and Vocalist sang with such fine effect? Into what particular corner of utter oblivion have faded the Premier Song and Dance Artist and the wonderful Professor of the slack wire?

In a short walk along Allen Street on a pleasant afternoon, one would likely see most of Tombstone's celebrities. Wyatt Earp, the lion of Tombstone, six-shooters on, keen eyes restlessly on watch. Town Marshal Virgil Earp, dour, silent. Morgan Earp and Doc Holliday laughing together in front of a saloon over some dry witticism of the humorous doctor, as agreeable a fellow as ever looked over the barrel of a gun. Sheriff John Behan bustling importantly. Deputy Sheriff Billy Breakenridge, neatly groomed and smiling. The Clanton and McLowery boys, sworn enemies of the Earps, just back probably from a cattle-stealing raid with Curly Bill. But as these breezy fellows swing past the Earps, they salute pleasantly instead of shooting, and the Earps respond with "Hello, boys." Which seems surprising. Sombre John Ringo, outlaw with a haunted past, who drinks hard, unlike other bad men, who take their liquor sparingly to keep their trigger fingers steady. Billy Grounds, Zwing Hunt, and Billy Claibourne dropping into the Oriental at "second drink time" for a social glass with Buckskin Frank Leslie, the genial bartender, looking innocuous in a white apron. Frank Stilwell who, it is said, has robbed the stages so often the drivers know him by his voice. Jeff Milton, government immigration officer, tall, dashing, a native of Florida with the manners of a cavalier. Dick Gird, Ed Schieffelin's old partner. John Slaughter, cattle baron, who is some day to clean up Tombstone, a small man with notably piercing black eyes. E. P. Gage, wealthy mine owner, and former Governor Anson Safford, banker, walking arm in arm. Henry C. Hooker, picturesque proprietor of Sierra Bonita ranch in the Sulphur Springs Valley, at which Augustus Thomas in later years wrote his famous play, *Arizona*. Or Walter L. Vail of the Empire ranch with his brother, Ed Vail. Or perhaps old Pete Kitchen, known as the Daniel Boone of Arizona, in from the Portrero for a visit.

Tombstone had plenty of money to spend and spent it in these boom times. The saloons equalled the silver mines as sources of quick wealth, and stores of all kinds prospered greatly. Visitors expressed astonishment at the quality and variety of the merchandise sold over the counters. The prosperity of the town was reflected in the habiliments of its citizens. Tombstone was dressy. Men of the wealthier class might have looked at home in a metropolitan club. The women kept abreast of the styles, and the fashion edicts of the Rue de la Paix, as set forth in the town papers, were echoed in the Arizona deserts. Though Allen Street was not Fifth Avenue or State Street, many of the costumes to be seen on this frontier boulevard were not lacking in smartness. Dances were held at the Cosmopolitan, Grand, and Occidental hotels, and it was the vogue for hostesses to entertain at dinner at the Can Can or Maison Dorée, where food and service were more or less distinguished.

Tombstone read the news of the great world with its morning coffee. The President's message to Congress, an ultimatum by the German Kaiser, or Wall Street's market quotations were discussed in the same breath with a stage hold-up at Robbers' Roost or Curly Bill's last attack on a smuggler train. Four newspapers, the *Nugget, Epitaph, Expositor,* and *Evening Gossip,* not only kept the town well informed, but the political pot furiously boiling. The *Nugget,* Tombstone's first newspaper, was established in the fall of 1879 by A. E. Fay and Thomas Tully, who brought from Tucson the primitive hand press on which had been printed the Tubac *Arizonian,* first newspaper ever published in Arizona. The Tombstone *Epitaph,* unique as the only paper of its name in the world, came out May 1, 1880, its owners John C. Clum, afterward postmaster and mayor, Charles D. Reppy, and Thomas R. Sorin. Antiquarians still argue over the origin of the name. Some say John Hays Hammond, famous mining engineer, suggested it in an after-dinner speech at the Can Can. Others attribute it to Ed Schieffelin, who with such happy inspiration had christened the early mines and the town. Mr. Clum, it is said, coming in with Schieffelin on the stage from Tucson, asked the passengers to suggest a name for the paper he was about to start.

"The *Epitaph,*" said Schieffelin quickly. "That's the

name for a paper that will celebrate in enduring print the deeds and fame of Tombstone."

"But," replied Mr. Clum dubiously, "epitaphs are usually mere chiselled lies."

"Well," declared Schieffelin philosophically, "they tell the truth about as often as newspapers."

Pat Hamilton, Sam Purdy, Harry Brook, John O. Dunbar, Harry Wood, Dick Rule, William O'Neill, and O'Brien Moore were the editorial thunderers of the Tombstone press, later achieving some celebrity in politics and journalism in other parts of the country. The *Nugget*, the political organ of Sheriff Behan, and the *Epitaph*, the champion of the Earps, were constantly at war, and journalism in the pioneer camp was not devoid of acrimony and personal bitterness. Pat Hamilton and Sam Purdy, having arranged a duel to the death, marched with seconds, doctors, and supernumeraries to the field of honour and then marched back again without fighting, to be chaffed unmercifully thereafter by the citizens.

S. C. Bagg of the *Prospector*, one of Tombstone's later papers, criticized a decision rendered by Judge W. H. Barnes of the District Court and was fined $500 for contempt. Bagg, a man of means, refused to pay the fine and was committed to jail, editing his paper for several weeks from his cell and revelling in his martyrdom. When his friends at last paid his fine, Bagg was indignant and refused to accept his freedom. The sheriff had to throw him out and lock the jail door to prevent his return. Several years later, Judge Barnes, having retired from the bench, was sent to jail in Tucson for contempt by Judge R. E. Sloan. As he passed through the prison doors, he was on the point of collapse and was only sustained, as Historian McClintock points out, "by the sympathy and stimulants of his partisans." His spirits were greatly revived when a messenger brought a telegram. "Friends from afar," remarked the former jurist to the little band of sympathizers gathered about him, "have heard of this damnable outrage." He tore open the telegram triumphantly. The message read: "Are you there, Moriarty?" It was signed by S. C. Bagg.

Old files of the Tombstone papers are filled with small-beer chronicles which retain some flavour of the life and spirit of the town:

The Rev. Endicott Peabody, educated at Cheltenham and Cambridge University in England, and now rector of the Tombstone Episcopal Church, is anxious to have the churchyard fenced and takes up a collection for the purpose. His congregation gives meagrely. Gamblers playing poker in the Crystal Palace learn of the good pastor's disappointment and, with their compliments, send the Rev. Peabody the kitty from the night's play, the kitty comprising chips taken out for all hands above two pair. The Rev. Peabody returns a note of polite thanks and the church fence is built.

Miss Nellie Cashman, running the Russ House at Fifth and Tough Nut streets, having for years followed stampedes and kept boarding house in mining towns from Montana to New Mexico, is known to every miner and gambler in the Western country. Her hotel is always crowded; if a fellow has no money, Miss Nellie gives him board and lodging until he makes a stake. She is one of the angels of the camp, held in an affection akin to veneration. Stranger or tenderfoot who gets uppish with Miss Nellie takes a long chance. A drummer, served with beans in Miss Nellie's restaurant, loudly and harshly demands food more pleasing to his cultivated appetite. A tall miner unlimbers his six-shooter and steps over to the drummer's table. "Stranger," he says grimly, "eat them beans." Which, with sudden gusto, the drummer does, to the last bean.

Dutch Annie, a figure in red-light society, is deeply mourned at her death by all Tombstone. Dutch Annie has been distinguished by great kindness of heart and many generous charities. A thousand buggies and carriages filled not only with women and men of the underworld but with business men and town officials follow her body to the grave in Boot Hill Cemetery. This is the town's only burying ground and is to remain so for many years. On the unfenced, desolate, windswept slope north of town, men who died with their boots on and the town's best citizens find a common resting place. Possibly some Tombstone matron of wealth and position will some day sleep side by side with Dutch Annie.

Bradshaw and McIntyre are business partners. Bradshaw goes shopping and buys a gorgeous shirt with black, green, and red stripes. When he appears on Allen Street in this portentous garment, he creates a tremendous sensation. But having acquired his ideas of smartness in attire out in the sage-brush, he takes his shirt seriously and feels that it is the last word in sartorial elegance. As he strolls along as proud as a peacock, all who meet him burst out laughing. He is unable to figure out the joke until boisterous citizens on the boulevard begin to shout at him, with uproarious guffaws, "Where did you get that shirt?" Bradshaw is vexed by

such ribaldry, but his show of displeasure only incites
his tormentors to new derision. He flies into furious
anger at last and declares flatly, "I will kill the next
man who makes fun of my shirt." The next man is
McIntyre. The shirt strikes McIntyre as excruciatingly
ridiculous. He laughs so immoderately that for a time
he cannot speak. He bends double in unholy glee, he
twists, he squirms, all the while pointing a finger at
Bradshaw but unable to articulate a syllable. Finally,
between gurgling outbursts, he manages to ejaculate
the fateful words, "Where did you get that shirt?"
Whereupon Bradshaw, beside himself with rage, draws
a six-shooter and kills him, the bullet entering Mc-
Intyre's mouth, which is wide open with merriment.
Tombstone takes this murder lightly, holding McIntyre
fortunate in that death comes to him as a sort of joke
and that he goes out into the other world holding his
sides with laughter.

Julius Cæsar rises to fame as the greatest of Tombstone restaurateurs and the Maison Dorée over which
he presides has dimmed the original prestige of the Can
Can. Portly, rubicund, with triple chin, he rubs his
hands unctuously, welcomes his patrons with smiles
and bows, suggests epicurean dishes, and tours the
crowded tables, inquiring solicitously as to the cookery.
His steaks and chops are especially celebrated among
Tombstone gastronomes, and a quail on toast at the
Maison Dorée is an event. Julius Cæsar grows comfortably rich but falls finally, not beneath dagger stabs
at the foot of Pompey's statue in the Capitol, but beneath the fascinations of faro. He is last heard of
running a cheap lunch counter at Benson.

A coroner's physician "performs assessment work"

Spurring his pony to a gallop, the corpse dragging and bouncing at the end of the rope, he races toward the grave.

on the remains of an unfortunate gentleman who has been badly shot up and finds the body "rich in lead but too badly punctured to hold whisky."

Johnny Blair of Double Dobe ranch comes to Tombstone to see the sights with a bunch of cowboy comrades and is taken down with the smallpox. His friends quarantine him under care of a Mexican woman, immune from the plague, in a cabin out on the mesa, themselves occupying another cabin a half mile away to lend whatever long-distance assistance they may. After five days, the Mexican nurse approaches within earshot and announces that Señor Juanito is very dead. To bury the victim of the dreaded disease without endangering the lives of the other cowboys becomes the immediate problem. Having scooped out a grave, they play seven-up to determine who will officiate as mortician. The loser at the game saddles his pony and, riding to the open door of the cabin where the dead man lies on a blanket on the floor, throws the loop of a riata about the feet. Spurring his pony to a gallop, the corpse dragging and bouncing at the end of the rope, he races toward the grave, into which the dead man flounces headlong. The other cowboys, rushing up with spades and making the dirt fly as they fill the grave, establish doubtless a world's record for lightning speed in funerals.

A sheriff's posse has a fight at the Stockton ranch with two outlaws. A member of the posse is killed. Also one outlaw. The other outlaw is wounded and brought to Tombstone, where he is placed in the hospital, the authorities declaring him too badly hurt to be locked in jail. In a week or two, the outlaw strolls out of the hospital and is seen no more. The townspeople view the official laxity with indignation. A little afterward a

crowded audience greets the amateur performance of
Pinafore in Schieffelin Hall. When Ralph Rackstraw
in his tuneful farewell to the captain's daughter, sings
"I go to a dungeon cell," Dick Dead-Eye interrupts.
"Say, Cap," says Dick Dead-Eye, "have you got a
dungeon cell on board this ship?" "No," replies the
captain, "but we have a hospital." This suggestive quip,
you understand, brings down the house.

Martin Costello, a shrewd fellow, runs the St. Louis
Beer Hall. He is the first saloon-keeper to sell St. Louis
beer in Tombstone, and as he handles a famous brand,
his bar does a land-office business. Costello in a little
while accumulates much money, but is always looking
for opportunity to make more. He grubstakes a prospector who makes a lucky strike in the Mule Mountains,
locating the copper mine afterward known as the Irish
Mag. Costello sells his interest in this mine a few years
afterward to the Calumet & Arizona Company for
close to a million dollars. So Martin Costello bids good-
bye to his Tombstone saloon and establishes himself in
a handsome residence in Los Angeles and lives there in
princely style for many years. One day he is found dead
in a lodging house, a pistol beside him and a bullet
hole in his head. Though some suspect murder, his
death, it seems pretty clearly established, is suicide,
but why he should have been in a lodging house, or why
he should have killed himself, remain mysteries. Costello
had invested in much Tombstone realty which his widow
owns to-day.

Miss Ethel Robinson, now Mrs. Macia, hostess of
the Arcade Inn, joins the choir of the Episcopal Church
upon her return from graduation at the University of
Arizona at Tucson. A handsome young tenor also sings

ïn the choir, and his voice at Sabbath services greatly impresses the congregation. The young choir ladies grow perturbed when they learn that this gentlemanly young fellow goes by the name of Dead-Eye Dick and sings for a living in the Alhambra saloon. Afterward they treat him with discreet politeness at choir practice but cut him dead on the street.

While a lawyer, "noted for his eloquence," is soaring in a flight of spell-binding oratory before a jury in Judge Wells Spicer's court, a burro beneath a window sets up a tremendous braying. Lawyer Marcus A. Smith, afterward United States Senator from Arizona, arises gravely. "If it please the Court," he says, "I object to the two attorneys speaking at the same time."

A visitor ships a burro to his home in Philadelphia for his small son to ride. The animal is billed as a burro, but the shipping clerk in Philadelphia, never having heard of such a beast and finding no furniture in the consignment, thinks a mistake has been made and turns in a report which reads: "One bureau short, one jackass over."

Mayor Robert Leatherwood of Tucson calls a meeting to celebrate the completion of the first telegraph line and the inauguration of wire service between his city and the outside world. This is early in 1880. A delegation of Tombstone citizens journeys to Tucson to be present on the memorable occasion. Mayor Leatherwood reads telegrams of congratulation from many distinguished men. President Hayes sends greetings. Mayor Leatherwood invites the crowd into the Palace Hotel bar and buys a round of drinks. Senators and Congressmen wire their compliments. After each message, Mayor Leatherwood buys another round of drinks. The crowd grows hilarious. But messages became fewer, rounds of drinks less frequent. Suddenly, congratulations begin to pour in mysteriously from all over the world. There is a message in French from the President of France. Mayor Leatherwood is a bit puzzled but buys again. Another message reads:

> Her Majesty, Queen Victoria, feels honoured at the opportunity to felicitate the Hon. Robert Leatherwood, mayor of the ancient and honourable pueblo of Tucson, upon the enterprise that has at last connected this famous city with the world at large and expresses the hope that this will be one more tie binding together the two great English-speaking nations.

This is signed "Beaconsfield." There is tremendous cheering. Mayor Leatherwood, without batting an eye, orders up champagne. Mayor Leatherwood is game. Then comes this message, signed "Antonelli,"

> His holiness the Pope desires to convey to the Hon. Robert Leatherwood, Mayor of Tucson, the assurance of his apostolic joy that communication by telegraph between the pueblo and the Eternal City has been established. But the Holy Father, in hope of further enlightenment, desires to learn of the Hon. Robert Leatherwood where in hell Tucson is anyhow.

The hill back of Tombstone was now thickly dotted with mines, workshops, and office buildings, and smoke boiled into the sky from towering chimneys. Mining machinery had been hauled in from Yuma across deserts and mountains by teams of thirty mules to a wagon, and an army of miners was busy night and day working three shifts. Companies organized by Eastern capitalists had acquired control of the mining properties—the Contention Consolidated, Grand Central, Tombstone Mining and Milling, Vizina, Empire, and Stonewall companies. Charleston and Contention, on the San Pedro River, had grown about stamp mills into booming towns. Benson, twenty-six miles to the north, came into existence early in 1880, when the first railroad was built through Arizona. With a rich copper strike in the Mule Mountains to the south, Bisbee, in its deep, narrow cañon, developed with the miraculous speed of Tombstone.

The Southern Pacific reached Tucson in 1880, and the following year established connection with the Santa Fe at Deming, opening a new transcontinental route. The first train went through March 20, 1881. Meanwhile, Tombstone had become the largest town in Arizona. At the end of its second year, it had a population estimated by some at 15,000, by others at 12,000. Tucson, its nearest rival, had at this time only 7,000, Prescott 2,074, and Phœnix 1,800.

CHAPTER III

WYATT EARP, who was to achieve sinister eminence as the six-shooter boss of Tombstone, and whose name, for good or bad, was to be bruited more widely, perhaps, than that of any other man in Tombstone's history, was born in Monmouth, Illinois, March 19, 1849. He went West as a youth, when Kansas and Nebraska were the frontier and Omaha and Kansas City were border towns. As a freighter, he drove bull teams on the Overland and Santa Fe trails. He hunted buffalo for a living when the prairies were black with the wild herds. He had experience as an Indian fighter. He became a professional gambler in the days when euchre was giving way to faro and draw poker on the frontier. He served as a policeman from 1874 to 1876 in Wichita, when that town was as hard boiled as any west of the Missouri. He was town marshal of Dodge City from early in 1877 to late in 1879.

Dodge City was then in its palmy days. It was the last of a succession of Kansas railroad towns that rose to lurid prestige at the end of the cattle trails from Texas. Abilene, Caldwell, Wichita, Newton, Ellsworth, and Hays had had their crowded hour and passed into peaceful obscurity. Farmers had spread over eastern Kansas and the old Texas trails were blocked by fenced fields of corn and wheat. Texas, still without railroads, was the West's only great cattle preserve. The cattle business in New Mexico and Arizona was still in its infancy. Northern ranges in Wyoming, Montana, and the Dakotas, in later years to swarm with cattle, were still wilderness. Millions of longhorns pastured half wild over the vast pampas between the Rio Grande and Red River and to Dodge City poured the Texas herds for shipment over the Santa Fe Railroad to Eastern markets.

While Wyatt Earp was marshal, Dodge City was as rough a village as ever welcomed the old, wild breed of Texas cowboys storming in after hard weeks on the trail to refresh and enjoy themselves in riotous pleasures. Among the notable fighting men whose exploits sent the town's fame swirling to the frontier skies in clouds of six-shooter smoke were Sheriff Bat Masterson, Doc Holliday, Mysterious Dave Mathews, Charlie Bassett, Bill Tilghman, Luke Short, Ben Thompson, Clay Allison, Pat Shugrue, Prairie Dog Dave Morrow, Neil Brown, Bob Wright, Ben Daniels, Dave Black, Charley Coulter, and Shotgun Collins. A man was a man who in such fighting company managed to escape the oblivion of Boot Hill. But during his three years as a peace officer in this toughest town of the Kansas prairies, Wyatt Earp became famous for personal force and desperate courage. After Dodge City, he was ready for Tombstone.

When the glories of Dodge began to fade and the fame of the bonanza silver strike at Tombstone was spreading over the West, Wyatt Earp set out for the new boom camp in Arizona. At Prescott, where he stopped to visit his brother Virgil, he met C. P. Dade, United States Marshal of Arizona, who, impressed by

the veteran's record at Dodge City, offered him an ap-
pointment as federal deputy marshal for the Tombstone
district. Wyatt Earp declined. He had had enough, he
declared, of a frontier peace officer's thankless hardships.
But, under Marshal Dade's persuasion, he at length
accepted, and when Wyatt Earp first set foot in Tombstone, December 1, 1879, he wore the badge of a United
States deputy marshal pinned on his breast. He held this
position from first to last during his Tombstone career.

Wyatt Earp was thirty years old when he arrived in the
city of silver and six-shooters. His face was long and of
pronounced pallor; his deep-set eyes were blue-gray;
his chin was massive; a heavy, tawny moustache hid his
mouth and drooped beneath the edges of his jaws. His
hair was as yellow as a lion's mane, his deep voice was
a booming lion-like brool, and he suggested a lion in the
slow, slithery ease of his movements and in his gaunt,
heavy-boned, loose-limbed, powerful frame.

He had been roughly moulded by the frontier and he
had the frontier's simplicity and strength, its sophisti-
cation and resourcefulness, its unillusioned self-suffi-
ciency. He followed his own silent trails with roughshod
directness. He was unaffectedly genuine. Whatever he
did, he did in deadly earnest. He was incapable of pretense or studied pose; he had no genius for the heroic
gesture. He was cold, balanced, and imperturbably calm.
If whirlwinds slumbered deep in the soul of him, no
hint of emotion showed in his face, which had the cold
stillness of sculptured stone. There was no swashbuckler
bluster about him. Nothing marked him as a desperate
man. But in his blue-gray eyes was a calm unafraidness,
as of a man not to be frightened by phantoms or realities
or anything else in the world.

With the turbulent conditions Wyatt Earp found in Tombstone, he had been familiar all his life. He was a natural master of such conditions. Probably no man of his day in the West was more logically fitted to become the man of Tombstone's hour. Brains, courage, and dominant qualities as a leader carried him quickly to the top; a myriad enemies pulled him down. He rose to power in romance and fell from power in tragedy, and the story of his rise and fall is one of the most dramatic in the history of the frontier.

Doc Holliday, the fighting ace of the Earp faction and considered by connoisseurs in deadliness the coldest-blooded killer in Tombstone, had accompanied Wyatt Earp from Dodge City. He was a rather tall, extremely slender, ash-blond, gray-eyed fellow, immaculate in attire, fastidious in his habits, temperamental, hot tempered and cold blooded, querulous and sometimes a little quarrelsome, a wit as well as a desperado. He might become quite excited if his breakfast eggs were not just so, but no man was cooler when bullets were flying. He was a consumptive, and the malady had left his face emaciated and very white and given it a look of refinement that might have passed for spirituality. One might have been tempted to suspect that this quiet, pale man with the fine gray eyes was a poet or a scholar who pored over erudite volumes under midnight lamps. But except for a few elegies done with finished elegance with his six-shooter, the doctor never displayed any poetic or literary leanings.

He was, after a kind, a cynical philosopher, and his passing observations were spiced with a dry, acrid humour. Life seemed a bitter joke to him. He was reconciled to tuberculosis, he said, because it had left him so thin that it took mighty good shooting to hit him. He was still ready to bet, however, that in the home-stretch drive, a bullet would nose out consumption at the wire.

He was an excellent shot. Buckskin Frank Leslie was the only man in Tombstone credited with being his equal in quickness and accuracy with a six-shooter. When deputized to assist the Earps in any little emergency that happened to arise, the doctor appeared with a sawed-off shotgun, deadliest of weapons, swung to his shoulder under his coat; he was not one to waste time, energy, or ammunition; when any shooting was to be done, he shot to kill.

He had been educated as a dentist. He sometimes dug out of his trunk to show to an intimate friend a souvenir that he had carried through all his peregrinations in the West. It was an old tin sign on which was painted "Dr. J. D. Holliday—Dentist," and it had once swung in front of his office in Dallas. The doctor often laughed to think that a true knight-errant and adventurer like himself ever had engaged in filling cavities and crowning molars.

A Southern man, well born and well educated, his speech was the soft slurring drawl of the South, and he could play the polished gentleman when he chose. No scruples of any kind handicapped the doctor in his busy life. Though square with his friends, who would have trusted him with their last dollar, his honesty had various shades and nuances. If honesty was convenient, he was honest; otherwise, he used a cold deck.

His courage was his one outstanding virtue. He was afraid of nothing. Despite his delicate appearance and his physical weakness, there was something in the calm, cold look of him which warned of danger. Men of gun-handle notches, whom everybody else feared, themselves feared Doc Holliday.

Holliday was born in Valdosta, Georgia, of a fine and very old Southern family, members of which still live in the little town just north of the Florida line. His ancestors had been cotton-planters and slave-holders for generations, and his father served through the Civil War as a major in the Confederate Army. The white boys of the town had reserved a swimming hole in the Withlacoochee River for their own exclusive use, and when they went to swim one day and found it filled with Negroes, young Holliday emptied his revolver among the darkies. One story says that he killed three and another that he only wounded that number. But as a result of this escapade, he disappeared from Valdosta and was never seen there again.

He was next heard of practising dentistry in Dallas. Having abandoned dentistry for gambling, he killed a man over a game of cards in Jacksboro. He killed a soldier a little later in another Texas town, and, to avoid capture by the military authorities, he rode alone across eight hundred miles of wild, unsettled country, swarming with hostile Indians, and arrived in Denver in 1876. There, in a knife duel, he almost killed Bud Ryan. He shot and seriously wounded Kid Kolton in Trinidad. He quarrelled with Mike Gordon in Las Vegas and shot him dead. He drifted then into the Texas Panhandle, where he fell in with Wyatt Earp.

"I first met Doc Holliday in Fort Griffen, Texas, in 1877," said Wyatt Earp. "I was down in that country from Dodge City after a bunch of cow thieves. There was a woman in town—well, you can call her Doc's

inamorata. Her name was Kate Fisher, but in that refined town they called her Big Nose Kate. A name like
that might suggest a big, coarse female, but Kate wasn't
like that; she was what you might call handsome, in a
way. I liked Doc; he was a witty fellow and good company; he asked me a lot of questions about Dodge and
thought he and Kate might like to come there. I had to
go to Fort Clark for a few days, and when I got back to
Fort Griffin, I found the town buzzing with excitement
over Doc and Kate.

"Doc had sat in a game of poker one night with a
fellow named Ed Bailey. This Bailey was a crooked card
man, and he was always monkeying with the deadwood, which is to say, the discards, and Doc admonished
him once or twice to quit this and play poker. Finally,
a pretty nice pot came along. Doc called and Bailey
spread down three kings. Doc didn't say a word but just
quietly pulled down the pot and threw his hand away
without showing what he held. Of course, Bailey started
a big holler.

"'I saw you palming one of those kings,' said Doc.

"'Give me that money,' roared Bailey. 'I won it and
I'll have it.'

"Doc was stacking the chips in front of him as
Bailey reached for them. Doc knocked his hand away.
Bailey went for his six-shooter and was coming up
with it when Doc drew a long knife from under his coat
collar—he had it hanging by a cord down his back—and
with a sidewise swipe below the brisket ripped Bailey
wide open.

"Doc was arrested. While he was being held in the
hotel office under guard of the town marshal and two
policemen, Bailey's gambler and cowboy friends gath-

ered in the street. The crowd kept growing and getting uglier. There was talk of getting a rope, and things began to look pretty bad for Doc. Big Nose Kate got word of what was going on and hurried to the hotel. The officers let her in, and she had a little talk with Doc and went away. Now a big nose generally means a strong, bold character—at least, so I've heard tell— and right now Big Nose Kate lived up to her nose.

"She ordered a couple of horses saddled at a livery and hitched them in an alley. Then she started a blaze in a shed back of the hotel and ran into the street yelling, 'Fire!' When, just as she had figured, the mob deserted the front of the hotel and rushed to the burning building, Kate walked into the hotel office. This time she had on a man's pants, coat, boots, and hat. From a satchel she was carrying she jerked a pair of six-shooters. Doc grabbed them and ordered the marshal and the two deputies to throw up their hands. While Doc kept the marshals covered, Kate disarmed them, and, stowing their artillery in her bag, she and Doc backed out of the door.

"When the mob got back from the fire, madder than ever and still talking about a lynching, Doc and Kate were galloping hard across the prairies on a four-hundred-mile ride to Dodge City. I found them there on my return, living in style at a hotel, and they laughed as they told me about their adventure and seemed to regard it as a fine joke."

Between Wyatt Earp and Doc Holliday, as cold, deadly men, perhaps, as the frontier knew, existed a friendship classic in its loyalty. For his friend, the coldest-blooded killer in Tombstone risked his life time and again, and only the accidents of the fighting prevented his making friendship's last supreme sacrifice. And what Doc Holliday gave in friendship, Wyatt Earp returned in a friendship as staunch.

"Doc Holliday saved my life in Dodge City once," said Wyatt Earp. "I had arrested a man known to be dangerous. His friends surrounded me to rescue him. Doc saw one of these cutthroats draw a gun and throw down to shoot me in the back. 'Look out, Wyatt,' Doc shouted. But before the words were out of his mouth, he jerked his six-shooter and shot the man who in another second would have murdered me. Lifelong friendships on the frontier were founded on such incidents as this. Doc was my friend and I was Doc's friend until he died. Many a man told me this and that about Doc Holliday —and he was no saint—but nobody on earth could knock Doc Holliday to me. He was one of the finest, cleanest men in the world, though, of course, he was a little handy with his gun and had to kill a few fellows."

So these two friends stood side by side through good and evil report, through fortune and misfortune, through thick and thin, and back to back they fought in the swirling gloom of the final storm that threatened to engulf them.

Virgil, Morgan, James, and Warren Earp, his brothers, soon joined Wyatt in Tombstone. Of the five Earps, Virgil was the eldest, Wyatt, Morgan, James, and Warren following in descending age sequence. Though Wyatt was the second born, he was the undisputed leader of the fraternal quintette by right of brains, initiative, and force of character. All were stalwart blond men, the family resemblance strong in every face, all plainly whelped in the same lion's litter. Wyatt,

Virgil, and Morgan alone played important rôles in Tombstone's colourful drama, James and Warren being looked upon by their elder brothers as mere cubs, promising, perhaps, but of an age too tender for the game of fang and claw.

Virgil Earp, who rose to historic importance as town marshal of Tombstone, had fought through the Civil War in the Union Army, was old to the frontier, and had himself served as early marshal of Dodge City. He had the stern look of a soldier and a soldier's stern sense of duty. He was a taciturn man of rough simplicity and blunt honesty, moving toward whatever destination he had in view with crushing inevitability and stolid, blind fearlessness. Morgan Earp was more headstrong and impetuous and mentally keener. With the cool poise that was a distinguishing mark of the breed, he, too, was slow to wrath, but when once aroused, fought with the same desperate, merciless courage that distinguished his two older brothers. He also had been schooled to the frontier in Dodge City.

When the railroad went through Arizona and the new town of Benson became the depot for all incoming and outgoing freight for the entire Tombstone region, Wyatt Earp for seven months rode as shotgun messenger for the Wells-Fargo Company on the Benson stages. With stages being robbed with startling frequency on all the other lines centring in Tombstone, it might be suppose that these seven months were crowded with thrilling adventures. But, on the contrary, nothing at all happened. When highwaymen saw the grim Dodge City fighter sitting up on the box with a shotgun across his knees, they left that stage alone. Not a single

Benson stage was robbed during Wyatt Earp's term of service. Bear this fact in mind. It will prove an illuminating footnote to certain events that happened later.

While Wyatt Earp was guarding Wells-Fargo treasure boxes, the Oriental saloon and gambling house, then the largest in Tombstone, got into difficulties. Dave Rickabaugh, one of the owners, had offended a clique of gamblers who were trying, by threats and gunplay, to run the proprietors out of town. Luke Short, an old-time Dodge City friend of Wyatt Earp's, was dealing in the Oriental. He was a quiet, gentlemanly fellow who, despite his diminutive stature, had a reputation as a gun fighter. Charlie Storms, formerly of Deadwood, one of the opposition gamblers, ugly and half drunk, came in.

"Any man who'll work for Rickabaugh is a yellow coyote," he snarled at Luke. Luke slid a case card out of the box and said nothing.

"You goin' to sit there and take that?" sneered Storms. Luke took a yellow stack off the five-spot and set it in the rack.

"These Dodge City fighters ain't deuce high here in Tombstone," taunted Storms. Luke paid off a bet on the queen.

Friends dragged Storms away; Luke went out to lunch. When Short returned, Storms stood in the doorway of the Oriental with a six-shooter in his hand.

"Say, you Dodge City killer, come on and fight," roared Storms. "I'll give you the first shot." Short took the first shot. Then two more for good measure. Storms fell dead.

But the killing, for which Short was acquitted in Tucson—he never returned to Tombstone—did not stop the campaign of intimidation. As a last resort, the proprietors of the Oriental offered Wyatt Earp a partnership in the place. He accepted. The new partner took over the management of the house. He moved among the patrons with a genial smile and a pair of big six-shooters buckled around him. He sent this message to the firm's enemies:

"If you fellows are still looking for trouble, drop into the Oriental and I'll fill you so full that it'll run out of your ears. I aim to please."

The sight of the gaunt old lion ready and perhaps eager for battle, discouraged the gamblers of the hostile faction. They thought him, as one expressed it, "too gosh-darned accommodatin'." There were no more attempts at terrorism. The Oriental became the most orderly place in town. Also one of the most popular and prosperous. As part proprietor of a big saloon and gambling house, Wyatt Earp seemed on the road to affluence. He resigned his position with the express company, and Morgan Earp succeeded him as shotgun messenger on the Benson stages.

Bat Masterson, former sheriff of Dodge City, joined Wyatt Earp in Tombstone but remained only a few months. Bat returned to Dodge City when he learned that his brother, Jim, was having trouble with George Peacock and Al Updegraft. Peacock and Jim Masterson were partners in the Lady Gay saloon and dance hall in Dodge, and Updegraft was their bartender. Bat went by stage to Deming, where he struck the railroad. As he dropped off the train in Dodge, he saw Peacock and Updegraft coming toward the depot and opened fire. Updegraft got a bullet through the lungs and staggered back into the dance hall. Peacock dodged behind a

calaboose across the railroad tracks, and Bat behind a
box car, and they shot it out until their ammunition was
exhausted. Neither Bat nor Peacock was injured.
Updegraft was in bed for two months, and when
pneumonia set in, he died.

"Bat Masterson was a brave man," said Wyatt Earp,
whose estimate of the famous sheriff is of interest. "As a
peace officer he deserved all the celebrity he ever had,
but as a killer his reputation has been greatly exag-
gerated. Old stories credit Bat with having killed
twenty-seven men. The truth is, he never killed but four
in his life.

"I knew Bat when he was a kid in Wichita and he
and I were bosom friends in Dodge. I hunted buffalo
with him when he was hardly big enough to handle a
rifle and I've been with him on many a round-up after
outlaws. I shared the same home with him in Denver
after my Tombstone days were over and kept up a correspondence with him until his death a few years ago
in New York. I know his career from beginning to end.

"Bat killed his first man at Sweetwater, Texas, when
he was eighteen years old. While he was serving as a
civilian scout with the army, a dance-hall girl in Sweetwater took a shine to him. A cavalry sergeant named
King grew jealous. When King went into the dance hall
one night and saw Bat and the girl dancing together, he
drew his gun. The girl saw him first and threw her arms
around Bat to protect him. King's bullet killed her and,
passing through her body, wounded Bat in the thigh.
As the girl fell, Bat put a bullet through King's heart.

"When I was marshal of Dodge in 1877, I went out
with a posse to hunt some train robbers who had held
up a Sante Fe express at Kinsley, and in my absence,

Ed Masterson, Bat's brother, acted as marshal. Some Texas cowboys were raising cain in a dance hall, and Bat and Ed went to quiet the disturbance. At the door, Jack Wagner, one of the cowboys, shot and killed Ed Masterson. As Ed reeled out into the street, Bat killed Wagner. When Alf Walker, the ringleader of the cowboys, came rushing out of the hall with a six-shooter Bat shot him twice. Walker ran up the street and through a saloon and dropped dead in an alley. Bat went into the dance hall and opened up on the other cowboys, but they piled out through the windows and got away.

"The next man on Bat's list was Updegraft. Bat showed me the message he received in Tombstone and it was not from his brother. It didn't say what kind of trouble Jim Masterson was mixed up in. It only said that Peacock and Updegraft were threatening to kill him. Bat had had a quarrel with Jim and was hardly on speaking terms with him at the time but he took the first stage out of Tombstone to go back to Dodge and help his brother. That was the old frontier's brand of loyalty. These four—King, Wagner, Walker, and Updegraft—are the only men Bat ever killed, and there has always been a doubt whether Updegraft died of pneumonia or the wound from Bat's bullet."

The Tombstone stage was set and the drama getting under way when John H. Behan, his entrance slightly delayed, as befitted that of so important an actor, made his bow as the first sheriff of Cochise County. He was appointed to the position by the governor when Cochise County was organized out of Pima County in the winter of 1880–1881, and Tombstone was made the county seat. Behan had lived in Arizona since 1863, having come across the plains from Missouri, had had varied frontier experience, and had served as recorder and sheriff of Yavapai county.

Already in middle life, he was a bustling, self-important man, never too busy to stop and shake hands or clap somebody on the shoulder with a great show of friendliness. Everybody in Tombstone was soon calling him Johnny Behan.

Johnny Behan was a good man misplaced in a tough mining camp, his life and character twisted by circumstances into which he had been hurled by one of destiny's unfortunate accidents. In a happier environment, he would have been considered a splendid character. He was sunny, companionable, kindly, honest, generous, loyal. But in Tombstone he was a twenty-two calibre man in a forty-five calibre town. Tombstone thirsted for strong waters; John Behan had only sarsaparilla and lemon pop on tap.

He was not devoid of courage or initiative. But his indecision left an impression of timidity, and he lacked the force to finish what he started. He was vacillating, flustered, impulsive. He darted at a problem instead of calmly thinking it out. He had energy but clouded vision. He was a man of words rather than action. He blustered and failed to live up to his bluster. He talked like a big man and acted like a little one. He was perhaps not wholly inoffensive and free from guile but, judged by his Tombstone career, he seems to have been rather futile. However, Johnny Behan was nobody's fool. He knew a cholla from a prickly pear when the desert wind was southerly.

But if, as a man, Johnny Behan was small potatoes, as a politician he was some pumpkins. Canny and sly and very crafty was the sheriff at the deep and subtle game of politics. He knew every crook and turn and sharp angle of it and was a wizard at all the tricks. When he smiled a little more than usual, people used to say, "Johnny's probably up to some top-and-bottom trick or dealing from a marked deck." Or if his face was particularly lamblike and innocent, he was suspected of having an ace up his sleeve. No amateur politician had any business sitting in at Johnny Behan's game. The man who gambled with the sheriff at politics had to nurse his chips and play his cards close to his belly, or he would find himself pushing his chair back from the table without bed money or the price of a breakfast. As a politician, Johnny Behan was a foxy, dangerous boy.

Sheriff Behan was hardly more than comfortably settled in office when Wyatt Earp announced himself a candidate for sheriff at the next election. So the two men were political rivals from the first, and political rivalry developed into personal enmity. Friendly with Sheriff Behan and solidly arrayed against the Earps were Curly Bill and his outlaws. After Wyatt Earp had on one occasion knocked Curly Bill about the head with the butt of a six-shooter and dragged him off to jail, the freebooter chieftain nursed his wrath and thirsted for revenge. Sharing his deadly antipathy were such leading figures in the outlaw confederacy as Ike, Finn, and Billy Clanton, ferocious Old Man Clanton, their father, Tom and Frank McLowery, John Ringo, Pete Spence, and Frank Stilwell.

A power to be dreaded and reckoned with were these outlaws. They were strong in numbers, and most of the dwellers up and down the lonely reaches of the San Pedro, Sulphur Springs, and San Simon valleys were either their avowed friends and allies or maintained a

show of friendliness through fear. If the Earps ruled in
Tombstone, all the wild region in which Tombstone
was an oasis lay under the shadow of outlaw dominance
and was, it might be said, in fief to these murderous and
powerful bands. The hostility of the outlaws, counte-
nanced, it might seem, by Sheriff Behan's friendly attitude toward them, finally brought in the day when
the power of the Earps was broken and they withdrew
from Tombstone forever, leaving behind them a crimson
trail to mark their vengeance.

This, then, was the line-up in a situation that rapidly
developed into hair-trigger tension. On one side Sheriff
Behan and his puissant political machine, with murderous outlaw hatreds in the snadowy background; on
the other side, Wyatt, Virgil, and Morgan Earp and
Doc Holliday, as the fighting force of the Earp faction,
entrenched in power in Tombstone but ringed with
enemies who watched and waited unseen in the deserts
and mountains.

Wyatt Earp cleaned up Tombstone. His motives may
have been those of an honest champion of good government, or they may have been those of a self-seeking
politician establishing a record on which he might
stand for election in the shrievalty contest. One's choice
is optional in the matter. But the fact remains that he
did a good job. His faction became known as the Law
and Order party. He had the support of the best citizens.
The Tombstone papers of the period were outspoken
in his praise.

Sheriff Behan's administration, on the other hand,
was repeatedly and severely criticized. His complacent
relations with the outlaws particularly brought about
his head the protests of citizens and the denunciations

of the press. It is not surprising, in view of the bitterness of the political situation, that all the charges made against the Earps had their origin in Sheriff Behan's faction. The desperate character of Wyatt Earp and his colleagues was pointed out. It was hinted that the Law and Order party was controlled by gunmen bent only upon their own aggrandizement. Vague rumours were set going that the Earps were in collusion with stage robbers. Suspicion was aroused in the public mind, but with the machinery of the law in his control, Sheriff Behan took no steps to arrest or bring to trial the men against whom these whispered insinuations were directed.

The long-smouldering feud between the two men might have been comic if its results had been less tragic. Wyatt Earp ignored the little sheriff or roused himself only occasionally to make a lazy gesture as if brushing a fly from the end of his nose. It was as if a truculent pigmy with twanging bow were shooting pins at some drowsy old saga giant. But when Johnny Behan fell back upon the ingratiating tactics of a politician, the advantage was all on his side. Johnny Behan was friendly, Wyatt Earp was grim; Johnny Behan smiled, Wyatt Earp shot from the hip; Johnny Behan was the personification of the glad hand, Wyatt Earp the personification of the trigger finger. . . . A lion stalks with measured stride through the dewy shadows. Back of him is the darkness of the donga. The moon is a sickle of silver in a glowing green sky against which a tall palm leans blackly. The grunting roar of the old wilderness monarch rolls with dim, menacing clamour across the veldt. From the mimosa thickets a fox fills the twilight with a thin uproar of shrill, savage barks.

CHAPTER IV

M R. HENRY SCHNEIDER sat at a pine-board table in the Chinaman's in Charleston and ate his breakfast in silence. Mr. Schneider was the chief engineer at the stamp mill of the Tombstone Mining and Milling Company. He could see through the front window of the restaurant the big plant on the other side of the San Pedro just across the bridge, its stacks pouring out a steady stream of smoke that went drifting over the hills. The January morning was cold; a heavy frost still covered the ground; the current of the narrow river looked almost black between the snowy ice sheets projecting from the banks, and the tracks of teams were still visible in the white rime on the plank flooring of the bridge. Mr. Schneider was an engineer of some note and a high-salaried employee at the stamp mill, which was kept busy day and night reducing ore from the Tombstone mines. He was a rather haughty, aloof man whose morning mood was usually morose and disagreeable and who required a good strong cup of coffee and several hours of sunlight to thaw him out into ordinary business urbanity.

At a near-by table Mr. Robert Petty, the village blacksmith, and Mr. John O'Rourke were devouring ham and eggs with some gusto. Mr. O'Rourke especially seemed in a mood of cheerfulness.

"I didn't make no killing last night," Mr. O'Rourke was saying. "But I done pretty good. The deuce stood by me. That card is certainly good to me."

Mr. O'Rourke was a gambler of the variety sometimes referred to as tin-horn. He was what might be termed, if one wished to be brutally frank, an insignificant little runt, wizened, undersized, colourless, with a prominent nose and huge ears that stood out from his head. He hung around Charleston gambling houses and saloons and dealt stud or monte when he had a chance and played faro if he happened to be in funds. The card on the faro layout for which Mr. O'Rourke showed a particular predilection was the deuce. He stacked up his chips on the deuce; he was never known to copper it, always played it open, and the deuce rewarded his blind faith by winning for him with startling frequency. Few people had ever been sufficiently interested in him to learn his real name, and because of his mania for backing his favourite card, he had become commonly known among the gamblers of Charleston and Tombstone as Johnny Behind-the-Deuce.

It happened that Mr. Schneider, Mr. Petty, and Johnny Behind-the-Deuce arose from breakfast at the same time and, having paid their bills at the front counter to Hop Sing, stood for a few moments warming themselves about the stove in the corner of the restaurant. To the engineer, Johnny remarked pleasantly that it was a cold day. Schneider gave him a sour look and did not reply.

"I say it's a cold day," Johnny repeated, on the chance that the engineer had failed to hear his shrewd observation.

Mr. Schneider preserved a scowling silence.

"Go to hell!" snarled Johnny. "I wonder if you are too deaf to hear that?"

Mr. Schneider heard that quite distinctly and, flaring into a rage, snorted out profane abuse. Mr. Petty pulled Johnny by the sleeve out the door into the street. But the cold air outside had no effect on Johnny's anger, which grew hotter.

"I guess that feller thinks he's too big to talk to the likes of me," he growled.

"What do you care?" soothed Mr. Petty. "Leave him alone."

The two men stopped near the end of the bridge. While Mr. Petty was still trying to calm Johnny, Mr. Schneider came bustling along on his way to his office at the mill across the river.

"I got a notion to learn you some manners," snapped Johnny as the engineer passed.

Mr. Schneider halted and, glaring furiously, reached into his trousers pocket. Johnny jerked out a revolver and killed him. An unopened pocketknife was found in the dead man's hand.

Constable George McKelvey placed Johnny under arrest. As he started for the calaboose with his prisoner, the mill whistle burst into a long-continued roar. The mill hands began to pour from the buildings. "I guess they've heard about it over there," said McKelvey, and began to revolve emergency plans. The crowd at the mill started toward town. McKelvey headed for a livery stable instead of the calaboose. The mob stormed into the streets. "Get a rope," was the cry. "Hang him to the bridge." McKelvey smuggled his prisoner out of the livery stable by the back way into a buckboard to which a span of mules had been hastily hitched.

"This is a pretty mess," remarked McKelvey as the two men settled themselves into the buggy. "Tombstone is nine miles away, but I'll get you there if I can."

A moment later the mob, yelling and shaking fists in disappointed rage, saw Constable McKelvey and Johnny Behind-the-Deuce thundering across the bridge and pointing out on the road for Tombstone, the team of mules at a dead run.

The flight of the prisoner presented a problem, but the workmen whose engineer had been so ruthlessly shot down were in earnest and were not to be so easily cheated. They hurriedly prepared for pursuit. They searched Charleston for saddle horses; they commandeered buggies and spring wagons; they armed themselves with six-shooters and rifles. This cost time, and the two fugitives were laying the miles behind them. But at length the crowd was ready. Fifty men on horseback set out on the trail at breakneck speed. Others in wagons, clattering far behind in a straggling procession, hoped at least to be in at the death.

Constable McKelvey and Johnny Behind-the-Deuce had passed quickly out of sight through a gap in the hills that border the San Pedro. From a height near the old Brunckow mine, Johnny Behind-the-Deuce had a last distant glimpse of Charleston. He could detect no great stir or confusion; the town seemed quiet enough.

"Maybe they gave it up," he said.

"Maybe," replied McKelvey.

McKelvey pulled his tired mules to a trot. He would conserve their stamina. He might have to call on them yet for all the speed they had to give. The Tombstone road was no boulevard. All the way it wound with a thousand crooks and turns through a roughly broken country covered with cactus and mesquite. It climbed over high hills, skirted the edges of ravines, came down abruptly into sandy arroyos and climbed steeply out again.

When the buckboard had clambered out of Twin Gulches past Robbers' Roost, Johnny Behind-the-Deuce saw far back a long, trailing veil of dust sweeping up from behind a ridge in filmy whorls against the sky. He watched it with the fixity of fascination. A horseman galloped out of the dust over the crest of the road. A swarm of others came riding hard after him. Small in the distance, they looked like menacing goblins to his frightened eyes. He half rose from his seat, his hand clutching McKelvey's shoulders.

"Here they come!" he yelled in McKelvey's ear.

McKelvey lashed his mules into a run. Of a sudden came a soft tiny noise like the smothered popping of a cork. A sharper metallic ping like the vibration of a taut, mile-long wire. Then the distinct and unmistakable thin whine of a bullet. Spouts of dust shot into the air beside the wheels. The road behind began to dance with dusty puffs as under a thunder shower. The faint clatter of hoofs grew into a rushing storm of sound. McKelvey and Johnny Behind-the-Deuce bent forward in their seats with white, tense faces. Around the flanks of the plunging mules McKelvey wrapped his rawhide whip. Down the slopes, up the grades flew the swaying buckboard, taking the curves on two wheels. The pursuers were gaining rapidly, firing at every jump, yelling like savages. For Johnny Behind-the-Deuce it looked like cases in a losing deal; a skeleton hand seemed reaching out for his last stack of chips.

Two miles out of Tombstone stood Jack McCann's Last Chance saloon. McKelvey and Johnny saw the long adobe roadhouse looming ahead with one last flicker of hope.

"Guess McCann's is our last chance all right," said McKelvey between clenched teeth. "We'll never beat 'em into Tombstone."

"If we get inside, maybe we can stand 'em off," replied Johnny desperately.

McCann had just mounted a race mare that stood saddled in front of his saloon. This filly was a thoroughbred named Molly McCarthy and had won local fame by showing her heels to the best horses around Tombstone. McCann had her entered for a race over at the Watervale track on the Contention road and was preparing to give her an exercise gallop to tune her up for this event. A slim, spirited beauty was Molly Mc-Carthy, and her satin skin sparkled as she champed the bit and pranced about on her clean, antelope legs in her eagerness for the run. McCann had turned her head to the road, when he caught sight of the pell-mell chase bearing down upon him. He stared in amazement. Well, what the divil?

"Take this lad behind you quick and get him into Tombstone before those fellows lynch him," shouted McKelvey as he brought his mules back on their haunches.

McCann didn't know Johnny Behind-the-Deuce, but he numbered many outlaws among his friends and had a lurking sympathy for fellows in trouble with the law. Many an all-night carouse Curly Bill and his merry men had had in the Last Chance saloon. And here was a

sporting proposition that might stir the blood of any
sporting man. McCann wasted no time in questions,
but brought Molly McCarthy alongside the buckboard.

"Pile on," he said.

As Johnny Behind-the-Deuce wrapped his arms around
McCann's waist, the mare broke at a bound into racing
speed as if at the drop of a starter's flag and went skim-
ming over the road with long, frictionless strides.
Drawing his jaded mules off to the side of the road,
McKelvey watched McCann and Johnny Behind-the-
Deuce dwindle in the distance. As the lynching party
roared past, McKelvey rubbed his chin and grinned.

"You'll play hell catching him now," he yelled cheerfully.

As McCann and Johnny Behind-the-Deuce rode into
Tombstone, the mine whistles on the hill began to
boom. News of the murder of the engineer had been
telegraphed ahead from Charleston. Miners flocked from
the shafts and streamed down the hill toward town.

Wyatt Earp was dealing faro in the Oriental. Doc
Holliday lolled in the lookout chair. Virgil Earp lounged
against the bar. Business was dull. The place was as
quiet as a prayer meeting. McCann and Johnny Behind-
the-Deuce burst in upon the peaceful scene.

"Mob coming," McCann broke out breathlessly.
"Going to lynch this boy. Hurry up. Do something, for
Christ's sake. No time to lose."

Wyatt Earp slid one card off the deck and then another. He took in a bet or two. He paid a few winning
wagers. With the skill of old habit, he levelled off the
tops of the stacks of chips in the check-rack and carefully evened them along the sides with the backs of his
fingers. He overlooked no detail of customary routine.

Then he turned up his box. The game, for the present, was over.

"Hold on to your chips, boys," he said to the players. "I'll cash 'em as soon as I've finished with this little business matter."

As a gambler, he pushed back his chair. He rose as an officer of the law. Stepping to the front door, he saw a block west, at Fifth and Tough Nut streets, an excited crowd gathered about the newly arrived horsemen from Charleston. On beyond, the hill was swarming with miners. The situation impressed him as having possibilities. But the Oriental, facing on two streets and with great doors and windows, was no place in which to stand off a mob. There was a bowling alley across Allen Street in the next block to the north, narrow and wedged between stores and with doors only at front and rear. A handful of determined men might hold it against a multitude. Wyatt Earp escorted Johnny Behind-the-Deuce to the bowling alley. He posted Virgil Earp at the rear and Doc Holliday behind the locked front door. He was ready now.

He had never met Johnny Behind-the-Deuce before. He had seen him a few times around Tombstone gambling houses and had chuckled over his strange nickname and the origin of it. He knew nothing of the right or wrong of the killing of the Charleston engineer. But now this little shrimp of a fellow had been placed in his custody; it was his duty as an officer to protect him. This sense of official duty—nothing else—actuated him. If he had to die in performance of his duty, he would die.

An ominous confused murmur rose from the direction of the hill, a deep moaning bellow like that of brutes stirring to fury, the note of menace unmistakable. The mob was starting. Here it came in a rushing, crushing mass eastward through Fifth Street. It surrounded the Oriental. A yell went up like a rocket—"He's in the bowling alley." With a roar, the mob turned for the rush to the bowling alley. As it changed front, it came face to face with Wyatt Earp at a distance of twenty paces. He stood alone in the middle of Allen Street, a double-barrelled shotgun resting in the crook of his elbow.

"Hold on, boys." Wyatt Earp raised his hand and for a moment kept it poised in air. "Don't make any fool play. There ain't no sense in this."

The mob halted in its forward sweep.

"Where 've you got that murdering rat hid?"

"He's right in there." Wyatt Earp jerked his thumb at the bowling alley. "And he's going to stay in there. He's my prisoner now, and you fellers ain't goin' to get him."

"The hell we ain't."

"You boys better disperse." Wyatt Earp said it as calmly as he might have said "Tut-tut" to naughty urchins in school. "Go on home. Go on back to work. I'm here to take care of this prisoner. And I'm going to take care of him."

The silence was shattered by sudden fierce yells.

"Ki-yi-ki-yi-yip!"

"Wa-wa-wa-wa—wa-hoo!"

The shrieks were broken into wild staccato by tapping the mouth with the hand. There were old Apache fighters in that crowd. The front ranks began to stamp up and down like savages doing a war dance.

"Here we go, boys."

"Smash in the bowling alley."

"String the dirty varmint to a telegraph pole."

Wyatt Earp cocked both barrels of his shotgun.

"Come on, then, you yellow curs. Let's see you get him."

His booming voice was like the roar of a lion at bay as he flung the challenge in the mob's teeth. Again the crowd stood still in wavering indecision.

One foot advanced, his shotgun held tensely across his breast ready for instant action, Wyatt Earp stood, one man against five hundred. Grimly alone. Hopelessly isolated for the moment from all the rest of the world. No help to fall back on, no chance to run, no shelter, no place of refuge. Just a man out there in the middle of the street, all by himself with only his own strength to depend on and only his own courage to save him. Before him a mob thirsting for blood, closing in for the kill, its victim almost within reach. The front line, stretching across the street from wall to wall, bristled with six-shooters and rifles, every face twisted and flaming with passion. One solitary man blocked the road to vengeance.

"That fool's bluffing." The shout was vibrant with impatient resentment. "Call his bluff and watch him quit."

Wyatt Earp brought his shotgun to his shoulder with a snap. At the level of a man's heart, he swung its muzzle very slowly across the crowd from one side of the street to the other and very slowly back again.

"Don't make any mistake," he flung back. "I'll blow the belly off of the first man that makes a move."

The storm was working to the bursting point. This was ridiculous. One man hold back five hundred? Rush him, disarm him, brush him aside.

"What's the matter out there in front?"

"Go on!"

The men behind began to push and shoulder forward.
Flickering waves of movement told of gathering momentum for a fresh start. A powerful thrust made the front
ranks bend and sway. It was like a ripple presaging the
final rush.

"Kill him!"

Wyatt Earp's jaws set. His eyes blazed. His face in
that tense moment was so marble-white that his tawny
moustache looked black against it. Again he swept the
crowd with his levelled gun, and death lurked in the
black depths of those twin muzzles.

"Kill me." His voice had a conversational steadiness.
"I'm ready. Ought to be easy; there are enough of you.
But I'll do a little killing myself. You can get me; but
I'll take a few of you to hell with me."

The drama had rushed to crisis. Here was a proposi-
tion. They could take it or leave it. He was ready to die.
If they were, too, all right. Yes, they could kill him.
One shot would do the business. They couldn't miss him.
But he would take some of them to the grave with him.
He might get two or three. Or half a dozen might
crumple down under the scattering double charge of
buckshot. It was sure death for some of them. Did they
want to gamble? Were they willing to take the chance?
Well?

Silence fell. For a space the mob stood motionless,
hesitating, undecided, weighing the odds. Then abruptly
the tension snapped. Some men in front, looking a little
sheepish, drew back into the crowd. Others followed.
The front line grew ragged; it was breaking up. Not
much sense, after all, in getting killed for a dirty little
blackguard like Johnny Behind-the-Deuce. The law
might hang him anyhow. This lynching business was,

pretty wild and crazy if you stopped to think about it. Just as well to let the law take its course. Men at the outer edges began to walk away. Gaps and lanes opened in the thinning ranks. Throngs began to bustle through the side streets like flood waters draining off through sluiceways. Soon all had disappeared except a few small groups that still hung about the corner. The storm had passed; peaceful sunlight once more bathed the empty streets. Wyatt Earp, leaning on his shotgun, stood in silence and watched the mob melt away. Then he stepped with an air of leisureliness over to the sidewalk.

"Go down to the O. K. corral, Doc," he said to Holliday in the casual voice of one arranging a detail of business routine, "and see if Johnny Montgomery can let us have a spring wagon. I guess I'll send Johnny Behind-the-Deuce over to Tucson."

Johnny Behind-the-Deuce was taken in the spring wagon under strong guard to Tucson. Ten heavily armed men on horseback accompanied him as far as Dennis's ranch but, as no attack developed, turned back to Tombstone. Johnny broke jail at Tucson before his trial, and though Papago Indian trailers were used to track him, he was not recaptured. He disappeared from the Southwest, and whatever became of the murderous little scalawag with the funny pseudonym no one in that country knows to this day.

CHAPTER V

CURLY BILL, most famous outlaw in Arizona's history, came from Texas, but when or how or why is one of several mysteries in his life, his end being as enigmatic as his beginning. He was a mediæval robber baron in the blue flannel shirt and white sombrero of a cowboy. He rode at times with thirty or forty tall fellows at his back, and it was said he could gather a hundred men-at-arms within a day if needful occasion arose. All the outlaws of southeastern Arizona owned some sort of allegiance to him. He lived boldly and jovially. After the dangers and hardships of a cattle-stealing raid or an attack upon a Mexican smuggler train in some mountain defile, he took his ease in his strongholds, with wassail and high revel and his merry men around him.

He was, to the eye, a good-natured, rollicking chap, heavy-set, black-eyed, with a shock of curly black hair. But for all his roly-poly look and the dimples that showed in his round, swarthy face when he laughed, he was a powerful fellow and as quick and tricky and dangerous as a panther. Though his career is a tale of romance, he was strictly a business man with no romance in him. He planned shrewdly, and murder was a routine detail in his trade of adventure. Some might tell you that John Ringo was his brains. This is not true.

Curly Bill had brains of his own, and sharp, resourceful brains they were, amply sufficient for all the generalship necessary in the life he led. Moreover, Curly Bill had the decisiveness in action that Ringo lacked. Curly Bill led, Ringo followed.

Curly Bill, in his earlier days, was the scourge of the Arizona ranges. He stole cattle from the scattered ranchers. He ran off horses from army posts and frequently had the soldiers on his trail. He soon found a more lucrative field in Mexico. Millions of longhorn cattle pastured half-wild on the vast ranges of Sonora and Chihuahua. Some of the wealthy hacendados of these two states just over the international line owned so many cattle they could not estimate the number within a hundred thousand head. Rich quarry were these countless herds for Curly Bill and his buccaneers who, stealing across the border, rounded up cattle from plains and foothills and brought them back in rushing stampedes, sometimes a thousand head at a single eagle swoop. But these forays were not without danger. The border Mexicans were hardy fellows, seasoned in warfare against Yaqui and Apache, and not infrequently the rustlers had stiff brushes and running fights with rurales or vaqueros and had to battle for their lives before they won to safety on American soil.

Markets for his stolen cattle were plentiful. Curly Bill did a thriving trade, it is said, with contractors who supplied San Carlos and other Indian reservations with beef. Other buyers, equally unscrupulous, shipped the pilfered steers East or sold them to frontier slaughter houses. And, it may be whispered confidentially as a deep, dark secret known only to everybody in Arizona, wealthy stockmen newly established in the country

swelled their foundation herds with cattle that Curly
Bill had stolen below the line.

So it will be seen Curly Bill was no cheap horse thief,
but a robber operating on a scale of wholesale mag-
nificence never known before along the international
border. He rose in time to prestige as an international
menace, and his depredations became a subject of discussion in Congress and of diplomatic correspondence
with Mexico.

Curly Bill's first recorded exploit in Tombstone's
history was not impressive. Frederick White, Tombstone's first town marshal, a two-fisted fighting man,
kept sleepless vigil over the town and was fearless in
his efforts to preserve order. He had taken counsel
with Wyatt Earp who, out of the wisdom of Dodge
City experience, cautioned the marshal against permit-
ting any shooting off of firearms within the city limits.

"The fellow who finds himself safe in shooting holes
in the atmosphere," said Wyatt Earp, "will, the first
thing you know, be shooting holes in citizens."

So Marshal White issued a ukase that anyone who
against the peace and dignity of Tombstone presumed
to fire a gun in town would suffer the full penalty of
the law, which meant a fine and the calaboose.

Curly Bill, new to Arizona, was just beginning to be
heard of as an outlaw. Mere reputation for lawless
deeds out in the mesquite jungles was not regarded as
just cause for arrest in the silver camp, and Curly Bill
came and went at his sweet will, and was a familiar
figure in saloons and gambling places. Wherever he got
it, he had money in plenty and spent it with a free hand.
Saloon loungers were sure of free drinks as long as Curly
Bill was in town, and when Curly Bill sat down at a

faro table, the dealer dropped his customary air of languorous indifference and straightened up for swift, stiff play.

With some roistering cowboy companions, Curly Bill emerged from a saloon on Allen Street one midnight, and it seemed fitting to the company to wind up the evening's entertainment with a salvo from their six-shooters, the same being an amusement dear to the cowboy heart. So everyone took a random shot at the moon, except Curly Bill, who refrained from wasting lead, having theories of his own on the advisability of keeping a six-shooter constantly loaded against all emergencies. When Marshal White came running to investigate this breach of the peace, the cowboys scattered, and Curly Bill, dodging across the street, stood in the shadow of a building in an open lot. Spying him out, Marshal White rushed over and demanded his gun.

"I didn't do none o' that shootin'," snarled Curly Bill.

"Gimme that gun o' yours," ordered the marshal.

Curly Bill slid his weapon from its holster and was in the act of handing it over when Wyatt Earp ran up behind and threw his arms about him. Marshal White at the same instant seized the gun, but, as he was wresting it from Curly Bill's grasp, the weapon was discharged and the marshal fell with a mortal wound. As the gun flamed, Wyatt Earp bent his six-shooter, as they say, over Curly Bill's head and, knocking him down, hustled him off to jail, where the outlaw nursed his split scalp and flamed into bitterness against Wyatt Earp for this abrupt manhandling—a bitterness that grew bitterer through the years and never died until Curly Bill himself died.

Marshal White was dead within a few hours, and
when the news of his death spread through the town, a
crowd gathered at the jail and threatened to lynch Curly
Bill, but was persuaded to disperse by Wyatt Earp
who thus saved the life of the man who was to become
one of his relentless enemies.

After a preliminary hearing before Justice Gray,
Curly Bill, who gave his name as William Brocius, as
appears by the official records, though old-timers who
knew him say it was William Graham, was removed to
Tucson where he stood trial before Justice Neugass.
Curly Bill testified that Marshal White had caused his
own death by the violence with which he had seized
the outlaw's six-shooter. This view of the fatality was
sustained by Wyatt Earp on the witness stand and by a
dying statement made under oath by Marshal White
and submitted in court. Thus exonerated by the two
officers concerned in the affair, Curly Bill was acquitted,
Justice Neugass holding the tragedy "a misadventure."

Curly Bill afterward boasted that he had killed
Marshal White intentionally. The outlaw declared that
he had presented his six-shooter butt foremost but,
slipping a forefinger inside the trigger guard, had trickily
whirled the weapon around end for end and fired as
Marshal White seized it. This story may possibly
have been true, though the details of the tragedy as
they came out in court seemed to discredit it. If Curly
Bill fired with malice aforethought, the trick was so
deftly performed that it deceived not only such a six-
shooter expert as Wyatt Earp but also the man who
died from the bullet.

The tragedy that deprived Tombstone of its first
town marshal was effective, it may be mentioned in

passing, in advancing materially the fortunes of the
Earps. Marshal White was killed October 27, 1880, and
at a general election a few days later, Virgil Earp was
chosen without opposition to fill the vacancy. With
Virgil Earp at the helm of police affairs and Wyatt Earp
in an important Federal position, the Earps were in a
way to become politically powerful.

Much more characteristic of Curly Bill than this
early Tombstone adventure was a later one in which
the principal rôle was enacted by the only man who
ever played a joke on the outlaw chief. Dick Lloyd was
an old cowboy as seriously stupid as a range steer and
perfectly harmless until he came to town and got drunk
enough to imagine himself a bad man. When he rode
into Fort Thomas one hot dusty day from Bear Springs
Valley over in the Grahams, he was dry with a five-
months' thirst. Tying his paint pony to a mesquite tree,
he clanked into E. Mann's saloon, where, as it happened,
Curly Bill was playing poker. Around the table with the
outlaw leader were such convivial spirits as John
Ringo, Joe Hill, Tom and Frank McLowery, Ike Clanton, and Jim Hughes, and the game had been roaring
for two days and nights without interruption. After a
few rounds of raw whisky with the genial E. Mann,
Dick Lloyd wandered with a sunrise smile to the poker
table. These rustlers were old friends of his. As a cowboy
in off the range to spend his money, he had had many a
social glass with them in Charleston and Galeyville, and
he greeted them with boisterous goodfellowship. "Hello,
Curly. . . . Howdy, Ringo. . . . Put her there, Hill. . .
How's all the boys?"

"I've knowed old Dick ever sence he worked for the
Diamond A over in the Animas," remarked Curly Bill

when Lloyd had gone back to the bar, "and a better hand never punched cows."

After Dick had had a few more drinks with E. Mann, the two men walked to the front door. There the cowboy, with no apparent reason, pulled his six-shooter and hauled up and threw down, as they say, on the genial E. Mann. The bullet creased the saloon-keeper's neck as he dodged behind the bar, leaving a scar that became a lifelong mystery, E. Mann being too drunk ever to remember why he was shot, and Dick Lloyd being past the point of explanations. This was the beginning of the affair.

Reeling across the street, Dick climbed on his pinto pony. Drawing his Winchester from its saddle scabbard and sticking the muzzle high over his head, he fired a shot by way of advertising the show, securing Fort Thomas's instant and undivided attention.

"Whee-e-e-e-e!"

Raising a war whoop, he went charging through the street, shooting up the town with fine abandon, his devastating course marked by crashing windows and splintered store fronts and citizens running madly for cover. When he chanced to spy the fine-looking horses of the Curly Bill outfit hitched in a corral, he abandoned his sorry pinto and mounted a rangy bay. This animal belonged to Joe Hill, now sitting in the poker game in E. Mann's saloon, as dangerous an hombre as rode with Curly Bill, and incidentally the black sheep of one of the best-known families in Arizona, Joe Hill not being his name.

Mounted now in style, Dick came curving out of the corral on the dead run and again went careering up and down the street, yelling and pumping lead at everything in view. But all the citizens having ducked out of sight, Dick, as an actor giving a high-class performance, felt the loss of his audience. Tearing up and down an empty street with nobody to shoot at wasn't much fun. A brilliant inspiration flashed upon him. He would ride into the bar and break up the poker game. That would be a great joke on Curly Bill. His stupid drunken face twitched in a gargoyle grin as he drew rein in front of the saloon. Guiding his stumbling horse up on the board sidewalk, he bent low in the saddle as he rode through the door.

For an instant there was profound silence. Then the saloon seemed to explode with a roar of six-shooters. Out of the door the horse lunged, snorting and wild-eyed, saddle empty, pommel shot away. Blue smoke drifted out into the street. The old cowboy's joke had been a riot. Laughing with huge enjoyment, Curly Bill and the rustlers settled back to their card game. The humorist lay sprawled in the middle of the floor, shot all to pieces.

"Old Dick," remarked Curly Bill, "was a good feller. Gimme three kyards."

"But what gits me," drawled Joe Hill, "is why that bughouse rep-tile—two to me—as soon as he gits his war paint on . . ."

"Bet you ten," said Curly Bill, shoving in a stack.

"I shorely never would have suspicioned nohow that that locoed tarantler, with me a-settin' here playin' poker and him knowin' it——I call."

"Aces up," said Curly Bill.

"Good hand. But what I can't figure out is how in the hell that simple-minded pifflicated centipede ever had the cold guts to come ridin' in here on my own hoss."

"Old Dick never meant no harm," said Curly Bill, skinning down his cards and reaching for the pot. "He was jest drunk and havin' a little fun."

They dressed old Dick in a brand-new suit of black clothes with white shirt, white collar, and black bow tie, Curly Bill contributing the money and insisting on such mortuary regalia.

"Them old duds of Dick's," he said, "wuz good enough fer ridin' range, but now he's dead, he oughter look stylish like a regular corpse."

The spring-wagon hearse went at a gallop out of town, the outlaws clattering behind and firing at every jump. At the grave in the cactus on the hill, Curly Bill tucked a pint of whisky beneath the dead man's folded hands.

"You might, maybe, need a swig along the trail, Dick," he said.

Beer bottles popped as the body was lowered to its rest on rawhide riatas.

"Here's how, old cowboy," said John Ringo, holding up his bottle. "You went out crazy drunk, but you'll have a hell of a long time to sleep it off."

They set the empty beer bottles around the mound and placed a quart whisky bottle at the head. Then, with a last six-shooter volley over the grave, the outlaws swung into their saddles and galloped back to their poker game in E. Mann's saloon. The man who played a joke on Curly Bill had passed into history.

Curly Bill, it was said, never forgot a kindness or an injury and never failed to repay either when opportunity offered. Sandy King, one of his rustlers, having been shot in a brush with officers, Curly Bill was nursing him in the hills near Fort Bowie. A lieutenant at the fort, out one day chasing jackrabbits with greyhounds, rode

into the outlaw camp and explained the accident of his
presence under cover of Curly's gun. When the officer
learned of King's wound, he offered to ride back to the
post and fetch an ambulance.

"What then?" asked Curly suspiciously.

"The man will be given proper surgical attention,"
replied the lieutenant.

"That all?"

"That's all."

The lieutenant brought out an ambulance and took
King to Fort Bowie, where, in the post hospital, the
outlaw recovered from his injury and went his way in
peace.

Several months later, Curly Bill raided the army cor-
rals at Fort Bowie and ran off a number of horses. The
same lieutenant was placed in charge of a squad of
soldiers that took the trail. He found the stolen horses
at Hughes's ranch in a corral surrounded by a high
adobe wall behind which stood Curly Bill's outlaws with
rifles.

"What do you want?" challenged the outlaw.

"I've come for those stolen horses," replied the lieutenant.

"Try to take 'em," shouted the outlaw, and the
rustlers cocked their guns.

Curly Bill took a second look at the lieutenant.

"Hold on, boys," commanded Curly. "That's the
man who saved Sandy King's life."

Curly Bill threw open the corral gate and helped the
soldiers cut out the stolen army horses. He shook hands
with the lieutenant.

"You can have anything you want from Curly Bill
any time you want it," he said in parting.

Curly Bill's outlaw kingdom had two capitals. The first was Charleston on the San Pedro. The second was Galeyville in the San Simon. When it seemed to King Curly that Charleston was a little too close to Tombstone and the reign of law and order Wyatt Earp had set up, he moved his headquarters eastward across the Chiricahuas to Galeyville.

Charleston was a town of five hundred people, under the shade of great cottonwood trees on the west bank of the San Pedro and half-encircled by that pellucid stream. To get drunk and shoot up this quaint village now and then was only to show one's self a public-spirited citizen. When one drew near Charleston at night, one estimated the distance by the definiteness of the revolver shots of inebriated revellers. C. L. Cummings, who now owns half of Tombstone and who was then ditch tender for the Charleston stamp mill, had to do sentry duty without a light along the mill flume because so many shots were fired from the town at his lantern. An ordinary form of salutation was, "Well, how many dead ones have they got on ice this morning?"

Jack Swartz, a Charleston saloon-keeper, buried his Mexican wife in the morning, killed a Mexican man at noon, and married another Mexican woman before sundown. Jim Wolf, catching a tramp robbing his house, resolved himself into a one-man lynching party and hanged the thief to an apple tree, relenting and cutting him down just before his life was extinct. Jerry Barton, a saloon man noted for his strength, was said to have killed seventeen men, three in handkerchief duels and two with his fist. When Jim Wolf inquired how many men Jerry had in his private graveyard, the giant pursed his brows reflectively. "Do Mexicans count?" he asked.

Justice of the Peace Jim Burnett, erratic czar of the town, having trouble with the Board of Supervisors over his fees, announced that in the future "this court will take care of itself," and thereafter remained in rebellion against the county authorities and put all fees in his own pocket. A coroner's jury, under instructions from the justice, brought in a verdict that "it served the Mexican right for getting in front of the gun." Justice Burnett issued his own warrants and served them with a shotgun. No matter where he arrested a prisoner, in street or saloon, he at once declared court open, assessed the fine, and usually collected it then and there. When Jack Haarer, a ranchman, was drunk and shooting up the town, the justice dragged him from his horse and fined him twenty head of three-year-old steers. Having fined Jaw Bone Clark, who ran a dance hall, fifty dollars for being drunk, Justice Burnett lost the money in a poker game. Then the Court left the table long enough to arrest Jaw Bone again on the additional charge of disturbing the peace, and having fined him another fifty, bought a fresh stack of chips.

The Rev. Tuttle came over from Tombstone and held religious services one evening in the schoolhouse, Charleston being shy on churches. Curly Bill, having some curiosity to see what church was like, rounded up Ike Clanton, and the two outlaws went to the meeting. As these noted robbers and desperadoes stalked up the aisle with their six-shooters on and took front seats, the congregation became panic-stricken. One slipped out and then another until the minister was left with Curly

Bill and Ike Clanton. Preacher Tuttle, sharing in the general consternation, was edging toward the back door when Curly Bill drew a bead on him.

"Come back here," shouted Curly. "We've took out chips in this game and we aim to see the deal through to the last turn."

The reverend gentleman, keeping a dubious eye on Curly's gun, came back.

"Me and Ike was feelin' low-spirited," Curly explained, "and we 'lowed we'd come in and hear you preach, thinkin' maybe yo' sermon might cheer us up. Yo' congregation's done sneaked out on you fer no speshul reason clear to us, but we'd admire to have you open up yo' game regular and," Curly added with an off-hand gesture with his six-shooter, "ef this here sermon don't come off on the square, it'll come off in the smoke."

Whereupon the minister launched into a pulpit oration of regulation length. But he took occasion as he went along to give his congregation of two outlaws some pretty hard digs, and did not fail to paint a telling picture of the hell of fire and brimstone that awaited all robbers and murderers who perished in their sins.

"Now," said the preacher with a sly smile at the conclusion of his discourse. "If the congregation will rise, I will pronounce the parting benediction."

"None whatever," declared Curly Bill. "This here round-up ain't over by no means. Yo' sermon's done got me and Ike millin' round and pintin' the right way but we ain't saved yit. However, in the present excited state of our feelin's, we allow a hymn might shove us on into the gospel corral."

Preacher Tuttle, who had a sonorous baritone voice, sang a hymn. He sang it so well that Curly Bill suddenly

developed a great taste for religious music and, casually
fingering his six-shooter, demanded more. And for an
hour the preacher sang hymn after hymn loudly and
with great fervour before Curly's new passion for
psalmody was appeased.

"You've done give us a good show," said Curly Bill
finally. "Ef me and Ike ain't got enough religion now to
git us through the pearly gates, it shore ain't no fault
o' your'n. Seein' as how yo' throat must be tolerable
dry, we'd be plumb pleased ef you'd step down to
Schwartz's bar with us. The drinks will be on me."

Dozing in a chair next morning under the alamosas in
front of Charlie Tarbell's Eagle Hotel, Curly Bill
opened his eyes to see Justice Burnett pointing a double-
barrel shotgun at his head.

"Curly Bill, hear ye, hear ye," intoned the justice
solemnly, "this honourable court is now in session and
you are hereby tried and convicted on the charge of il-
legally, unlawfully, and without warrant of law breaking up the church services in the schoolhouse last night.
And it is the judgment of this here court, to wit: that
you be fined twenty-five dollars, and that you pay this
here fine forthwith, immediately and at once."

"All right, Jim," said Curly good-naturedly, getting
out a roll and peeling off several bills. "Here's your
money, and the fun was cheap at the price."

Curly Bill used to tell this story on himself with great
glee. "And that low-down ornery old robber," he would
say, "who didn't know no more 'bout law than a range
bull, kept them two barrels of his'n p'inted right between my eyes till I paid him that fine."

Charleston's famous justice of the peace met a tragic
death years afterward. He had gone to ranching near

Hereford, a few miles up the San Pedro Valley from Charleston, and his land adjoined that of W. C. Greene, principal owner of the Cananea copper mines in old Mexico, and a multimillionaire. A dam Greene had built across the river for irrigation purposes was blown up, and in the flood that followed, Greene's little girl was drowned. Greene became convinced that Burnett had wrecked his dam and, encountering the former justice at the Allen Street entrance of the O. K. corral in Tombstone, shot him to death. Some of the most distinguished lawyers of the Arizona bar were engaged in Greene's defense at his trial in Tombstone, and he was acquitted. Greene, dead now many years, was popularly supposed to have been the original of the Old Cattleman of Alfred Henry Lewis's Wolfville tales. Burnett, who was unarmed at the time of his death, always denied blowing up the dam, and the evidence seemed to establish his innocence. "It is singular," remarks Historian McClintock, "that his killing was for one crime that in all probability he did not commit."

Galeyville, Curly Bill's last capital, sprang up in the fall of 1880 as a boom silver camp in Turkey Creek Cañon on the east side of the Chiricahuas. It was named for John H. Galey, a Pennsylvania oil man, who owned the discovery mine and established a small smelter there. The town was totally deserted by the latter part of 1882. Nothing of it remains. Few people in Arizona know where it was.

The site of the famous old place is a mile from Paradise, which itself was a boom camp that went up like a rocket and came down like the stick in the early years of the present century, and is now only a huddle of dilapidated houses deep in the wilds of Silver Creek

Cañon. From Paradise you pass to Turkey Creek and come to a point where the mountains open out into an amphitheatre. Here you climb to a stony mesa sparsely covered with juniper and live oak. You see a number of rectangular mounds that suggest unconvincingly the foundations of old buildings. But you stumble on a whisky bottle clotted with dirt, empty probably for nearly half a century, drained possibly by Curly Bill himself, and you know you stand on the site of Galeyville. The main range of the Chiricahuas towers to the west. Down in the lowland by the creek is a tangle of ash and sycamore timber. Through the mouth of the cañon, a few miles away, you catch a glimpse of the San Simon Valley. Where once stood the drunken, roaring outlaw stronghold, the romantic beauty of the lonely mountain bowl is steeped in peace and deep silence.

"I lived in Galeyville two years," said James C. Hancock, now postmaster of Paradise. "The main street ran along the edge of the mesa, and all the saloons and stores stood on one side of it facing Turkey Creek bottoms. All except Nick Babcock's saloon, which had the opposite side of the street all to itself. Curly Bill used to sit in a chair under a live oak in front of Babcock's with a bottle of beer in one hand and a six-shooter in the other and, between drinks, shoot at lizards, chipmunks, and tin cans. . . . Larry Garcia didn't stop when Jim Johnson called to him but walked on behind a coal dump down by the smelter. Johnson saw a hat bobbing behind the coal and, supposing it was Garcia's, sent the hat flying through the air with a bullet. When the face of a stranger, greatly astonished, rose above the coal, Johnson apologized. 'Excuse me, mister,' he shouted. 'I evidently made a mistake.'

. . . I remember how the bullets whistled up the hill
when Al George shot at a butcher who had waved a
paper at George's pony. Little things like that were
always happening in Galeyville. Every five minutes or
so, day and night, somebody was firing off a gun. Galeyville was one of the most healthful spots in Arizona, but
three doctors did a fine practice patching people together. . . . While showing what an expert he was at
whirling a six-shooter, Jim Johnson shot himself in the
leg. Blood poisoning set in, and the doctor said ampu-
tation was necessary. But Jim wouldn't have it. 'I
ain't worth more'n a dollar and a half with two legs,'
he said. 'With one leg, I wouldn't be worth a drink of
Nick Babcock's booze.' So Johnson saved his leg and
lost his life. . . . Galeyville put on metropolitan airs
when a weekly paper started up. But there weren't but
three issues. A pony, tied to the ridgepole of the shanty,
ran away and wrecked the printing plant."

When Cherokee Jack Rogers rode into Galeyville one
day, leading a mule by a rope, Curly Bill addressed him
in tabasco language.

"You ten-cent pickpocket," said Curly Bill, "you
stole that there mule from a widow woman in Pinery,
and you take that there animal straight back to her.
Head west mighty quick and burn the wind, or I'll fill
your cheap carcass full of lead."

And Cherokee Jack did what Curly Bill told him and
did it pronto. Cherokee had been four-flushing about
Galeyville for some time pretending to be a hard
hombre, and being called by Curly Bill in this way
stung his sensitive spirit. The first time he got drunk
he started in to convince a skeptical community that
he was bad.

He ran into Bob Williams in Jack Dall's saloon and made him get down on his knees and say a prayer. Then he wandered into Shotwell's store, and poking a six-shooter into Pat O'Day's ribs, ordered him to dance. Though a genial soul, Pat had conscientious scruples against doing a hornpipe under threat and, grabbing a sledge hammer, he stretched Cherokee out senseless on the floor. He was about to take another swing but Shotwell stopped him.

"Don't mess up the place, Pat," said Shotwell. "Take him outside and kill him."

So Pat dragged the unconscious Cherokee out into the street. A crowd of citizens assembled. Milt Hicks, one of Curly Bill's men, spoke feelingly.

"The reputation of our town for law and order," said Milt, "has suffered from the depredations of this here Cherokee Jack, and it's time he was learned a lesson."

These sentiments seemed to be unanimous and old Jim Hughes, who was also a member of Curly Bill's gang, made a suggestion to Pat O'Day.

"Thar ain't no use in us citizens gittin' mixed up in this here affair," said Jim Hughes. "We'll withdraw down to the smelter and inspect the machinery. You've done started the job, Pat, and you might as well finish it. You'll find my old long-tom rifle leaning behind the bar in Jack McConaghey's saloon."

So the citizens retired to the smelter, which was just off the mesa down by Turkey Creek, and devoted themselves to a careful inspection of the machinery until they heard a shot. Then they went back up town and, inviting Pat O'Day to join them, refreshed themselves with much liquor at Nick Babcock's bar.

It was a little after this incident that Curly Bill took

charge of the election in San Simon. San Simon was a
railroad station twenty miles from Galeyville consisting
of two or three dwellings, a saloon and general store,
some stock pens, a water tank, and a section house.
There weren't more than thirty people living there,
including the women and children and ten or twelve
Chinese section hands. Charles Shibbell was running
against Bob Paul for sheriff of Pima County, Cochise
County not yet having been organized. As Paul had
been a stagecoach shotgun messenger, Curly Bill and
his men, who sometimes dabbled in stage robbery, were
strong for Shibbell.

San Simon's legitimate voting strength, of course,
wasn't a drop in the bucket in the returns of any general
election, but as the political boss of the San Simon
Valley, Curly Bill wanted to make a big showing for
Shibbell and demonstrate to Paul the contemptuous
estimate the San Simon placed on all shotgun messengers.

Curly brought the Chinese section hands in from their
labour on the railroad and voted them. He voted the
women and children. Still the ballot box looked pretty
empty. Then he dropped in ballots for all the livestock,
giving names to all the horses, mules, burros, goats,
dogs, and poultry. The saloon-keeper's dog became Shep-
herd W. Towser; Hiram J. Gander was the lordly bird
belonging to the mistress of the boarding shack; and
Dominick R. Crow was the section boss's speckled
rooster. San Simon piled up a rousing majority for
Shibbell. The election commissioners in Tucson were
startled when they counted the great number of ballots
from this insignificant way station in the desert. An

investigation followed, and the San Simon precinct was
thrown out.

Galeyville never had more than three or four hundred
people. When the mine closed down and the smelter
was moved to Benson, the town emptied like a circus
tent after a ring show. In two weeks the only persons
left were Rube Hadden and Seward Smith, who had
been a justice of the peace. For twenty years these two
lived in the empty town alone, and then Smith moved
away. But for five or six years longer, Rube Hadden
remained as Galeyville's last and only inhabitant. He
did a little mining and assessment work in the hills,
and when he sat in the evening by his front door, he
could see from one end of the main street to the other.
The old saloons where Curly Bill and his outlaws had
once caroused were falling into decay, the bars still
standing and the mirrors behind the bars reflecting only
cobwebs and empty darkness. The dance hall where the
rustlers used to shoot the French heels off the slippers
of ,the girls whirling in a waltz or a quadrille was tumbling down. The store windows were black with rain-
spotted dust, the rotting wooden sidewalks were caving
in, and grass and weeds were growing in the street.
But Rube Hadden didn't seem to mind the silence and
loneliness. He grew old and gray as Galeyville's entire
population, and he might be there yet if it hadn't been
for the new silver strike in Silver Creek Cañon. Then
he moved a little closer to Paradise, and you'll find him
there to-day living alone in a log cabin under the pines
and edging along toward ninety. What was left of Galeyville was finally torn down, and the lumber used for
buildings in Paradise.

Charleston, like Galeyville, passed into oblivion in the full tide of its iniquities. When the stamp mill was closed, the town was abandoned. The place that knew Charleston in its glory is now a haunted desolation. The tall cottonwoods that shaded the village still stand by the San Pedro, but buried in thick underbrush beneath them are only a few crumbling adobe walls. Stark and ghostly in the mesquite tangles, the old ruins stand like grim skeletons in lonely vigil above a scene of crime.

CHAPTER VI

THE AFFAIR OF SKELETON CAÑON

GHOSTS? Well, why not? But you don't believe in them? Then you are unfortunate and may miss some delicious thrills. If you believe in ghosts, Skeleton Cañon is haunted; if you don't, it's not. That's the way Ross Sloan seems to look at it. But, after all, that may be the wrong point of view, and Skeleton Cañon may have its ghosts, faith or no faith. Who knows?

Skeleton Cañon winds through the wildest part of the Peloncillo Mountains from the Animas Valley in New Mexico to the San Simon Valley in Arizona. The Animas Valley in the old days used to be a main place for outlaws. Curly Bill had a ranch there, and Old Man Clanton and Dick Gray and Billy Lang. Down in this farthest angle of the southeastern corner of New Mexico, jam-up against the Mexican border, still stand the old Cloverdale ranch house, the Roofless Dobe, the Double Dobe, and other old weather-beaten places of refuge famous in outlaw tales. Where Skeleton Cañon opens out into the San Simon Valley on the west stands Ross Sloan's ranch house with high hills of red rock towering above it and back of it, only a few miles, the main range of the Peloncillos. Across the valley loom the Chiricahuas, and you can see from Sloan's front door the far-off, shadowy mouth of Silver Creek Cañon that leads up to Paradise and Curly Bill's old haunts around Galeyville.

Ross Sloan's ranch is a sort of romance preserve. Just below his house is the spot where old Geronimo surrendered. Near it is a spring hidden in the cliffs known as Geronimo's Seep, where, in summers of drought, when all the streams were dry, the Apaches always found plenty of cold, clear water. Smuggler trains coming up from Mexico by way of San Luis Pass through the Animas range and across the Animas Valley used to thread the gorges of Skeleton with their jingling mule bells on their way to the San Simon. Two murderous encounters between outlaws and smugglers took place in the cañon within a mile of Sloan's house, one almost in his front yard. Down in a corral beyond the stables still stands the Outlaw's Oak and the scars of bullets are plain on the live oaks and sycamores under whose shade Skeleton Creek is forever singing its pleasant song. Skeleton Cañon has, too, a tradition of buried outlaw treasure that drips with romance and rivals the wild tales of Cocos Island and the Spanish Main; and all up and down the cañon are the holes dug by treasure-hunters who have come with high hope and gone away empty-handed.

The men murdered in Skeleton Cañon were left unburied. Coyotes and buzzards picked their bones, and the place became a charnel house. For years these grisly relics made the ground white at the places of battle and massacre. Some of the bones were washed away by storm waters in the creek, some were taken as curiosities by travellers, and some of the skulls picked up by cowboys became soap basins in San Simon Valley ranch houses. But fragments and shards of the skeletons remain scattered through the grass in ghastly abundance. If you go to gather the wild flowers that enamel the banks of the stream and the little vega in the park-like space at the Devil's Kitchen where the steep walls open out, you may find as many bones as blossoms— knuckle-joints, a tibia, the broken arch of a rib; and, likely as not, you may stub your toe against a skull. The cañon that once echoed to cries of battle and death is now a place of brooding stillness that seems almost uncanny, and the deep silence is past understanding.

So it is perfectly clear that, according to all the rules, a wild, lonely spot like this, where so many tragic things have happened, must be haunted; and if you cannot find a ghost in Skeleton Cañon, you had best stick to your office or business back home and go on footing up dollars and cents, making collar buttons or automobiles, clipping coupons or selling groceries.

As you sit at night in Ross Sloan's comfortable ranch house listening as he spins yarns of Skeleton Cañon's strange, romantic history, you will hear, perhaps, through the silence and darkness a shriek that will suddenly make your blood run cold. It rises in a shrill, shivery crescendo and dies in an eerie wail. There seems something human in its note of poignant agony. It is like the death cry of some murdered man. It is like the scream of some poor devil who falls in his tracks with a bullet through his heart and leaves his unshriven bones for the wildcat to polish.

"That's a cougar back in the mountains," says Ross Sloan easily. "Those varmints holler around every night. They get a calf or a pig once in a while. We call 'em lions out here—mountain lions. They've got a funny yell. Yes, it might sound a little ghostly if you, happen to be superstitious. There was a lady out here to visit us once, and she went all to pieces when she heard one of those panthers scream like that. 'I know that's a spirit,' she said. 'A lost spirit that went into the other world without book or bell or holy sacrament. Oh, dear,' she says, 'that's the tortured ghost of one of those men murdered in the cañon by outlaws and doomed for his sins to haunt the spot of his bitter death.' We had a lot of trouble calming her down. She was going to stay a week, but she packed up and went home next morning, and we never could get her to come back to see us any more.

"They say Skeleton's haunted. A lot of people think there's no doubt about it. But I don't pay much attention to the queer noises around here at night. Sometimes the wind in the trees sounds like voices babbling and sometimes, if you didn't know it was the windmill, you might think a human being was whimpering just outside the door. The creek that just murmurs along like any other creek in the daytime seems at night trying to tell you something in some strange language you can't understand. If a fox barks on the hill, it sounds mighty lonesome, and the catamounts have a peculiar wailing cry; there's a lot of these prowlers around, and you've got to keep your chicken-house locked.

"Now and then you'll see a light up the cañon moving slowly. That may be a will-'o-the-wisp in a marshy spot, or maybe a stray traveller with a lantern cutting across to the Animas. I've never seen anything. Once at dusk up at the forks of the cañon I thought I saw a dim figure step out of some bushes and disappear in the Devil's Kitchen. But I wasn't sure; it was pretty dark. One night, two cowboys came riding down the cañon hell-bent and swore that, up at the Devil's Kitchen, they had seen a band of skeletons dancing in a ring and could hear their bones rattle and see the moonlight shining through their ribs. Those two fellows were scared half out of their wits, and their hair was standing on end, but I think maybe they'd had one pull too many at their bottle. I'm not saying Skeleton's haunted, and I'm not saying it's not; I'm just a plain cow man and know more about branding irons than ghosts. But I'll bet a two-year-old steer you can't find a Mexican in the country with nerve enough to ride through the cañon after dark."

Don Miguel Garcia was a gallant figure with a touch of the hidalgo as he rode at the head of the long mule train winding down through Skeleton Cañon toward the San Simon Valley. His steeple sombrero was ornamented with silver bangles, his bell-shaped buckskin pantaloons were set with pearl buttons down the seams, and his striped resplendent *sarape* was swung with loose grace across his shoulders. Except for the six-shooter in a scabbard at his side and the rifle that rested across the pommel of his saddle, he looked just the fellow to stand in some dim, moonlit patio and strum a guitar beneath a lady's balcony. Doubtless Don Miguel was dreaming of some dusky beauty who had taken his fancy in the last village in which his caravan had stopped among the mountains of old Mexico, for these smugglers were jolly fellows and, like sailors, had a sweetheart in every port.

Behind, in single file, came the mules, small, lithe, clean-limbed, of ancient Andalusian stock, each with a jingling bell at its throat and each half-hidden be-

neath great rawhide aparejos—pack sacks called by
cowboys kyacks, that did not stand out from the animal
squarely like panniers, but fitted snugly around the
curving sides and were strapped securely beneath the
belly. Along the flanks of the train trailed heavily
armed outriders, swarthy, hard-faced men, alertly vigi-
lant, their sharp black eyes searching rocks and coverts
for sign of lurking danger.

Many a smuggling expedition had Don Miguel led
over the international line to trade at Tucson for merchandise upon which customs authorities never levied
duty and on which he made fat profits. If the saints to
whom he prayed blessed him now with a prosperous
journey, Don Miguel, after leaving Skeleton Cañon,
would turn north through the San Simon, round the
northern end of the Chiricahuas, and passing through
Dragoon Gap and across the San Pedro, arrive in Santa
Cruz Valley where at trail's end he would pitch his camp
among the desert cholla thickets in the environs of
Tucson. Here the merchants, who grew rich on this
trade in contraband, would gather to meet him, and
Don Miguel's aparejos would soon be empty of their
wealth of silver dobe dollars and packed to bulging
fullness with goods and commodities of many kinds.
Then at last, the trading over, Don Miguel and his
men, before setting out on the long return journey to
Mexico, would revel for a while in the Mexican dance
halls of the old pueblo and refresh their weary souls
with much wine and tequila.

While the smuggler train moved slowly through the
cañon, up and down over the rough trail, in and out
among trees and giant boulders, around many a corner
of towering precipices, a solitary horseman lounged

easily in his saddle in the sequestered coolness of the
tall cathedral rocks that form the Devil's Kitchen.
He was a burly figure, with bull neck, round swarthy
face, and a shock of curly black hair, and from his appearance might have been a wandering cowboy resting for a while in the shade of the deep recess. His hat
was pushed back from his brow, and he had a look of
carefree good-nature as he gazed with calm indifference across the level grassy floor of the cañon and
heard the gurgle of the creek on the far side rippling
over sand bars under the green shadows of willow trees.
Though one might have wondered at his purpose in this
lonely place, one who had ever seen him before would
have been in no doubt as to his identity. This was Curly
Bill.

From far up the cañon through the golden, sunny stillness came the faint tinkle of a bell.

There was seeming magic in the dim, silvery shiver
of sound. Curly Bill was instantly transformed from
listlessness into electric animation. He straightened
tensely in his saddle. His dark face froze in the rigidity
of sculpture. His black eyes gleamed like those of an
ambushed panther that suddenly on a slant of wind
scents prey. He drew his six-shooters from their holsters
and gave them close scrutiny. He carefully adjusted
the magazine rifle that hung in its sheath at his side.
Then, with a satisfied air of preparedness, he touched
his pony lightly with his heel and moved off up the
cañon at a walk.

He had gone only a few steps from the Devil's Kitchen when he shot a swift furtive look from beneath
the brim of his sombrero to the broken rocks and
tangled chaparral along the rim of the cañon wall. In

the fraction of a second occupied by that rapid glance, a man's hand that seemed as if detached from its body was thrust from a thicket, opened, and closed in a lightning-quick signal, and disappeared. That was all. Except for this strange, sudden apparition, the canõn's rim seemed as peaceful as the blue sky against which it was outlined.

The jingle of bells was growing rapidly more distinct. It became a loud, confused tintinnabulation. From round a bend the long mule train swung into view. When Don Miguel beheld a horseman riding toward him, a look of surprise came into his face. With commanding uplifted hand, he brcught the caravan to a halt. The music of the bells went out in sudden silence.

"*Como esta usted, señor?*" said Curly Bill with an easy smile, reining in his pony.

Don Miguel's air was one of guarded aloofness.

"*Buenas dias,*" he returned with a touch of chill in his voice.

"Fine day."

Curly Bill threw one leg nonchalantly over the pommel of his saddle and drawing a sack of tobacco and a package of yellow paper from his pocket rolled a cigarette.

Well, yes, Don Miguel agreed, it was a fine day. But just a little hot. So for a moment they exchanged casual courtesies. Curly Bill spoke Spanish with all the inflections and vernacular idioms of a Mexican. Don Miguel began to thaw.

"I thought it possible," he said apologetically. "Well, never mind. It imports nothing. But, by the Virgin, one cannot be toò careful when travelling these wild trails. I have never yet met with misadventure. But

I have been warned that sometimes robbers lurk in these lonely mountains."

Curly Bill threw back his head and laughed.

"Robbers, eh? No, señor. What few people there are over here on this side of the line are all right. Just plain honest people trying to make a living."

Curly Bill himself, if Don Miguel happened to be curious, was just a cowboy looking for stray cattle. The headquarters ranch of his outfit was way up yonder—he waved his hand—way up yonder to the north. If, possibly, the señor was going in that direction, he might see the ranch buildings with the windmill off to the right. Don Miguel would keep his eye out. He was bound for Tucson.

"Ah, Tucson," returned Curly Bill with a sly chuckle, "is *muy bueno* town. You bet. Plenty pretty girls. A *baile* every night. Good hard liquor. You and these hombres of yours will have one high old time. Eh?"

Don Miguel smiled. This rough-looking stranger after all was a very pleasant fellow. But the caravan was losing time. It must be moving.

"*Vaya con Dios*." Don Miguel lifted his sombrero with the courtly politeness of a Spanish gentleman. "Go with God."

"So long," said Curly Bill.

As the mule train, with a huge clashing of bells, got under way, Curly Bill again shot a swift furtive glance to the rim of the cañon wall. Nothing stirred. Rocks and chaparral thickets, bathed in peaceful sunshine, were as still and silent as death.

Riding slowly along the length of the caravan, Curly Bill gave genial salutation to the dusky outriders as he passed each one in turn.

"*Como le va?*" he called jovially to the two Mexicans trailing behind as rear guard.

"*Bien y usted?*" they shouted back gaily through the dust.

But while their friendly looks still rested on him, Curly Bill's dimpling geniality vanished with the suddenness of an extinguished candle. His face darkened like thunder. His eyes sputtered fire like twin black devils. With the quickness of a wildcat's spring, he snapped out his six-shooter. Twice he pulled the trigger. The two shots were so close together they sounded almost as one. With the smile of greeting still on their lips, the two Mexicans slumped from their saddles, thumped upon the ground, and lay still.

As if the report of Curly Bill's gun had been a signal, a dozen rifles spouted flame from along the rim of the cañon wall. Among the rocks and tangled chaparral, steeped a moment before in wilderness stillness, ambushed outlaws rose against the sky as by devil's necromancy. Through drifting blue veils of smoke they loomed like phantom demons, pumping lead from their rifles with the steadiness of death machines.

"Get 'em all, boys."

"Give the greasers hell."

Death leaped upon the Mexicans in the cañon as a mountain lion springs from a tree upon the back of a deer. Caught in the trap, with no chance for their lives, the smugglers, here, there, yonder, pitched to headlong death from their plunging ponies. Their death cries went up in poignant tumult to the still mountains. The mules, stampeding, swept over the bodies in a whirlwind of terror. . . . Throwing his hands aloft in wild death spasm, a bronzed horseman dived to the ground and rolled over in a somersault. . . . Another, wounded to the death, fought hard to the last against dying; tottering weakly he clenched his saddle pommel; he bent down slowly, his eyes glazing, his face stricken gray, contorted in agony; as he fell, he wrapped his arms blindly around a foreleg of his flying pony and was jerked to the earth, his body sprawling with a thud at full length. . . . One was carried by his maddened horse to the top of a high embankment against the cañon wall; a bright red spot leaped out upon his forehead. "Mother of God," he screamed as, plunging twenty feet downward, he crashed through the tops of willow trees into the creek. . . . Don Miguel, borne down the cañon in the hurly-burly, was struck by a bullet between the shoulder blades; he was flung to the ground, his rifle whirling in mad parabola. But Don Miguel had knightly courage as well as knightly courtesy. Staggering to his knees, he pointed his six-shooter in a weakly wobbling hand toward the heights of flaming death; his bullet whistled harmlessly. But this was the smuggler chieftain; he must be killed quickly. A concentrated fire was turned upon him; he sank gently to the ground as if composing himself for sleep. . . . A handsome stripling —he was only sixteen—raced in wild flight up the cañon. Curly Bill himself from his place of concealment behind a rock at the edge of the massacre fired a half-dozen shots after him, cutting leaves from the trees about the lad's head. "José," shouted the boy at the top of his voice, "Pancho, Manuel." These were his brothers. But they will not hear his frantic calls to them. They lay crumpled in the bear grass. Darting up a fork of the cañon, the youth lost himself in the far purple shadows. He alone of all the smuggler band escaped.

Down into the pit of death, the outlaws swarmed on their horses, picking their way along the steep declivities. Curly Bill rode out among them, a smile of triumph on his round, dark face. He had never seen a trick turned in handsomer style. Nothing had gone amiss. The thing had come off from beginning to end like clockwork.

"Here's a greaser still breathing."

"Well, finish him off."

There was a shot. Another over there. A third. But there was no time to lose. The buzzards and coyotes would attend to these fellows. Whatever loot in dobe dollars there might be was in the aparejos on the runaway mules. Off down the cañon, Curly Bill and his outlaws clattered in pell-mell pursuit, leaving behind nineteen dead Mexicans on the little vega in front of the Devil's Kitchen.

The pack mules were overtaken in the San Simon Valley and, having been rounded up, were driven to Al George's cienega at the mouth of Cave Creek Cañon where $75,000 in Mexican silver rifled from the aparejos was divided in equal shares. For riotous weeks, the outlaws squandered their spoils among the bars of Galeyville and Charleston. What they had left at the end of their debauch was won from them at poker at Roofless Dobe ranch by John Ringo and Joe Hill, reputed the most expert card sharks in the lawless crew.

This murderous foray took place in July, 1881. Those who, it is said, shared with Curly Bill in the sickening glory of it were Old Man Clanton, Ike and Billy Clanton, Tom and Frank McLowery, John Ringo, Joe Hill, Jim Hughes, Rattlesnake Bill, Jake Gauze, Charlie Thomas, and Charlie Snow.

CHAPTER VII

BILLY BREAKENRIDGE MAKES GOOD

WILLIAM M. BREAKENRIDGE had come to Tombstone half tenderfoot. When Sheriff Behan appointed him a deputy, folks in Tombstone had misgivings. Everybody liked Billy Breakenridge. He was a dapper, smiling, handsome young fellow, who looked upon the world with a pair of the friendliest eyes in it. He carried a six-shooter and a rifle, and was pretty expert with both, but his most effective weapon was his friendliness. The town people seemed to think it required more nerve than he possessed to ride deputy sheriff in that rough country. "He'll never make good"—that was their prediction. Billy Breakenridge's official career at the outset seemed darkened by the ominous shadow of his smile. But what Tombstone prophets failed to take into consideration was the daredevil courage behind the smile.

"Billy," said Sheriff Behan one day, "I want you to go over into the San Simon and collect the taxes. You'll have to make your own assessments and collect the money on the spot. That's our way in Cochise County. When can you start?"

"Just as soon as I can saddle up," replied Deputy Breakenridge without blinking an eye.

The sheriff had given his order as if he were telling the young deputy to drop into the Can Can for a dish of corned beef and cabbage. But Billy Breakenridge was in no way deceived. He knew all about the dangers he had to face. The San Simon was a no-man's land, with Curly Bill its overlord and Galeyville its capital. No taxes had ever been collected there, for the reason that no sheriff's deputies, single-handed or in posses, had ever had the nerve to invade this retreat of outlaws and murderers. Sheriff Behan had failed to mention these few simple facts, but Billy Breakenridge made up his mind that he would bring those taxes back in his saddlebags or come back himself nailed in a pine box.

He rode out of Tombstone alone, looking as unperturbed as if he were on his way to serve an innocuous subpoena. But he was thinking hard. If the people of the San Simon refused to pay their taxes, how was he going to make them pay? Suppose he succeeded in collecting a few dollars, how far would he ride before a gang of cutthroats robbed him? These questions were only some of the perplexing angles.

As he looked across Sulphur Springs Valley from the summit of the Dragoons, a big idea came to him. It was a daring idea, perhaps desperate and a little hopeless. But it was worth trying. By jingo, if he could only put it over! He headed straight for Galeyville.

The mining town on Turkey Creek was at the peak of its boom. His big idea was dependent on a certain man, and when he reached Galeyville he set out at once to find him. He stepped into a saloon. Some rough-looking customers were absorbed in a poker game; five or six cowboys were shooting pool. On a table a burly fellow with curly black hair and round, swarthy face lay sprawled, his head propped by his elbow. He seemed/

in philosophic meditation. Deputy Breakenridge had never seen him before, but it came to him in a subconscious flash—that this man was the fellow he was looking for.

Just then the saloon-keeper came in carrying a pail of water. He dipped up some water in a tin cup and laughed as he waved the cup aloft.

"Here's fun, boys," he shouted.

The burly man on the table stirred indolently, drew his six-shooter, and, without apparent aim, shot the tin cup out of the saloon-keeper's hand.

"You'll git away with no sech low-down skullduggery as drinkin' water," he drawled.

Deputy Breakenridge required no further enlightenment. He stepped up to the six-shooter adept.

"Curly Bill," he said, "I want to introduce myself to you. Sheriff Behan has sent me over to the San Simon to collect the taxes, and I want you to help me do the job."

That was Deputy Billy Breakenridge's big idea.

Curly Bill looked for a moment flabbergasted. Soon he began to smile. Then he laughed. At last he roared.

"Well, I'll be damned," he said. "You've got guts, young feller. But, by gosh, I'll do it. Come on and take a drink. Me and you are deputy sheriffs together from right now."

Curly Bill thumped on the bar.

"Line up, boys," he called out. "Nominate yer pizen. I'm gittin' into politics. Here's a young he-wolf from Johnny Behan's office, and me and him are goin' to collect the taxes in this end of the county. Ef any gent holds out a cent on us, I'll shoot him full of holes, and don't you fergit it."

For weeks the chief of the outlaws and the young deputy sheriff rode together from one end of the San Simon to the other. They shared crusts beside camp fires, they drank from the same canteen, they exchanged confidences as they lay on their blankets side by side under the stars, and they got on terms of intimate friendship. And they collected the taxes. Nobody said a bitter word or made a hostile gesture. Everybody paid with a smile. Curly Bill, sitting in his saddle with rifle and six-shooter, was better than a Fourth of July oration in convincing the people of the importance of fulfilling the obligations of good citizenship.

Deputy Breakenridge's saddlebags were bulging with tax money when he and Curly Bill arrived at the crest of the Dragoons. Tombstone was in sight.

"I reckon I'll be turnin' back here," said Curly Bill. "Ain't no danger of yer gittin' robbed now. Ef I can ever do anything more fer you, let me know. So long."

So Deputy Sheriff Billy Breakenridge made good, received his accolade as a hero, and assumed an honoured place at the Round Table of Tombstone's knighthood.

Deputy Breakenridge, sitting on his horse in the darkness, lifted a loud halloo. The door of the Mc-Lowery ranch house at Soldier Holes in Sulphur Springs Valley opened warily; a kerosene lamp shone through the narrow slit. A challenging voice came from within. The deputy recognized that voice.

"It's me, all right, Curly," he said.

The big front room was filled with men—Frank and Tom McLowery, the Clanton boys, and half a dozen other members of the Curly Bill federation. Deputy

Breakenridge was friendly with them all. But his cheery greeting met cool reception. The outlaws were suspicious of this unexpected night visit, and a little guilt perhaps was mingled with the suspicion. They sat puffing at cigarettes in sullen silence. The deputy's attempts at familiar small talk fell flat. Curly Bill drew him into another room.

"What's the trouble?" asked Curly.

"Well, it's this way," began Deputy Breakenridge. "A horse belonging to the superintendent of the Contention mines has been stolen; fine animal; racing blood; Kentucky bred. I've traced the horse here."

Curly nodded.

"I'd like to find this horse."

Again Curly nodded.

"And I'd like to take it back to Tombstone in the morning."

"That all?" said Curly. "Well, I can't see no speshul reason for givin' up this hoss. What fer? A hoss thief is a business man. He aims to make money. No good hoss thief steals a hoss fer the fun of givin' it back."

"But," argued Deputy Breakenridge, "Sheriff Behan is very anxious to recover this animal. It would set him in right with the Contention people, and they control a lot of votes. It might help put him over at the next election."

Curly ruminated for a while.

"You're invitin' me to bite off a purty big chaw," he said. "But, to heip Johnny out, I reckon I'll see what I kin do. But it's goin' to kick up a hell of a fuss.

Deputy Breakenridge saw Curly Bill and Frank McLowery in the kitchen arguing by candlelight across a table. Curly talked coldly and with an air of de-

cisiveness. McLowery looked ugly, scowling, shaking
his head and snapping out his words viciously.

When bedtime came, Deputy Breakenridge curled
up on some blankets on the floor and slept peacefully;
the law of hospitality was sacred; an enemy would
have been safe under the outlaws' roof. After breakfast
next morning, Frank McLowery touched him on the
arm.

"You'll find the horse you're after," said McLowery
with a wry smile, "hitched out at the corral."

Deputy Breakenridge saddled his own horse and,
leading the stolen thoroughbred, set out on his return
to Tombstone. He had not gone far when, off at the side
of the road a half mile or so, he saw six outlaws on
horseback. They were riding slowly, but this meant
nothing unless confidence that they had him trapped.
If he continued to follow the road, they would run into
him on their angling course a mile or two farther on.
He jogged along, pretending to have no suspicion of
danger. But he knew he must do something pretty
quickly if he was to escape. No law of hospitality would
protect him now.

A wagon train coming over from the Chiricahuas
turned into the trail a little ahead of him. The wagons,
piled high with lumber, were almost broadside to the
outlaws. He rode unhurriedly behind the train. But as
soon as he had disappeared from the view of the outlaws, he was suddenly transformed into a dynamo. He
dismounted. Keeping both his horses at a walk he performed the difficult task of transferring his saddle from
his pony to the thoroughbred. Throwing his pony's
halter rope to a teamster and telling him to lead the
animal to Tombstone, he sprang on the clean-limbed

racer and took it on the run. He shot into the clear past the head of the wagon train, and the dumbfounded outlaws saw him flashing across the valley like an antelope.

Tricked but not yet defeated, the outlaws came thundering after him. As they saw the thoroughbred drawing rapidly away, bullets began to kick up dust around the deputy. Bending over in his saddle, he urged his horse to more desperate speed. The sound of the firing began to grow faint. As he climbed the southern slopes of the Dragoons, he looked back. The outlaws had given up the chase. They were riding slowly back to the McLowery ranch. He watched them until they disappeared in the distance in a dusty glare of sun.

When Deputy Breakenridge and Frank McLowery met on the street in Tombstone a week or so later, they greeted each other cordially. The affair of the stolen horse apparently was forgotten. Two good gamblers had played shrewd poker and the game was over. McLowery had lost. Billy Breakenridge had won. That was all.

Curly Bill's friendship for Billy Breakenridge once came near costing the outlaw chief his life. Curly was carousing in Galeyville with some of his men, among whom was Jim Wallace. Wallace was a rough fellow himself and had been with the outlaws for five or six months. He was from the Pecos River country and was said formerly to have ridden with Billy the Kid, the famous New Mexico outlaw reputed to have killed twenty-one men when he was twenty-one years old. Deputy Breakenridge was in Galeyville on some civil business for Sheriff Behan. When he saw Breakenridge wearing his deputy's star, Wallace made some slurring remark and drew his six-shooter. This threw Curly Bill into a fury, and he made Wallace apologize.

"No Lincoln County hoss thief kin come in here and abuse Breakenridge," said Curly Bill. "Breakenridge is our deputy and he suits us."

When a truce had been patched up, Curly, Wallace, and Breakenridge went into Phil McCarthy's saloon where a band of cowboys was drinking. After a few rounds, Curly grew ugly. He pulled his gun from its holster.

"I reckon," he said, glowering at Wallace, "I'll jest kill you fer luck."

The other boys interfered, and Wallace went across the street to a corral and saddled his pony. He brought the pony into the street in front of Babcock's saloon. Standing behind his pony, Wallace was evidently waiting to kill Curly Bill. A henchman took word to Curly of these hostile preparations. Bursting out of McCarthy's place, three fourths drunk and boiling with rage, Curly Bill caught sight of Wallace and, drawing his gun, started across the street toward him. Wallace rested his six-shooter coolly across his pony's neck and fired. Curly Bill fell in the middle of the street with a bullet through his jaw. Wallace jumped on his pony, but the cowboys, pouring out of McCarthy's, dragged him from the saddle and would have strung him up to the nearest live oak if it had not been for Harry Elliott, a Silver City lawyer, who managed to calm them. Then Wallace was taken before Justice Ellingwood and bound over. Curly Bill had a close call and was in bed for several weeks but he finally recovered. Wallace disappeared and was never tried.

The attempted robbery of the Charleston plant of the Tombstone Mining and Milling Company was a

bunglingly murderous affair. Mr. Austin, mill manager,
M. R. Peel, chief engineer, son of Judge B. L. Peel,
George W. Cheney, and F. F. Hunt, assayer, were in
the office at eight o'clock in the evening. Peel stood in
front of a counter idly drawing a picture on a piece of
paper. The others stood behind the counter watching
him. Austin noticed the lever handle of the door turn.

"Well," said he, "am I seeing things or are there
ghosts about?"

As all four looked at the moving handle, a heavy rap,
which might have been made with the butt of a gun,
sounded on the door.

"Come in," shouted Austin.

The door flew open. Two masked men entered with
rifles. Without a word, one of them fired, killing Peel
instantly. Austin, Hunt, and Cheney dodged below
the counter as the bandit fired a second time, the bullet
burying itself in the wall. Apparently seized with panic,
the two intruders made no attempt at robbery, but
rushed out and disappeared.

An alarm sounded by the mill whistle called Charleston citizens to the plant, but no trace of the bandits
was found. Two rockets went up into the sky in the
direction of Tombstone and were answered by a third
in the direction of the Huachuca Mountains; the meaning of these signals was never solved. The two bandits,
it was established later, were Zwing Hunt and Billy
Grounds.

Late that same night, Hunt and Grounds arrived
at the Stockton ranch near Antelope Springs nine
miles southeast of Tombstone. The Stockton ranch, on
the road between Tombstone and the Chiricahuas, was
a favourite stopping place for the freighters hauling

lumber and also for outlaws in their frequent trips between Tombstone and Galeyville. It was originally
owned by Eugene Edmunds who, as one of the survivors of the Stockton Indian massacre, was known as
Stockton Edmunds. It was now a dairy ranch owned by
Jack Chandler. At the ranch were Bull Lewis, Jack
Elliott, and a man named Caldwell. It was evident to
these men that Hunt and Grounds were under great
nervous tension. Keeping their horses saddled and
bridled, the two outlaws went out on the hills the next
morning and searched the country with field glasses.

"I'd rather see my grave than the inside of Yuma
penitentiary," Hunt said.

Hunt dispatched Elliott to Tombstone with a note
to Jack Chandler asking for $750 which Chandler owed
Hunt. With this money, the two outlaws proposed to
escape from the country.

When Elliott presented the note to Chandler in
Tombstone and told of the suspicious actions of the
two outlaws at the ranch, Chandler laid the facts before
Deputy Sheriff E. A. Harley, in charge of the sheriff's
office in the absence of Sheriff Behan. Harley at once
organized a posse which he placed in command of
Deputy Sheriff Breakenridge and which comprised
County Jailer E. H. Allen and Deputy Sheriffs Jack
Young and John A. Gillespie. Deputy Breakenridge
protested.

"Let me go out to Chandler's ranch alone," argued
Breakenridge. "I know Hunt and Grounds well, and
I can persuade them to surrender without bloodshed.
If I take a posse out there, there is going to be a fight
and several men may be killed."

But Harley was unconvinced.

"Friendship will cut no figure with those boys now," he said. "They have committed a murder. They won't submit peaceably. They know, if they give up, they must swing or go to Yuma. It would be foolish to go alone and try to argue with them. Go with a posse at your back and bring them in dead or alive."

Deputy Breakenridge and the three others of the posse started from Tombstone for the Stockton ranch at one o'clock in the morning. A bloodless capture was still in Breakenridge's mind. He planned to surround the place in the darkness and wait until morning, when he hoped to arrest the outlaws as they came outside to feed their horses or get wood for the breakfast fire. Near the ranch, the four posseman hitched their horses in the mesquite brush and closed in on foot. The first white streaks of dawn were showing above the distant Chiricahuas, and the ranch house stood dark and silent. Breakenridge posted Gillespie and Young behind a wood pile commanding the back door with strict instructions to remain in their hiding place until daylight. Breakenridge and Allen started for the front of the house to go into ambush beneath the low bank of Shoot-'Em-Up Creek that ran among oak trees past the front door.

But Breakenridge's careful plans went quickly to smash in anticlimax when Gillespie disobeyed orders. Breakenridge and Allen had not reached the creek bank when Gillespie thumped loudly on the back door.

"Who's there?" asked a startled voice inside.

"The sheriff," thundered Gillespie. "Open the door."

There was silence for an instant. Breakenridge and Allen sprang behind oak trees in front of the house. The back door flew open and from the cavernous darkness

Hunt fired twice. Gillespie fell dead. Young dropped with a bullet through his thigh. At the same moment the front door was flung wide. Bull Lewis came marching out holding his hands above his head.

"Don't shoot me," he shouted. "I've done nothing."

From behind him Grounds fired. The bullet struck Allen in the shoulder and knocked him down the creek embankment. Grounds' second bullet peeled the bark from the tree behind which Breakenridge was standing. Breakenridge returned the fire and Grounds fell lifeless in the doorway.

Hunt darted out the back door, leaping over Gillespie's body, crying to Grounds, "Come on, Billy." As he ran up the creek over a bit of rising ground, he came out in momentary black relief against the white dawn in the eastern sky. Breakenridge and Allen, who had clambered back up the bank, both fired at him. One bullet—Breakenridge's, it was believed—struck Hunt between the shoulder blades and passed through the lungs, bringing him down. But the outlaw was up in a flash and, dashing on, was quickly lost to sight in the brush. The fight had lasted less than thirty seconds, according to Breakenridge, and two men had been killed and three wounded.

Breakenridge and Allen, accompanied by Bull Lewis, began a slow stalk up the creek on Hunt's trail. They had gone a hundred yards when Breakenridge heard a rustle in the bear grass.

"Come out of there," he cried, with his gun at level, though he saw no one. "And come with your hands in the air."

"I'm dying," a feeble voice answered. "Come and get me."

Then, in the dim light, Breakenridge saw Hunt lying on the ground.

"Roll over on your face," ordered Breakenridge, "and stretch your hands out beyond your head."

This was a new way of making a man throw up his hands, but Breakenridge was taking no chances. Hunt did as he was told and Bull Lewis went up and disarmed him.

The dead and wounded were taken to Tombstone in a ranch wagon, Breakenridge, alone unscathed, riding alongside. Allen and Young soon recovered from their injuries. Hunt, dangerously hurt, was placed in a hospital. Several weeks later, when Hunt was convalescent, Billy Hughes, one of his old San Simon pals, drove up to the hospital in a buggy. He would, he said, take the invalid for a pleasant little ride for his health's sake. Hunt was helped into the buggy, and the two drove off eastward. They never came back.

Much mystery enveloped Hunt from the time of his escape. A reward was offered for him. Buckskin Frank Leslie took the trail but returned to Tombstone in a day or two, and why this sleuth hound abandoned the pursuit was not known. A posse went out but came back, unable to trail an invalid who had to travel in a buggy, and the perfunctory chase was soon given over.

Billy Hughes and Hunt camped on a sugar-loaf hill above Antelope Springs for a day or two. Then Hughes and Coley Finley took Hunt in a covered spring wagon to Frank Buckles's ranch in Pole Bridge Cañon in the Chiricahuas. Here Hunt was joined by his brother, Hugh Hunt, who came out from Texas. After Zwing Hunt had recuperated for three weeks at Buckles's, the two brothers, mounted and with a pack horse, headed south, announcing they were going to Mexico. The next heard of them was when Hugh Hunt rode alone into Camp Price at the southern end of the Chiricahuas and told Lieutenant Clark that Zwing Hunt had been killed by Indians.

When the two brothers arrived at the Point of Mountains at the north end of the Swisshelms, according to Hugh Hunt's story, Zwing Hunt was fagged out, and they went into camp beside a spring in a cañon. Five Apaches coming through the Narrows between the Chiricahuas and the Swisshelms, saw the smoke of the camp fire and crawled upon the camp. Hugh was cooking breakfast. Zwing was struck in the pit of the stomach by a bullet at the first fire.

"Are you badly hurt?" asked Hugh.

"Never mind me," answered Zwing. "You fight."

Zwing rolled over on his breast and with his rifle killed an Indian running toward him just before he himself was killed by a bullet through the head. Hugh leaped on his pony hobbled near camp and escaped with lead singing about his ears. For two miles Hugh rode his pony with the hobbles on, and for a great part of that distance the Indians running on foot were able to keep within range of the awkwardly plunging animal. When he was out of danger, Hugh took the hobbles off and made his way to Camp Price.

Jim Cook, in command of a party of scouts, rode back with Hugh to the scene of the fight. They found a dead man at the camp, not mutilated in the customary Apache way, and buried the body in a grave at the foot of a juniper tree and on the tree they cut with a knife Zwing Hunt's name and the date of his death. The juniper tree still stands, the knife-carved epitaph still decipherable, and the cañon has been known ever since as Hunt's Cañon.

Jim Cook and his scouts followed the trail of the Indians, and in Half-Moon Valley in the Pedragosa hills to the south they found the Indian Zwing Hunt was said to have killed. The Apaches had carried their dead comrade off and had covered the body with a mound of stones.

Hugh Hunt's story of his brother's death seemed plausible and was apparently corroborated by all the evidence. But a rumour spread that Zwing Hunt had not been killed but arrived safely in time at his old home in Texas. There was a story that the man buried at the foot of the juniper tree had been killed by Zwing Hunt himself, and another story that the body had been obtained from an undertaker in Tombstone. These rumours became so insistent that Sheriff Behan felt called on to make an investigation, and, under his orders, Deputy Sheriffs Billy Breakenridge and Phil Montague dug up the body in Hunt's Cañon. Both these deputies had known Zwing Hunt, and both identified the body as his.

This, it might seem, should have settled the matter, but it did not, and years later, members of Hunt's family declared that Zwing Hunt survived the alleged Indian attack and died in bed at his Texas home of the old wound Deputy Breakenridge had given him in the fight at the Stockton ranch. And on his deathbed, according to this story, Hunt drew a map showing the location of a cache in which he and Billy Grounds had hidden the rich loot of their robberies, and this map became the origin and inspiration of one of the most interesting buried-treasure hunts in the history of the Southwest.

CHAPTER VIII

THE OLD MAN WITH A BEARD

SINCE the red day in Skeleton Cañon when Curly Bill and his outlaws had sent to death all the Mexicans of a smuggler train except one stripling youth, the cry for vengeance had run along the border.

"Death to the gringo robbers!"

Sound cause for deep and bitter hatred had the dusky little people below the line. They had been treated like dumb beasts by the desperadoes who had come riding gaily across the border to plunder and murder at free will and gone riding gaily back again. Stealing Mexican cattle had been as simple as rifling a bird's nest in a garden. It was so nowadays among these murderous bandits that to kill a Mexican was no more than to kill a yellow coyote in the hills; it was not a crime to be punished by any law; it lay lightly on the gringo conscience; it was even too contemptible a thing to count in the notched gun-handle records of bad men.

The Skeleton Cañon atrocity had fired the Mexicans with new determination and courage. They would submit tamely no longer to the cutthroat depredations. They themselves had some skill in war-trail strategy, death traps, and ambuscades. Their watch fires hereafter would burn on the mountains. Their gathering signals would fly among the valleys. They would fight to the last man. Woe to the gringo spoilers who in the fu-

THE OLD MAN WITH A BEARD

ture should come raiding across the border, unprepared for desperate battle.

The sixteen-year-old boy who had escaped from the Skeleton Cañon hecatomb leaving three brothers murdered upon the field burned from that day of death with a white-hot fire of hatred and became an apostle of vengeance among his people. His brothers, foully slain, cried out to him from the ground. He heard their voices in the mountain streams, in the winds that talked among the pines. They called him to a vengeance of life for life and blood for blood, which, according to the mystic sybils of the border, is the law of the dead.

Looking back as he fled from the massacre, this boy had seen along the top of Skeleton Cañon's wall a line of fierce, demon countenances glaring death among flashes of rifle fire and snakelike wisps of smoke. But the quick vision was a blurred nightmare in his mind. Only one devil face remained in his memory with distinctness. That was the bearded face of an old man—a full beard as white as snow, hard wrinkled cheeks tanned as yellow as saddle leather by the winds and suns of years, blue eyes blazing fiercely. The boy did not know who this old man was, but some of the boy's kinsmen knew at once by the description. The gorgon head of fear and death that haunted the boy's dreams was that of Old Man Clanton.

Old Man Clanton was a fiery, lawless, ruthless old wolf of the frontier. He was a Texan and, it is said, made the ox-team trek to California in the gold-rush days of 'Forty-nine. He failed to wash a fortune from the sands of Feather River, drifted back eastward into Arizona in the early 'seventies, and took up a ranch near Fort Thomas.

"Old Man Clanton's wife was dead in 1875 when I first knew the family," said Melvin Jones of Tucson. "He had four children—Phineas, known as Finn, Ike, Billy, and Mary. The girl married Jack Slinkard and went to live on the Little Colorado River. My father bought Old Man Clanton's ranch, and the Clantons moved to the San Pedro Valley near Charleston. Ike, Billy, and Old Man Clanton died with their boots on. Finn was the only man of the family who came to a peaceful death in bed."

Mr. Jones's Arizona memories date back only to 1875. That isn't so long ago. But Arizona then was almost empty. On his way overland from Kansas, when he left the steel-end of the Santa Fe Railroad at Las Animas, Colorado, in 1875, he did not see a railroad again until 1881 when Southern Pacific trains began to run across Arizona. His wife, who was Laura Frame, born at Gila Bend in 1867, was the second white child born in Arizona and missed being first by only a week or so—lost the honour by an eyelash, as racing people might say.

The ruins of the old Clanton home on the San Pedro, twelve miles or so from Tombstone, are still eloquent of outlawry. Roofless now and with great breaches in the crumbling walls, the old adobe house stands on a hill commanding a wide prospect of the San Pedro Valley. West are the Huachucas, southeast the Mules, north the Whetstones, and straight up the valley across the line in old Mexico the San José Mountains. The San Pedro River brawls among its cottonwoods at the foot of the hill. Charleston was five miles north. The little town of Lewis Springs is on the railroad a quarter of a mile away across a fine *vega* where many a stolen horse once pastured. On its commanding hilltop the house was a castle, its thick adobe walls bulletproof and pierced with portholes. With a pair of field glasses the Clantons could sweep the valley up and down for seventy-five miles and appraise every man on horseback, every bunch of cattle, every stagecoach. No enemy could approach unseen. One may be sure that every stranger who came to the Clantons' door had undergone careful scrutiny at long distance.

Old Man Clanton turned over his San Pedro ranch to his boys, and in the latter part of 1880 moved to the Animas Valley in New Mexico. To show his contempt for any possible danger from Mexicans whom he robbed and killed, his Animas Valley home was only a mile from the Mexican border.

Old Man Clanton took part a month before his death in the Skeleton Cañon atrocity. His ranches were places of rendezvous and refuge for stage robbers, cattle thieves, and all manner of fugitives from justice. Though his white hair and beard gave him a benevolent aspect, Old Man Clanton, even to the end, was a tough, rapacious, merciless fellow, quick on the trigger and not squeamish about blood. Ike and Billy Clanton were active members of Curly Bill's banditti and suspected of many stage robberies. They were intelligent men, pleasant to meet, rather genial, but of a geniality that smiles with the hand resting on a six-shooter. Misfortunes and tragedy have given their fame a halo of picturesque pathos, but the Clanton boys were true sons of their father, born and bred to outlawry, and in their desperate calling, as bold and unscrupulous men as ever rustled cattle across the line or murdered Mexicans from ambush in a lonely mountain pass. Finn

Clanton was reputed the mildest of the lot, but he served a ten-year sentence in Yuma for cattle stealing.

Six of Curly Bill's outlaws set out upon a cattle raid into Sonora in the summer of 1881. They were Milt Hicks, Alex Arnett, Jack McKenzie, John McGill, Bud Snow, and Jake Gauze. A hundred miles south of the line they rounded up three hundred head. When they had rushed the herd through San Luis Pass out into the Animas Valley, they felt they were out of danger and allowed the beeves to drift and graze. At Cloverdale ranch three miles north of the boundary, where were good grass and water, Milt Hicks was left to guard the herd while the others rode to Curly Bill's Roofless Dobe ranch only five or six miles away, where they found the outlaw chief and a dozen other members of his band.

Smoking a cigarette at the Cloverdale ranch house, Milt Hicks could see the mouth of San Luis Pass southeast across the valley. The wide low gap through the Animas range between the Playas and Animas valleys was swathed in blue mist. Magic water and verdure of mirage trembled in the heat waves over the intervening alkali flats. Gazing at the cañon's mouth, Hicks noticed a certain movement in the misty blueness, a certain shifting of colour from delicate azure to whitish yellow of dust. A shadowy colossal figure came surging across the shimmering silver leagues of a mirage lake. Then the giant dwindled into a Mexican in a steeple hat on a pony. Other Mexicans in steeple hats on ponies materialized until there were perhaps thirty. All came careering across the valley at a run.

Milt Hicks climbed on his horse and split the wind for the Roofless Dobe.

Far down in Sonora, when the news of the gringo raid

had spread, the Mexicans had quickly foregathered and taken the trail. In the distance they saw a dust cloud travelling along the horizon. That was the stolen herd. For three days the dust beaten to the sky by the stampeding hoofs was like a pillar of cloud to guide pursuit. The Mexicans had been only a few miles behind when the cattle plunged bellowing through San Luis Pass.

The Mexicans, all old vaqueros, rounded up the cattle left by the outlaws at Cloverdale ranch and, quickly lining them out into a column, rushed them close-herded across the valley. When they passed Double Dobe ranch, owned by Charlie Green and Charlie Thomas, they added to the herd two hundred more cattle belonging to these two men. The Mexicans had lost three hundred cattle; they were taking five hundred back into Mexico.

As soon as he had been informed by Milt Hicks of the coming of the Mexicans, Curly Bill got what men he had at the Roofless Dobe ranch into the saddle. His company mustered all told sixteen. He could have gathered more. There were others of his band at Lang's and Clanton's ranches and at the little town of Gillespie not far away. But if these cattle were to be saved from the Mexicans, it was necesssry for Curly Bill to make every move as well as every man count. So, with his sixteen men, he set out in pursuit of thirty. He did not lose time by going to Cloverdale. He guessed what had happened there, and he figured that the Mexicans were pushing the herd hard for San Luis Pass. He set his course for this gap in the mountains.

The battle opened in the wide-flung jaws of San Luis Pass. With the cattle streaming through the cañon at a run, urged on by three or four vaqueros, the other

Mexicans deployed as a rear guard. Without slacking pace, Curly Bill out in front, the rustlers rushed upon them. Out of the padding thunder of hoofs rang a few scattering rifle shots as prelude to the blaze and crackle of gunfire across the cañon's mouth. Mexicans began to tumble from their ponies. Under the whirlwind attack, the Mexicans were seized with panic. They turned tail and set out in wild flight after the cattle. Hard upon their heels pressed the outlaws, pumping lead among them. The Mexicans left the cañon and took to the hills, and many were killed as their ponies floundered among the gulches. For six or eight miles the running battle continued. When the last Mexican had disappeared over the ridges, the outlaws got the cattle under control and headed them back for the Animas Valley ranges. Fourteen Mexican saddles had been emptied. All the wounded were ruthlessly killed when Curly Bill took the back trail. The casualties on the side of the outlaws were three men slightly injured.

"I had the story of this fight from Milt Hicks and several others of Curly Bill's men when I met them in Gillespie a few days afterward," said Rube Hadden of Paradise. "All the accounts agreed that fourteen Mexicans were left dead in the pass. Besides the six men who had been on the raid into Sonora after the cattle, Curly Bill had with him John Ringo, Joe Hill, Jim Hughes, John and Charlie Green, Charlie Thomas, and Tall Bell, and one or two more whose names I have forgotten. The two hundred cattle stolen by the Mexicans from the Double Dobe ranch were returned there and the three hundred brought out of Mexico on the raid by Milt Hicks and his bunch were bought by Old Man Clanton at fifteen dollars a head."

Fifteen dollars a head was not all these cattle were to cost Old Man Clanton. These three hundred stolen beeves stampede in wild border story from one red romance to another, costing nineteen human lives before they attain their final phase as sirloins and roasts on comfortable home tables somewhere in the world.

Though the Mexicans were eager to avenge the Skeleton Cañon tragedy, fortune so far had been against them. The game of death stood thirty-three to nothing. Nineteen of their people had been left dead in Skeleton Cañon and fourteen in San Luis Pass and not a single gringo ghost had been sent to the nether shades in blood atonement. The boy who had escaped from the Skeleton Cañon massacre had apparently preached his gospel of vengeance in vain. But wraithlike he still haunted the frontier line. Border men told of seeing a horseman watching in lone vigil on the hilltops and melting into thin air at any attempt to approach or follow him. When Old Man Clanton decided to drive the three hundred cattle to market at Tombstone, his plan was known across the line in Mexico almost as quickly as among his own rancher neighbours. The Old Man with a Beard—Bewhiskered Old Devil Face of Skeleton Cañon—was to take the road. For this the boy had been waiting these long days. Here was his opportunity at last. The voices of his three dead brothers might now be answered. He laid his plans swiftly and cunningly. He would make the trail to Tombstone for Old Man Clanton the trail to death.

With Old Man Clanton when he set out on the drive were Dick Gray and Billy Lang, his neighbours, Bud Snow, Harry Ernshaw, and Jim Crane—the Jim Crane who with Bill Leonard and Harry Head made the murderous attack on the stage on the Benson road. Their route, as planned, was to pass from Animas Valley through Guadalupe Cañon across Guadalupe Mountains out into San Bernardino Valley, and then northward through Sulphur Springs Valley past the southernmost buttresses of the Dragoons to Tombstone. They made their first camp six miles within Guadalupe Cañon and a half mile below the line in Mexico.

Harry Ernshaw was on night herd when next dawn came gray and dim in a drizzle of rain. The cattle were bedded down; Ernshaw was standing on guard in the shelter of a bluff; his pony was grazing a short distance from him. Suddenly, the cattle got to their feet in an excited scramble and, facing toward camp a quarter of a mile away, began to sniff the air and give throat to low moaning bellows. Ernshaw saw nothing and heard nothing. He fancied the herd scented a coyote or a bear.

He walked back toward camp to see if he might discover the cause of this strange panic. The camp was astir. Through the rain which made a gray mist in the faint half-light of daybreak, he saw Dick Gray and Jim Crane kindling a fire for breakfast. A little blaze began to flicker up among the wet faggots. Old Man Clanton, who had made his bed in the bottom of the chuck wagon, rose from his blankets and stood upright, a shadowy figure that in the moist twilight seemed to tower above the sodden earth. He stood half awake for a moment and swept his snowy beard with a paw-like hand.

The sloping cañon walls, which went darkly up to the leaden skies, sparkled on the instant with leaping flames, and the detonations of ambushed rifles drowned the swishing whisper of the rain. Old Man Clanton plunged over the side of the wagon in a staggering fall and crashed upon his face in the mud. Gray gave a death shriek that echoed up and down the cañon as he fell. Crane measured his length across the camp fire and extinguished it. Bud Snow, aroused by the hubbub, lifted himself for a quick moment at arm's length on his blankets and sank back into them lifeless—asleep, awake, and dead in a twinkling. Billy Lang sprang from his bed and rushed upward among the giant rocks along the cañon wall. Sheltered behind a boulder, he began to churn his rifle. Bullets crashed about him as thick as raindrops. His foes remained hidden, but he fired at the flashes of their guns. But several of his enemies circled across the cañon and worked in above and behind him. Kneeling, he fired his last shot, toppled over, and lay still.

Ernshaw, at the first volley, had taken to his heels. Through the cañon he fled in the wake of the cattle that stampeded in headlong flight, his pony racing away in the midst of the herd. Half a mile from the camp, Ernshaw plunged into thick brush on a hill. Here he remained hidden. When the firing ceased, a dozen Mexicans rode past his place of concealment, talking excitedly in Spanish. Among them was a slight, youthful figure, looking hardly more than a child. This was the boy. He rode in silence, a glow of happiness on his face. Vengeance at last was his. He had paid his debt to his three dead brothers in gringo blood.

Next day, cowboys at the Cloverdale ranch saw through the mists of mirage over Animas Valley a solitary pedestrian approaching from where the blue Guadalupes shut in the horizon to the south. Haggard, exhausted, his clothes ragged from cactus and briars,

Ernshaw staggered up to the ranch house with news of the tragedy.

"The Cloverdale boys rounded up a gang of thirty to bring out the bodies," said Rube Hadden. "I went with a bunch of nine fellows from Gillespie. John Ringo and Charlie Green were at Roofless Dobe ranch, and they went along. We found the five dead men where they fell. There were a dozen empty rifle shells around Lang's body. He had been shot in the back by the Mexicans who had worked around behind him. The hammer of his rifle was down on a cartridge that had been fired. We didn't look for the cattle. The Mexicans had rounded them up and taken them on down into Mexico.

"We brought the dead men out across our saddles to a little mesa in Animas Valley midway between the ranches of Lang and Old Man Clanton and about ten miles east of Cloverdale. There we buried 'em in a row and heaped stones over the graves. I heard that the Clanton boys later took Old Man Clanton's body to Tombstone and buried it in the cemetery there."

The five graves on the little mesa in the Animas Valley represented the sum total of Mexican vengeance for the Skeleton Cañon tragedy. Thirty-three to five— that was the final score. But the murder of their father in Guadalupe Cañon inflamed the Clanton boys with hatred for the entire race of Mexicans. Within the next month or two, five dead Mexicans riddled with bullets were found from time to time in the San Pedro Valley near the Clanton ranch south of Charleston. No one ever knew who killed them. But it was generally believed in Tombstone that they gave their lives in vicarious atonement for Old Man Clanton's death.

CHAPTER IX

JOHN RINGO stalks through the stories of old Tombstone days like a Hamlet among outlaws, an introspective, tragic figure, darkly handsome, splendidly brave, a man born for better things, who, having thrown his life recklessly away, drowned his memories in cards and drink and drifted without definite purpose or destination.

As Curly Bill's right-hand man, he took part in the raids of his outlaw associates, drank and gambled with them, was one of them in crime and dissipation, but he remained a man apart. Tall, of sculpturesque physique and lean, saturnine face, he was a silent man of mystery who, in moods of bitter melancholy, sometimes spoke of suicide. He was held in fear by the outlaws and by everyone who knew him, and there was no doubt about his desperate courage. His recklessness, perhaps, was due to the small value he placed upon his life; if someone else killed him, he would be saved the trouble of killing himself.

His sombre eyes seemed brooding upon a fate that had changed a life of bright promise into a career of sinister futilities. He was plainly a man of some breeding and inherent refinement. The primitive speech of the frontier was not his language; he spoke literate English, and many believed, though it is improbable, that he had been educated at college. The other outlaws caroused

133

to satisfy an animal lust for riotous pleasures. Ringo apparently drank to forget, and the stinging tanglefoot whisky of the wild country was the only convenient nepenthe. He evidently had fallen far, but even in the tragic ruin of his life he retained something of the dignity and commanding qualities of his former estate.

He was, if ever there was such a thing in the world, an honourable outlaw. His word once given was kept inviolately. Those to whom he made a promise could be sure he would fulfill it to the last letter, or die trying. Old-timers still tell of his quixotic ideals regarding women. Womanhood to him was an ikon before which he bowed in reverence. No woman was so bad that she was ever outside the pale of his knightly chivalry. A man who in his presence made a disparaging remark about any woman, be she irreproachable maid or matron or red-light siren, had to eat his words or fight. That was John Ringo's way.

Ringo was born in Texas. While he was little more than a boy, he became involved in a war between sheep and cattle men. His only brother was killed in the feud, and Ringo hunted down the three murderers and killed them. His vengeance satisfied, he left the country to escape the law, and for years was a vagabond through the West, living by his wits, his six-shooter, and his dexterity at cards, and wandering finally to Arizona, where he threw in with Curly Bill. This was Ringo's own story of how he came to drift into outlawry. It was told in a rare mood of confidence to William Fyffe, a Mormon rancher on Five Mile Creek in the Chiricahuas, at whose home he often stopped overnight on his trips between Tombstone and Galeyville.

Ringo came by his reckless courage honestly. He was

a second cousin of the famous Younger brothers of Missouri, whose exploits as guerillas under the black flag of the bloody Quantrill and as bank robbers with Frank and Jesse James, fill a red chapter in Western history. The Youngers were of Missouri and Kentucky stock and were perhaps forced into lawlessness as a result of the savage hatreds that grew up on the Missouri-Kansas border during the war between the North and South. The Younger family is an extensive one, and numbers many men throughout the country of honourable and distinguished name in business and the professions. Ringo's three sisters, to whom he was devotedly attached, lived in San Jose, California, with Col. Coleman Younger, his grandfather.

Once, while riding through Sulphur Springs Valley with Deputy Sheriff William Breakenridge, Ringo drew a letter from his pocket. He had read the letter before, perhaps many times, but he read it again with an air of deep abstraction. When he had folded the missive and put it back in its envelope, he fell into momentary silent reverie. He shook his head sadly as he held out the envelope to Breakenridge.

"Seems strange," he said, "for a tough, no-good fellow like me to get a letter like this."

"Sweetheart?" queried Breakenridge, noting the superscription was in a woman's hand.

"My sister," said Ringo solemnly. "She writes to me regularly. Thinks I'm in the cattle business out here and doing fine. Doing fine. Humph! Dear little sister, I hope she never learns the truth."

Curly Bill, since the killing of Town Marshal White, had given Tombstone a wide berth. Ringo, the Clantons, McLowerys, and others among the outlaws still

dropped in occasionally, and as long as they conducted
themselves quietly, the Earps did not molest them.
The outlaws were Sheriff Behan's problem, and as long
as he saw fit to remain amiable and tolerant, Wyatt
Earp preserved an armed neutrality. Ringo did not approve of the Earps. Under the administration of these
six-shooter Puritans, the fatal peace of a New England
village seemed settling upon Tombstone. Things had
come to such a pass that, in the decadent serenity of
the camp, a man almost felt called on to explain his
thirst, and when decent outlaws, in the enjoyment of
their constitutional privileges, wished to shoot out the
lights, they must retire to such provincial places as
Charleston and Galeyville. This sort of injustice rankled
with Ringo. He stood for the wide-open frontier of old
tradition, and as an apostle of spiritual liberty, he felt
called on to regenerate Tombstone and restore it to its
lost prestige as the toughest town in the Southwest.
The whole question, it seemed to him, might be settled
by ordeal of personal combat between himself as champion of the outlaws and Wyatt Earp as champion of the
law and order crowd.

Ringo's appearance in Tombstone became a challenge.

"Everybody looked for a fight every time Ringo came
to town," said William Lutley, freighting lumber over
from the Chiricahuas in those days. "He was plainly
spoiling for a fight. He'd swagger up and down Allen
Street, looking mighty hostile with his big, ivory-
handled guns buckled around him. Or in cold weather,
he wore a great shaggy buffalo-skin overcoat, a six-
shooter, of course, in each pocket. Then he looked like
a giant. If he saw the Earps standing on a corner, he

made it a point to walk past them and stare them in the eye. Or he would stroll into the Oriental, the Earp hang-out, and take a drink as cool as you please with the place full of Earp men and maybe one or two of the Earps talking with Doc Holliday at the other end of the bar. It was fine, impressive swashbuckling, and the way everybody figured it was that Ringo was willing to get killed for the privilege of taking one or two of the Earps with him. His chances in a single-handed fight against the Earps would have been about the same a jackrabbit would have in a pack of lobo wolves. The Earps and Doc Holliday were as hard, desperate men as he was."

Wyatt, Virgil, and Morgan Earp and Doc Holliday stood one day in front of Bob Hatch's saloon and billiard parlour chatting with Mayor Charles N. Thomas. Directly across Allen Street John Ringo, Ike, Finn, and Billy Clanton, and Tom and Frank McLowery lounged in front of the Grand Hotel. The situation appealed to Ringo as ideal for putting into effect his obsession for settling the enmity between Earps and outlaws by personal combat between individual champions. He stalked across the street.

"Wyatt Earp," he said, "I'll make you a proposition. We hate you and you hate us. If this feeling keeps up, there's going to be a battle some day, and a lot of men'll be killed. You and I can settle this whole thing. Just the two of us. Come out into the middle of the street with me, and we'll step off ten paces and shoot it out, fair and square, man to man."

Wyatt Earp looked at Ringo for a moment in amazement.

"Ringo," he said, "I'm not given to makin' sucker

plays. If you're drunk or crazy, I'm neither one nor the other. I'd be a fine simpleton—a peace officer and candidate for sheriff—to fight a duel with you in the street. Go and sleep it off."

He turned on his heel and went inside the saloon. Doc Holliday, second only to Wyatt Earp in the affairs of the Earp faction, remained standing in the door, a cold little smile on his cadaverous face. Ringo drew a handkerchief from the breast pocket of his coat and flipped a corner of it toward Holliday.

"They say you're the gamest man in the Earp crowd, Doc," Ringo said. "I don't need but three feet to do my fighting. Here's my handkerchief. Take hold."

Holliday took a quick step toward him.

"I'm your huckleberry, Ringo," replied the cheerful doctor. "That's just my game."

Holliday put out a hand and grasped the handkerchief. Both men reached for their six-shooters.

"No, you don't," cried Mayor Thomas, springing between them. "You'll fight no handkerchief duel here. There's been enough killing in Tombstone, and it's got to stop."

That ended it. Holliday went into the saloon. Ringo withdrew across the street. The apostle of spiritual liberty had a rather crestfallen air, for all the fool's courage he had displayed. The first move in his crusade for a wilder, tougher Tombstone had been decisively defeated.

Sheriff Behan was sitting in his office with Deputy Breakenridge when news of this affair reached him.

"What do you suppose John Ringo's been up to now?" said the sheriff. "Go and bring him in."

Deputy Breakenridge found Ringo pacing up and down in front of the Grand Hotel, his spirit hot and disturbed, and conducted him to the office.

"What's the trouble, Ringo?" asked the sheriff.

"Nothing much," replied the outlaw. "I simply offered to shoot it out with the Earps—that's all. Wyatt Earp backed down, excusing himself on the ground of politics. Holliday was willing. Doc's game, all right. I'll give him credit for that. But I'm not keen about being locked up, Johnny. How about my making bail?"

"You're not arrested. Give up your guns and you can go."

Ringo unbuckled his two guns and handed them over. Sheriff Behan placed them in a desk drawer and went up town.

"That's a right sweet little trick Johnny's played on me," remarked Ringo after the sheriff had gone. "My life won't be worth a white chip if those fellows catch me without my guns."

Deputy Breakenridge sat for a while in deep thought.

"I don't see any way out of it," he said at length. "I guess the sheriff didn't think what it would mean. But, you know, he's the boss."

Deputy Breakenridge stepped over to the desk, opened the drawer, and left Ringo's guns in plain view. Then he went out the door. When he returned, Ringo and the guns were gone. Also Deputy Breakenridge had made John Ringo his friend for life.

Not long after this, Ringo and Dave Estes robbed a poker game in Evilsizer's saloon in Galeyville. It was not a heroic feat, but the two outlaws needed the money. Having played since morning with the luck against them, they arose at midnight as neatly cleaned as if they had been to the laundry. They held counsel together as they went to the corral after their ponies. A fellow named Webb was spreading down four aces on the table as Ringo and Estes reëntered at the front door.

"If I know anything about poker," remarked Ringo, covering the players with his gun, "a six-shooter beats four aces."

Having pocketed $500, the two outlaws rode off across the mountains. Ringo had perpetrated such little pleasantries before, and the gentlemen who had been robbed had always laughed heartily, feeling it a little unsafe to do anything else. So a week or so after this latest drollery, Ringo was back in Galeyville amusing himself in his saturnine way as if nothing had happened. Deputy Breakenridge rode in one morning and served him with a warrant charging robbery with a gun.

"So those fellows couldn't take a joke, eh?" said Ringo, greatly astonished. "The damned blacklegs have no sense of humour."

Deputy Breakenridge was in a hurry to get back to Tombstone. Ringo had some business matters to settle.

"Tell you how we'll fix it up, Billy," said Ringo. "You hit the trail, and as soon as I've straightened up my affairs, I'll catch up with you."

Deputy Breakenridge hesitated.

"You have John Ringo's word," said the outlaw, straightening.

So Deputy Breakenridge started home alone. Having made camp that night at Mormon Smith's, he struck across Sulphur Springs Valley next morning. Noontime came, with no sign of Ringo. The late afternoon shadows began to lengthen. Still no Ringo. Deputy Breakenridge began to fret and stew with anxiety. Sheriff Behan would raise cain if he came in without his prisoner. Ringo was an outlaw, after all. Maybe it had been silly to trust him. If Ringo had lied. . . . Far across the valley Deputy Breakenridge saw a little swirl of dust. A horseman came into view riding hard. When Ringo drew alongside, his horse was wet with sweat. The outlaw had ridden all night to keep his promise.

"Think I wasn't coming?" he asked.

"No," replied Breakenridge Deputy. "Never had the least doubt in the world about it. I had your word. That was enough for me."

That night, in Sheriff Behan's office in Tombstone, Ringo sent for Lawyer Ben Goodrich to arrange bail, and from the lawyer he heard disturbing news. Curly Bill was accused of having robbed the stage at Robbers' Roost single-handed, and the Earps, it was reported, had located him in Charleston and planned to capture him next day. This made it vital for Ringo to get to Charleston as quickly as possible. Curly Bill was probably drunk on the loot of the hold-up, and unless Ringo arrived in time to aid him, the outlaw leader would doubtless be caught in the Earp trap.

"Get my bail and get it quick," snapped Ringo to Lawyer Goodrich.

While the lawyer was hunting a bondsman, Wyatt Earp learned with keen satisfaction of Ringo's arrival as a prisoner. With Ringo in jail, the capture of Curly Bill would be simplified. Wyatt Earp called on the district attorney and obtained from that official a promise to keep Ringo locked up without bail for twenty-four hours.

Lawyer Goodrich, having arranged matters, returned to Sheriff Behan's office.

"Everything's all right, Johnny," he said. "I've got good securities. They'll be in court to-morrow. With the bail fixed up, I guess there's no need for detaining Ringo any longer."

"No, I guess not," replied Sheriff Behan, feeling that, under the circumstances, it would be unnecessary to await official approval of the bond. "You can go any time you like, Ringo."

A few minutes later, Ringo was on his horse and burning up the road to Charleston.

Wyatt and Virgil Earp and Doc Holliday set out for Charleston early next day. Riding past Robbers' Roost and the old Brunckow mine, they emerged from the hills. Bathed in crisp sunshine, Charleston was just below them across the San Pedro. They arrived at the bridge. As they started to cross it, they reined their horses to an abrupt halt.

At the far end of the bridge, John Ringo stood facing them holding a rifle as a hunter holds a gun when the dogs are at point and the quail are about to flush from cover.

"Come on in, boys," called Ringo. "The water's fine."

This was a surprising situation. Ringo was supposed to be securely locked in jail back in Tombstone, and just as the Earps were about to swoop down on Curly Bill, here was Ringo holding the bridge and blocking their way to Charleston. The Earp trio advised together. As Ringo was here, Curly Bill probably wasn't.

Moreover, it looked a little like suicide to go any farther. So, wisely it seemed, they turned their horses in the direction of Tombstone and rode off slowly.

"We'll see you some other time, Ringo," shouted Wyatt Earp. "Give our regards to Curly."

As John Ringo's famous victory at the Charleston bridge became history, Sheriff Behan appeared in the District Court in Tombstone.

"I'll be ready in a few minutes," said the judge to the sheriff, "to take up the matter of John Ringo's bail."

"Ringo's bail?" exclaimed Sheriff Behan, his eyes wide with astonishment. "Ringo's gone."

"The district attorney," returned the judge, "has declined to approve the bond offered."

"I thought," stammered the sheriff, turning red, "the bond was fixed up last night."

"The sheriff is well aware," replied the judge frigidly, "that a bond must be officially approved before a prisoner is released."

"Well," said Sheriff Behan helplessly, beads of perspiration popping out on his forehead, "Ringo's disappeared. That's all there is to it."

"You are mistaken, Mr. Sheriff, in thinking that is all there is to it," returned the judge in tones of ice. "I will continue this matter until to-morrow morning. If at that time you fail to produce John Ringo in court, I will hold you personally responsible."

It was a chapfallen sheriff who sat in his office a little later with Deputy Breakenridge.

"What in hell are we going to do?" said Sheriff Behan.

"I'm damned if I know," replied Deputy Breakenridge.

News of Sheriff Behan's predicament reached Curly Bill in Charleston. Curly Bill laid the matter before John Ringo.

"Johnny Behan's been our friend," said Curly Bill, "and they might throw him loose from his job with this here judge all het up that-a-way. There's no tellin' what a lawyer can do to a feller. 'Twixt a lawyer and a catamount, I'd take chances on the catamount. But seein' as how we got Johnny Behan into this hole, we got to git him out, and we got to do some mighty fast work. I don't aim to lay down and see no friend of ours take the worst of it."

When the District Court convened in Tombstone next day, the face of the judge was like a thundercloud. Lawyers looked grave. The crowd sat in hushed solemnity. Sheriff Behan stood before the tribunal with bowed head.

"Mr. Sheriff," said the judge, "are you prepared to produce John Ringo?"

"No, your honour," replied the sheriff contritely. "I owe this court a profound apology."

The door of the courtroom opened and Deputy Breakenridge entered. Behind him stalked a tall, dark man with lean, saturnine face and sombre eyes.

"Your conduct, Mr. Sheriff," the judge went on, "has been extremely reprehensible. This is a matter of very serious importance. This is——"

"John Ringo!" shouted Sheriff Behan, his face beaming.

The ridiculous anticlimax left the honourable Court looking sheepish, his jaw hanging open on the last thunder note of his carefully prepared diatribe. The crowd roared, and scandalized bailiffs rapped for order.

Through the merry tumult, Sheriff Behan, Deputy Breakenridge, and John Ringo passed out smiling.

"The friendship of these outlaws," observed Sheriff Behan to Deputy Breakenridge after it was all over, "is at times embarrassing. But," added Sheriff Behan, "at other times it makes a fellow feel like he was sitting behind an ace-full in a fat jack pot."

CHAPTER X

RUSSIAN BILL materialized out of blue space and swaggered for a time among Tombstone's saloons, attracting much curious attention. He was a mystery. Nobody knew him or had ever heard of him. Nor did he condescend to introduce himself by any other name. He was Russian Bill—that was all.

A remarkably handsome fellow was Russian Bill, with a cameo face, fine eyes, and golden-yellow hair that tumbled about his shoulders. He dressed in cowboy regalia, complete in every detail, from white, sugarloaf sombrero to high-heeled half-boots with fancy tops and immense spurs that clanked noisily when he walked. It seemed evident at first glance that here was a bold, desperate fellow who probably would think no more of killing a man than of eating his breakfast.

Russian Bill revelled luxuriously in his reputation as a bad man. He hinted darkly of a long career of outlawry and of having killed four men and, in ostensible corroboration of a tragic record, he exhibited four notches carved with a penknife, as neatly as you please, on the handle of one of the two big six-shooters that dangled from his belt. He scowled ominously, carried himself like a swashbuckler, and tossed off his whisky with a flourish. Also he played a good hand at poker, and his game at faro was not to be sneezed at. Certainly, Russian Bill had all the earmarks of a dime-novel hero.

Buckskin Frank Leslie and Doc Holliday looked him over as he passed on Allen Street.

"There goes Russian Bill," remarked the doctor. "Famous outlaw and desperado."

"Russian Bill?" repeated Leslie musingly. "I don't seem to place him."

"Nobody else can," replied Holliday. "But he's bad. He admits it."

Leslie studied the tall figure, the fleckless cowboy accoutrements, the polished guns, the bright yellow holsters, the golden curls shaking over the broad shoulders.

"The gent's got pretty hair," said Buckskin Frank with the air of delivering a verdict.

Russian Bill, it must be admitted, was extraordinary for an outlaw. He displayed an amazing familiarity—for an outlaw—with history, literature, and science. Tombstone saloons were not haunts of the intelligentsia, and it would have been possible for a man with even a smattering of book-learning to acquire a reputation as a sage. But Russian Bill spoke with authority on many recondite subjects, and though his unlettered hearers at times hardly knew what he was talking about, it was generally assumed in Tombstone that his scholarly attainments were genuine.

Evidently of foreign birth, his English was almost without a trace of accent, and he was reputed to speak three other languages equally well. Sometimes, when mellow with liquor, he recited poetry. "This is from Keats," he would say. Or "That is from Shelley." The saloon hangers-on wondered where Keats tended bar and for what brand Shelley punched cows, but they were impressed. And in discussing such commonplace topics as the double-out system at bank or the advantage of drawing one card to three of a kind at poker, Russian Bill was just as likely as not to drop in a phrase of Latin or a Greek quotation. He seemed to have difficulty in holding back his erudition.

Then, Russian Bill's manners were distinguished. He did his best to conceal this scandalous fact, but it stood out as plain as the nose on his face. If he failed to catch some remark, he would say "Pardon me," instead of "What the hell was that you said?" And he had a way of saying "Thank you very much," and "Very kind of you," which sounded queer out here on the desert. And when he invited a fellow to take a glass of tanglefoot, he would not blurt out, "Line up and nominate your pizen," in the usual outlaw way, but would say with a courtly bow, "Do me the courtesy, my good friend, to have a little drink with me." These absentminded lapses did his reputation in Tombstone no good. Try as hard as he might, he seemed unable to convince anybody that he was rough and tough. A subtle something about him set him apart even in a Tombstone saloon and marked him unmistakably as a gentleman to the manner born.

Naturally, Russian Bill fell under grave suspicion. Tombstone was not used to outlaws that talked like scholars and observed the punctilios of polite society. Moreover, the spick-and-span newness of Russian Bill's cowboy make-up caused remark. It smacked of the mail-order house and looked too new to be true. Tombstone puzzled for quite a while over Russian Bill. When it came to outlaws, the town was pretty hard to fool. It made an honest effort to accept Russian Bill for the bold, bad man he represented himself to be, but at last the conclusion was forced upon it that this Russian Bill was only a make-believe outlaw and all his quaint stories were only so much blood-and-thunder claptrap.

The truth was, Russian Bill was dramatizing himself in a little play of his own creation. He was a natural actor who, having missed the footlights, had made the world his stage. His life was a drama that he lived before the critical eyes of an invisible audience. It was not vanity, but the artist in him, that made him strut and pose. Every move, every smile, every frown, was a detail of his art. The rôle of outlaw had appealed to him as romantically fitting in this wonderful Arizona stage-setting of lonely deserts and mountains. If he enjoyed playing outlaw, where was the harm? It was a satisfying character part. There was good drama in it. It gave him an opportunity for some fine heroics and theatrical effects. But if in this picturesque rôle of outlaw he should ever meet death standing at a turn in the road, what then? This was a question that did not concern him. As an artist at make-believe, why should he worry about death? Death was reality. There was no art in death.

The Bird Cage Theatre was crowded. The evening's entertainment was of that excellence Tombstone was wont to expect in this home of refined vaudeville. In one of the upper boxes sat Russian Bill in the midst of a bevy of red-light beauties, and waiters were busy hustling bottles of champagne from the downstairs bar. When the Tombstone Nightingale tripped from the wings and stood smiling behind the footlights, the audience greeted this ever-popular queen of song with vociferous cheering and waving beer mugs. The orchestra struck up something soft and plaintive, and the beautiful cantatrice launched into a soulful aria. Her rich soprano was trembling on a top note when a rough, drunken voice roared from the end box directly above the stage.

"Rotten. Who ever told you you could sing?"

The Tombstone Nightingale cut short her melody. Indignation blazed from her eyes. Billy Hutchinson, theatre proprietor, rushed upon the stage, several hard-looking gentlemen known as bouncers at his heels.

"Hey you, up there!" Billy Hutchinson shook his fist menacingly. "What do you mean by this outrage?"

Raucous laughter was his answer. The man hidden from view of the audience behind the box curtains was plainly a tough hombre and doubtless far gone in drink.

"You cut that out," yelled Billy Hutchinson. "I'll stand for no more disturbance from you. Interrupt this lady again and you'll get what's coming to you."

The man in the box subsided. The Tombstone Nightingale, taking a step nearer to the footlights, resumed her song. Again the drunken voice:

"Awful. Rats. Take her out."

Out from the wings bounced Billy Hutchinson, plainly boiling with wrath.

"Hustle up there and throw that fellow out," he shouted to the bouncers.

The audience itself was worked up to a pitch of fury by this time. Cries of "Throw him out" rose all over the house. Up the stairs bounded the bouncers. Followed boisterous dialogue. The scuffling noise of violent tumult. Savage yells. Loud oaths. Then the crash of revolver shots. Smoke swirled from the box.

The excited audience leaped to its feet. Murder was

more than it had bargained for. Out of the box a body hurtled. It plunged through the air, arms and legs flying helplessly, hat sailing off across the theatre. There was a mad scramble to get from under. But in vain. The body came crashing down on the heads of several wildly ducking, panic-stricken men.

Horrified silence for a moment.

Then up went a great roar of laughter. It was all a joke. The murdered man was only a suit of old clothes stuffed with straw.

The red-light beauties in Russian Bill's box burst into shrill merriment. Thrilling. Ripping. That stuffed figure certainly fooled them. Looked exactly like a dead man. Hadn't they had the scare of their lives? Best joke of the season. Just like Billy Hutchinson.

"Wasn't it just too funny for anything?" Flashing eyes turned upon Russian Bill.

"Yes," responded Russian Bill, smiling feebly from a corner. "Yes, it was very funny."

"Why, Russian Bill," exclaimed the painted lady, "whatever's the matter with you? You're as white as a sheet."

Russian Bill, sitting at a table in the Alhambra, was entertaining his roistering companions with breezy, merry talk. Miners and cowboys were drinking at the bar. Faro and roulette tables were crowded. The place was filled with boisterous hubbub. Suddenly Russian Bill fell into a reverie. His eyes clouded. There was a look of sadness in them. Possibly just a suspicion of undue moisture. One of his half-tipsy comrades clapped him roughly on the shoulder.

"What's eatin' you?" he asked loudly.

Russian Bill seemed to wake out of a dream.

"I was thinking of my mother," he said simply.

Doubtless the bold, bad outlaw was often thinking of his mother. His moods of silent reverie were frequent.

Russian Bill had a curiosity to see Charleston. He had heard much of the free-and-easy doings in the fantastic little capital of the San Pedro. He arrived there when, as it happened, Jack Swartz had on his war paint and all signs pointed to blood on the moon. Russian Bill was enjoying a quiet drink at a bar when in staggered Swartz.

"I'm a curly wolf," yelled the inebriated hombre as he shot out the lights and all the hangers-on hunted cover. Deep darkness for a time was starred with spitting flames. When the lamps were relighted, Russian Bill was gone. He was travelling at an easy gallop on the road to Tombstone. Not frightened, you understand, but a little disgusted. He had no stomach for Charleston. The village plainly was lowbrow and vulgar.

Russian Bill rode east one morning alone. It was his farewell to Tombstone. The town never saw him again.

Curly Bill sat in a chair under the big live oak in front of Nick Babcock's saloon in Galeyville, drinking beer out of a bottle and amusing himself with a few practice shots from his six-shooter at lizards and tin cans. It was a quiet day. Few people were about the street. The Chiricahua ridges were steeped in sunshine. The murmur of Turkey Creek came up out of the belt of timber below the mesa. Curly Bill's black eyes opened wide as, across the street, he beheld a tall young man with a cameo face and golden-yellow hair falling on his shoulders, who looked, in his cowboy trappings, as immaculate as if he had just stepped out of a bandbox.

"Who the hell's that?" growled the rustler chief in amazement.

"Sh-h-h!" whispered John Ringo. "Don't you know who that is? That's Russian Bill, the terrible outlaw."

"Who the hell's Russian Bill?" snarled Curly. "We oughter learn that tenderfoot not to wear his golden hair hanging down his back that-a-way in these here parts. It's immoral."

Russian Bill just at that moment was smoking a cigar held at a jaunty angle between his teeth. The next moment he wasn't. The cigar had disappeared from his mouth as by magic. A thin wisp of smoke was twisting from the muzzle of Curly Bill's six-shooter under the live-oak tree. With his bottle tilted over his head, Curly Bill was taking a deep swig of beer.

That was Russian Bill's introduction to Curly Bill. The real outlaw and the make-believe outlaw had many drinks together that day. They seemed to get on famously from the first. Possibly Curly liked the easy good-humour with which the tenderfoot took the joke of the vanishing cigar.

"I want to be an outlaw and join your band," said Russian Bill with his usual simplicity after the new friendship had been sealed with many drink offerings.

"*Bueno, compadre,*" replied Curly, laughing. "Git your pony saddled. I'm ridin' fer the Animos *pronto.*"

It was as if a king had said, "Arise, Sir Knight," after laying on the sword. Naïve directness was often the way to Curly Bill's good-will. When the rustler captain started for his ranch in the Animas Valley late in the day, Russian Bill was riding by his side.

"My brother and I," said Melvin Jones of Tucson,

"were camped at a cow ranch we had just bought over on the Gila River side of the Mogollons. Sitting by our camp fire just after dark, we heard some horses coming. Thinking it might be Indians, we grabbed our rifles and got back out of the firelight. Then somebody hollered 'Hello' and said they were two prospectors, and we told them to ride on up and camp with us.

"When they'd unsaddled and sat down by the fire, I looked these two 'prospectors' over. They didn't know me or my brother, but I knew both of them. One was Curly Bill and the other was Russian Bill. I used to see Russian Bill around Tombstone. Curly had a bandage wrapped about his face. Jim Wallace, not long before, had shot him in the jaw in Galeyville and come near killing him. Right after the shooting, Russian Bill rode over to Galeyville from Lordsburg and nursed Curly. Now the two were looking for some quiet spot in the mountains where Curly wouldn't be hunted and could get well undisturbed. They found the spot at a deserted sheep camp on the Negrito and stayed there three weeks. On his way out of the mountains, Curly Bill met me on the San Francisco and rode into the brush with me and helped me gather up some cattle I was driving back to our new ranch. His wound was healed, and he was all right again. I asked about his companion. 'He's headin' back fer the Animas,' Curly said."

Russian Bill had made progress since his Tombstone exit. He had risen to a speaking part in the outlaw drama. He was a member of Curly Bill's band. He clinked the glass of brotherhood with all the outlaws when they met in Galeyville for a carouse. When he stalked through the street in Lordsburg or Deming, awed citizens nudged one another and whispered, "Russian Bill, one of Curly Bill's outlaws." He was recognized everywhere as an outlaw. He posed and swaggered to his heart's content. He bathed in glory.

But, for all his honours, Russian Bill was not happy. Though he had the reputation of being an outlaw, he himself knew he was not. Though his freebooter comrades treated him with consideration, he felt that secretly they must view him with something akin to contempt. They had records as outlaws; he had none. They rode on cattle raids into Mexico and plundered smuggler trains along the border. He stayed at the home ranch and tended the kettles or did a little nursing now and then. His spirit burned within him as he thought of himself as an outlaw who had never committed a lawless deed, a robber innocent of robberies, a lamblike bad man, a desperado guiltless of blood. He must achieve guilt of some kind—any kind so it was guilt. He must steal something, engage in some depredation, kill somebody. He did not wish to stain his soul too deeply. But if his career in the rôle of outlaw was to be saved from the rocks, a crime was necessary.

With his artistic future at stake, Russian Bill sallied forth and stole a horse. Very crude and amateurish and foolish was this first and last crime ever attributed to Russian Bill in the Southwest. But the horse was easy and convenient to steal. Of course Russian Bill was caught. As soon as he rode into Shakespeare, a mining town over in the Pyramids in New Mexico, Deputy Sheriff Tucker walked up to him and quietly placed him under arrest. Russian Bill was an actor. He knew nothing about stealing horses.

But, as it happened, on the same day Russian Bill was locked in jail. Sandy King, a real outlaw, who had

ridden on many a freebooting expedition with Curly
Bill, got drunk and shot up Shakespeare for the second
time in a week. Sandy's first performance had been ex-
cused as mere maudlin frivolity, but his second was one
too many for Shakespeare, which was tough. As Sandy
went galloping up and down the main street, whanging
away, by and large, with his six-shooter, a mere clerk,
wearing a white linen shirt with stand-up collar and
tie, stepped to the door of a dry goods emporium and,
with a rifle, tumbled Sandy neatly out of the saddle
with a bullet through the neck. Sandy was only stunned,
and as soon as he had been brought round, the Stranglers assembled in executive session in the dining room
of the Pioneer House.

"But," protested the hotel proprietor, "this ain't no
time for you boys to be deliberatin' on a lynchin' in my
dinin' room. I'm jest about to set supper on the table."

"The victuals can wait," snapped the chairman of
the vigilance committee. "We've got important business on hand."

With the vigilantes seated around the supper table,
the Court was called to order and Sandy King was
brought in.

"Tucker's jest took up a hoss thief," piped up a
member of the committee, "and I moves, Mr. Chairman, that we takes this hoss thief's case up at the same
time."

So, in this purely incidental way and as an after-
thought, Russian Bill was also placed on trial. The
evidence against both men was brief but convincing.
Russian Bill was convicted of horse stealing and Sandy
King of "being a damned nuisance," both capital
crimes in Shakespeare. The table and the chairs were

moved over against the walls to give the vigilantes plenty of room, and the nooses were adjusted.

The bell had rung for the curtain. Russian Bill's drama was ending. He had learned how an outlaw should swagger and pose but he had neglected to learn how an outlaw should die. His histrionic art had prescribed no rules for the proper gesture, the correct attitude, at the final tragedy. The big third-act climax had caught him unprepared. The artist in make-believe at last had come face to face with the grim, lonely reality of death.

The two men were asked if they had anything to say.

"Thar ain't no whisky whar I'm goin', they tell me," spoke up Sandy King, "and ef you fellers air agreeable, I'd like a drink o' licker before I hit the out-trail."

He was given a good, stiff drink fetched in from the hotel bar.

But Russian Bill, standing erect, shoulders back, his cameo face set, his steady blue eyes shining with calm courage, shook his handsome head so that his golden-yellow hair tossed about over his shoulders and said never a word.

"This here hoss thief," remarked one of the committee, "is so damned good-looking it seems 'most a pity to hang him."

But the ropes having been thrown over the rafters, Russian Bill and Sandy King were swung into the air half up to the ceiling and the counterfeit bad man and the genuine bad man went out together.

After all, Russian Bill had needed no art to teach him how to die. He knew. He had lived like an actor. But he met death like a man.

After the bodies had been cut down and the tables

and chairs set back in their places, the hotel landlord, still hot under the collar at this unwarranted interruption of his customary routine, hustled in the steaming supper dishes, and his patrons, chafing at the delay, fell with gusto upon the corned beef and cabbage.

This was all for the time being. But a few months later, Mayor Thomas of Tombstone received a letter from the United States Consul General at St. Petersburg asking information of Lieutenant William Tattenbaum, formerly of the Imperial White Hussars, who had disappeared from Russia after wounding one of his superior officers in a quarrel, and was last heard of, it seemed, somewhere in Arizona. The missing officer's mother, the letter said, was the Countess Telfrin, a lady-in-waiting at the court of the Czar and she was deeply worried and very anxious to locate him. A photograph was enclosed. Mayor Thomas showed the picture about among Tombstone gamblers and saloon men, who, without hesitation, identified Lieutenant William Tattenbaum of the Imperial White Hussars as Russian Bill.

But Tombstone kept its secret. A reply was sent back to St. Petersburg that Lieutenant Tattenbaum, long a prosperous citizen of these parts, honoured and respected by all, had recently been the victim of an accident resulting in his untimely death. This untruth was, perhaps, cold comfort to the bereaved mother in Russia, but at least it ended her long search for her lost boy and saved her from a broken heart. The unfortunate noblewoman doubtless remained in ignorance to the end of her life that her high-born, scapegrace son had been lynched.

Buckskin Frank Leslie arrived in Tombstone while the town was still young. He was a jovial fellow, full of boisterous fun, rather handsome and well set up, though quite small. He cut a dashing figure as he paraded about the streets in a costume of fringed buckskin with two six-shooters at his belt. Tombstone accepted this Kit Carson finery with a grain of salt, and was inclined to believe Buckskin Frank a tenderfoot in frontier masquerade.

Buckskin Frank met Mrs. Mary Galeen at a dance. Pretty Mrs. Galeen was the belle of the evening, and gallant Buckskin Frank, very susceptible to feminine charm, was notably attentive. But after his fifth waltz with the dainty lady, Buckskin Frank was tapped on the shoulder and called aside by a tall, serious, dark man.

"That lady," said the tall, serious, dark man, "is my wife. Don't dance with her any more. If you do, I'll kill you."

Mr. Michael Galeen, who tended bar at the Crystal Palace, had been separated from his wife for several months, but still watched her every movement with jealous eye. He had sent word to her not to attend this dance, adding that if she did, her elaborate ball gown would prove her shroud.

Mrs. Galeen, being light-hearted and very comely and something of a coquette, preferred to ignore this tragic warning, but she was greatly perturbed over it, and when the ball was over, she was afraid to go home alone and asked Buckskin Frank to escort her. Which Buckskin Frank did with great pleasure.

It was one of Tombstone's wonderful nights. The

moonlight immersed the silent houses in frosty silver and filled the deserted streets like white, transparent fog. Walking along Allen Street arm in arm and talking in low, lover-like tones, the couple approached the Cosmopolitan Hotel where Mrs. Galeen was in lodgings. Mrs. Galeen was gurgling dulcetly over some pleasantry dropped by her cavalier when Mr. Galeen opened fire from an upper balcony in front of the hotel. But Mr. Galeen had time to fire but once when Buckskin Frank had out his own six-shooter and pinked Mr. Galeen neatly between the eyes. A few weeks later, Buckskin Frank married the widow of the man he had killed.

In view of all these romantic happenings, Tombstone sat up and took notice of this Buckskin Frank. A gentleman who could shoot with such accuracy in moonlight seemed worthy of more than passing attention. It turned out that Buckskin Frank was not a tenderfoot after all, but a noted desperado who, it was said, had killed ten or twelve men. He was a native of Kentucky, his boyhood passed in that state in an atmosphere of mountain feuds. As a scout with the army, he had seen Indian fighting in Texas, Oklahoma, and the Dakotas and had taken part in one or two Arizona campaigns against the Apaches. Tombstone was amazed that a fellow with such a tragic record could take the world with such light-hearted gaiety. Geniality and deadliness seemed his most distinctive characteristics; his heart apparently was overflowing with fun and murder.

Buckskin Frank became in time one of Tombstone's six-shooter personages. He was unquestionably one of the quickest men with a Colt's in the country. He shot with the same accuracy at a tin can as at a man who happened to be firing at him. Which, it may be re-

marked, is one of the fine points of desperado genius.
There seemed, moreover, to be no doubt as to his game-
ness; he would take a chance face to face, but, it was
said, was not above shooting a man in the back. He
would kill a man, it was declared, for anything—or
nothing. It all depended on his mood, which was precarious. As far as anyone knew, he had never killed a
man merely to see him fall, but he was suspected of being capable of just such an amusing prank.

He was a sly, crafty, subterranean man, with many
deep secrets. His comings and goings were enigmatic.
He was soon on terms of intimacy with Curly Bill's
outlaws, especially with John Ringo, and indulged in
many drinking bouts with them at Antelope Springs,
Soldier Holes, Myers Cienega, Charleston, and Galeyville. Though he tended bar at the Oriental in which
Wyatt Earp acquired an interest, he never threw in
with the Earps. He remained always a lone wolf who
played his own dark, mysterious game. A very dangerous person was this Buckskin Frank Leslie and for all
his joviality, a fine fellow to let alone if one wished to
live in peace or even to live at all. He was to add several more notches to his gun-handle before Tombstone
saw the last of him.

After their marriage, Buckskin Frank and the Widow
Galeen set up housekeeping in a cottage and lived quite
happily for a time. But Buckskin Frank found domesticity dull, and sought to vary the drab monotony with
piquant novelties. As he sat in the mellow glow of the
family hearth of an evening, he would surprise his pretty
bride by shooting a rose out of her hair or a cup of coffee
out of her hand as she brought it in for supper. Or he
would stand her against the parlour wall and, with the

neatness of a pencil drawing, outline her figure with bullets fired from across the room.

With the air of an artist at an easel in his atelier, he would stand off and measure his subject—and the distance—with his eye and then, having rounded off the lady's head with bullets placed an inch apart, he would work downward to skirt hem, matching rapid pistol fire the while with rapid fire of comment and criticism.

"Stand perfectly still, my dear," he would say. "I am now doing your left ear. . . . Now for the other. . . . Ears are more or less difficult. . . . Three bullets on each side will do nicely for your throat. . . . Smile, darling. . . . You are prettiest when you smile. . . . My only regret is that I can't get the smile in my picture. . . . Your pose is charming this evening. Hold it one moment while I reload. . . . I am now at your waist line. I must not fail to bring out the fine curves. . . . The skirt is easy. Draperies offer no difficulty to a real artist. . . ."

The outline of the figure completed—a portrait of this kind usually required several boxes of cartridges—Mrs. Leslie was at liberty to step out of her bullet silhouette. Then, as finishing detail, the Michael Angelo of the six-shooter would touch in eyes, nose, and mouth with a few final shots.

"Ah, magnificent," he would say, cocking his head at his masterpiece with immense satisfaction. "Your friends will admire this portrait. It looks exactly like you."

All Tombstone, in fact, marvelled at the artistry of these mural portraits, which remained on the parlour walls for years and were shown with great pride by the citizens to visitors to town, the Leslie cottage serving

in lieu of a municipal art gallery. But Mrs. Leslie, being
of a purely domestic turn, showed her utter lack of
artistic appreciation by getting a divorce. She married Alex Derwood, a mechanic with no ambition to
be a portrait painter, and moved to Banning, California,
where at last accounts she is still living.

Nigger Jim, as black as the ace of spades, would say
with great seriousness: "Yes, suh, me and Sime White
wuz the fust white men ever in this camp." Nigger Jim
didn't date quite that far back, but he was among the
early arrivals. His name was Jim Young but he was
never anything but Nigger Jim in Tombstone chronicles. He had been a slave, a soldier in the regular army,
and a prize fighter. He was more than six feet tall,
straight and powerful, and looked as proud and dignified as a Zulu chief at the head of a war impi. He
worked in the Contention mine on the hill, and he staked
himself a claim near it. When one morning he discovered Frank Leslie had jumped his claim, Jim armed
himself with a shotgun.

"Bad man or no bad man," he said, "he ain't goin'
jump no claim o' mine."

"This claim's mine," said Nigger Jim, striding up to
Buckskin Frank. "You-all ain't got no business foolin'
round heah, and you better go on back to town mighty
quick."

So it wasn't so easy to jump a lone nigger's claim, after
all. Buckskin Frank smiled it off.

"I heard some fellers were about to jump your claim,
Jim," he said, "and I came out here to help you stand
'em off."

Nigger Jim didn't argue over the explanation and

Leslie went away. When the story went the rounds that Nigger Jim had bluffed one of the worst of Tombstone's bad men, Jim's prestige rose and Buckskin Frank's went off a point or two. But the show-down rankled with the desperado. When he met Jim unarmed in a store and the Negro's back was turned, Leslie slipped his gun out of its holster. But the woman who owned the place screamed and sprang between them. Again Buckskin Frank smiled it off. He was, he said, merely examining his six-shooter to see that the cylinder was in good working order.

With his ready wit and suave tongue, Buckskin Frank, it was said, could talk himself out of any situation. When his six-shooter was inconvenient, he always had his tongue to fall back on. Later, it is declared, he talked himself out of the penitentiary and into the heart of a woman at the same time.

Nigger Jim, past ninety, still lives in Tombstone. His memories of old days have faded to a misty blur, but he is still proud and dignified and as straight as an assegai, and still looks as if he might be capable of leading an impi out on a war trail.

CHAPTER XI

ON THE BENSON ROAD

BUD PHILPOT gathered up his lines. "Come on, boys," he said to his four horses. The leaders pranced and curvetted, the wheelers leaned soberly in their collars. The Benson stage went at an easy trot out Allen Street. Bob Paul, shotgun messenger, was in his seat beside the driver. Three passengers sat on top. Six others filled the seats inside.

The sidewalk crowds paid no attention. This was merely the regular Benson stage starting on schedule time. They would have taken only slightly more interest if they had known that in the boot was $80,000. It was an unusual shipment, but treasure was going out on the stages every day or two. And Bob Paul was a brave, dependable fellow as shotgun messenger. So the stage rumbled out of Tombstone almost unnoticed and disappeared over a hill, leaving a little cloud of dust hanging against the sky.

But the departure of this lumbering old coach, March 15, 1881, was, in its long train of tragic consequences, one of the momentous events in Tombstone's history. While the stage jogged peacefully out of the town, fate was waiting grimly on the Benson road.

At Contention, ten miles from Tombstone, Paul and Philpot changed seats. This change may have been a whim of Paul's. He would see what kind of stage-driver he was, just for fun. Philpot was willing; he could take

it easy for a time. When the stage swung briskly out of
Contention, Philpot was in the customary seat of the
shotgun messenger, and Paul was doing the driving, his
shotgun leaning between his legs.

Beyond Drew's ranch, six miles out of Contention,
the stage crossed a dry wash. The wash was broad and
deep, and on the far side, the road angled at a sharp
grade up a hill. Up this incline the horses went at a walk.
It was growing late; the sun was dipping toward the
Huachucas; long, cool shadows lay across the landscape.

Halt!

Three masked highwaymen stepped out of the mesquite with levelled rifles. Dropping the reins, Paul seized
his shotgun. As he threw the gun to his shoulder, the
robber on his side of the road fired. The bullet crashed
into the seat. Paul emptied both barrels of his shotgun
without apparent effect. At the same instant, the robber on the other side of the road sent a bullet squarely
through Philpot's heart. Philpot half rose and pitched
headlong beneath the heels of the wheelers. The terrified
horses leaped into a run and went rearing and plunging
up the grade. The bandits fired twenty shots after the
coach. Peter Roerig, a resident of Tombstone, sitting
on top at the rear, was killed and tumbled to the
ground. With bullets whistling about it, the stage
thundered over the crest of the hill out of range.

With the lines dragging on the ground, the horses left
the road and went tearing through the mesquite, the
coach careening over rocks and threatening every moment to upset. Clambering down on the tongue, Paul,
at risk of his life, retrieved the lines. The horses ran
away for a mile before he quieted them down and got
them back into the highway. With the $80,000 safe in

the boot, Paul brought the bullet-riddled coach into
Benson. Searching parties went out after nightfall and
took the two dead men into Tombstone.

Sheriff Behan and a posse took the trail at daybreak
the morning after the murderous fiasco. In the posse
were Wyatt, Virgil and Morgan Earp, Bob Paul, and
Marshall Williams, agent of the Wells-Fargo Company
in Tombstone. They found at the scene seventeen
empty rifle shells and three strange-looking masks made
of cloth to fit over the head like a wig and with an attached band to hide the lower face, wig and band covered with dangling strands of untwisted rope to simu-
late hair and beard. The trail of the robbers was followed east to the Dragoons. Wood choppers at the base
of the mountains said three riders had passed their
camp and turned northwest.

The fugitives were tracked to Tres Alamos, sixty
miles north of the scene of the crime, where they had
crossed the San Pedro. They had taken advantage of
a twelve hours' start to play every trick known to plains-
men to confuse their trail. They had travelled Indian
file. They had doubled back on their tracks and then
switched off at right angles on stony ground that left
no imprints. They had kept to long outcropping reefs
of rock. Once they had rounded up a bunch of horses
and, driving them before them, had hidden their own
tracks in the swarming hoof prints. Again they had ridden for a mile through the San Pedro River, emerging
in thick brush, and a little farther on had taken to the
stream once more.

The scent grew warmer at Wheaton's abandoned
ranch. Here a horse was found so badly tuckered out it
could hardly stagger, its back covered with saddle sores.

A few miles farther down the river, at the ranch of H.
T. Redfield, father of Leonard Redfield, who for thirty
years has been postmaster at Benson, the posse saw
a man in a field loaded with warlike armament and
milking a peaceful cow. This remarkable milkmaid
scurried for the brush as the posse galloped toward
him. Wyatt and Morgan Earp headed him off and took
him prisoner. He proved to be Luther King. Besides a
rifle strapped across his shoulders, two six-shooters,
and two belts full of cartridges, King had a dozen boxes
of cartridges stuffed in his pockets. He admitted the
exhausted horse found at Wheaton's belonged to him.

King had been a San Simon Valley cowboy but had
been working on the Redfield ranch for several weeks.
He lied fluently at the start. But maintaining his innocence of active participation in the attempted robbery,
he confessed finally that the bandits were friends of his,
he had had previous knowledge of their plans, and
had met them in their flight to replenish their stock of
ammunition. He named Bill Leonard, Jim Crane, and
Harry Head as the highwaymen. These were outlaws
associated with the Clanton-McLowery group of Curly
Bill's band. King declared explicitly that these three
men alone had been concerned in the attack on the
stage.

King was taken to Tombstone by Sheriff Behan
and Marshall Williams and placed in jail. His confession seemed unbelievable, and it was suspected that he
had held the horses for the three road agents while they
attempted to rob the stage. But nothing more of King's
connection with the crime was ever learned. He escaped under peculiar circumstances, two weeks later.
He had sold the horse that had been found exhausted

at Wheaton's ranch to John Dunbar, and to complete the transaction had been taken into the sheriff's office. Under Sheriff Woods, Dunbar, and Harry Jones were present, and Jones was drawing up the bill of sale when King slipped out the door, and mounting a horse saddled and waiting for him, rode out of town and out of any further knowledge of that part of the country from that day to this.

Meanwhile, the three Earps and Paul, joined near Benson by Detective Fred Hume of the San Francisco office of Wells-Fargo, pressed hard on the traces of the murderers. The trail led west along the northern flanks of the Rincon, Tanque Verde, and Santa Catalina mountains, south through Cañada del Oro, east past Tucson through the Santa Cruz Valley, and again across the San Pedro River. After travelling in a gigantic loop more than three hundred miles around, the criminals had come back to the Dragoons. Here, at Helm's ranch, Sheriff Behan rejoined the posse, bringing with him Deputy Sheriff Billy Breakenridge and Buckskin Frank Leslie.

Across the Dragoons and the Chiricahuas, the posse made its way to Galeyville. There Wyatt Earp, having been on the trail ten days, turned back for Tombstone. The others pressed on into the Cloverdale region of New Mexico, where Leonard and Head had a ranch. Finding the ranch deserted, the chase was abandoned. On the home trail, the posse encountered severe hardships. One could travel fifty or seventy-five miles through this semi-desert region—and can do it to-day —without sighting a ranch house. Food ran out. No water could be found. Virgil Earp's horse became exhausted, and Morgan Earp took his brother up behind him. Under the double load, Morgan's own horse was soon staggering from weakness, and the two Earps had to lead their horses and follow on foot far behind the others. When the possemen stumbled on a spring in the eastern edge of the San Simon, it was the first water they had had for forty-eight hours. Sheriff Behan, Deputy Breakenridge, and Buckskin Frank Leslie left the others here and, riding night and day, reached San Simon ranch a hundred miles to the north and sent back supplies by horseback messenger. When relief arrived, those left behind had been four days and a half without food.

Upon arrival in Tombstone, Sheriff Behan and his men received the plaudits of the press.

> The persistent pursuit of the murderers of poor Bud Philpot [said the *Epitaph*] is a credit to each individual member of the posse and will pass into frontier annals as a record of which all may be proud. Especially worthy of praise was the tireless work of Bob Paul and Virgil and Morgan Earp, who were in the saddle continuously for seventeen days and followed the trail from the morning after the Benson road murders.

In the aftermath of gossip that followed the attempted stage robbery, the bungling amateur touch which had seemed to characterize the work of the road agents came in for criticism. If these fellows had been old hands, it was pointed out, they would have shot one of the lead horses. That would have brought the stage to a halt. Then, if they could have finished off Bob Paul, they could have looted the coach at their leisure. It must have been humiliating to see $80,000 escape them and go galloping over the hill in a cloud of dust. . . . The strangely shifted positions of driver **and shotgun** messenger caused comment. No such thing, it was said, had ever been heard of before. Why had Paul and Philpot changed places? Some attached deep meaning to this; others regarded it as a casual coincidence. Paul, it was argued, must have had some inkling that a robbery was to be attempted or have received a warning of some kind, which was probably untrue. The opinion grew that the highwaymen had been especially anxious to do away with the shotgun messenger, possibly because of secret information he possessed, and believed when they killed Philpot, they were killing Paul. . . . Philpot was an old-time stage-driver, who had had long experience on mountain routes in California and been through many hold-ups. Once, so the story ran, when highwaymen ordered him to throw out the money chest, he threw out a green band-box belonging to a lady passenger and by the time the robbers discovered the trick, Philpot and the stage had passed out of danger. As reward for this heroic subterfuge, Philpot had been presented with a gold watch by the Wells-Fargo people. At his death, Philpot left a wife and four children in California.

While Sheriff Behan and his posse were scouring the country for the highwaymen, Tombstone awoke one morning to read in one of the papers this bit of startling news:

Positive proof exists that four men took part in the attack on the Benson stage. The fourth is in Tombstone and is well known and has been shadowed ever since his return to town. He is suspected for the following reasons: On the afternoon of the attempted robbery, he engaged a horse at a Tombstone livery stable stating that he might be gone for seven or eight days or might return that night. He left town about 4 o'clock armed with a Henry rifle and a six-shooter. He started toward Charleston and about a mile below Tombstone cut across to Contention. When next seen, it was between 10 and 1 o'clock at night, riding back into the livery at Tombstone. his horse

fagged out. He at once called for another horse, which he hitched in
the street for some hours, but he did not again leave town. Statements attributed to him, if true, look very bad and, if proved, are
most conclusive as to his guilt either as a principal or an accessory
after the fact.

The man brought under suspicion as the fourth highwayman was Doc Holliday. The suspicion against the
right bower of the Earp faction seemed to have a certain semblance of logic, and Tombstone was soon rolling the delicious tidbit of scandal over its tongue. Holliday's many friends were indignant at what they de-
nounced as a new trick of the Behan crowd. Holliday's
many enemies gleefully and promptly returned a verdict of guilty in the first degree. The insouciant doctor,
wit, and desperado, took the matter lightly.

"So I'm a stage robber," he remarked with cynical
good-humour. "Well, I don't believe it. They'll have to
prove this to me. If I had been there, you can bet a
stack of blue chips that eighty thousand never would
have got away."

The doctor seemed to resent the implied reflection on
his well-known artistry.

"And I've made incriminating statements, eh?" the
doctor smiled derisively. "Well, it's just like me to talk
the rope around my neck. I shoot up the stage, kill a
couple of fellows, and blab it all over the country. No
honest stage robber'll trust me after this, and serve me
right."

The doctor was noted for a pleasant garrulity, but he
had never been known to reveal any of his own secrets.
He was habitually too wise in the treacheries of the
underworld to place his own safety unreservedly in the
hands of any man.

"They seem to think being armed with a rifle and a six-shooter makes the case against me look pretty black," he pursued. "Humph! The next time I ride out into the brush in this outlaw country, I'll wear kid gloves and carry a bunch of Sunday-school tracts.

"But," added the doctor, "what's the difference? Let 'em talk their heads off. Talk's cheap. If I'm guilty and don't hanker to do a stretch in Yuma or cash out at the end of a rope, I ought to run away. Or you might think they'd arrest me. They know where to find me; I'm not hiding from anybody. They're making a hula-baloo because I happened to ride out of town the day of the hold-up. I might have gone to visit an old friend. I've done such a thing before but I never thought of it as a hanging matter. Well, I'll keep my mouth shut.

"A still tongue is the best policy. The Behan crowd are trying to frame me and if I told the gospel truth, they'd swear I was lying. But I'll wait for the show-down. If it ever comes, I'll spread better than a pair of deuces on the table. You can bank on that."

A little adventure that befell Mr. and Mrs. John Slaughter on the Charleston road that night added to the suspicion against Holliday. Slaughter, afterward famous as the fighting sheriff of Cochise County, had drawn $10,000 that afternoon from the Charleston bank. He had the money with him when he and his wife at 10 o'clock at night set out to drive to the dairy ranch of Amazon Howell, Mrs. Slaughter's father, at William Springs, between Charleston and Tombstone.

At a lonely spot in the road, a horseman rode toward them out of a dry wash. He may have had some sinister design. Or he may have been following the wash as a short cut from Charleston to Tombstone. But, at any rate, he had a drawn six-shooter in his hand, and Slaughter suspected the fellow meant to rob him.

"Look out, John," cried Mrs. Slaughter in alarm, "that man has a gun in his hand."

"Well," replied her husband calmly, "so have I."

And Mrs. Slaughter saw her husband's hand gripping a six-shooter held in his lap, its barrel grimly following the shadowy figure moving in the darkness. Whatever was in the mind of the man on horseback, he made no menacing move with his revolver, but riding on without a word, disappeared on the road to Tombstone. Slaughter recognized the horse. "That was Charlie Tribolett's blaze-face roan," he said. "I'd know that horse anywhere." Slaughter believed the man on the horse was Doc Holliday. Moreover, he always remained of this opinion.

Suspicion against Holliday grew when it was learned that he had been a close friend of Bill Leonard. This friendship, however, had been of several years standing. Leonard and Holliday had first known each other in Las Vegas. There Leonard was a prosperous jeweller and stood well as a business man. He came to Tombstone from Las Vegas and for a long time worked in a jewellery shop, and in Tombstone also, during this period of employment, his reputation was good. He was an expert watch repairer, and some of Tombstone's old-timers still recall his deftness at his trade. Gambling, drinking, and bad associates caused Leonard's fall. He became intimate with the Clantons and other Curly Bill outlaws, and was soon taking part in their criminal affairs. For several months before the Benson stage hold-up, Leonard, Head, and Crane had been "batching" in a cabin at a place called the Wells, ten miles from Tombstone, over toward Contention. It was bruited about that Holliday several times had visited Leonard there, and it was suspected that he had seen Leonard at the Wells a few hours before the attack on the stage.

Holliday admitted he had hired a horse in Tombstone on the afternoon of the attempted robbery. He said, however, that he had hired it, not from Charlie Tribolett, but from John Dunbar's corral. He denied that he had been in Charleston or that he was the man on the blaze-face roan whom John Slaughter had encountered at night on the Charleston road. He had returned to Tombstone, he declared, at dusk, at about the hour the attempted stage robbery was taking place some sixteen miles away. He had hitched his horse in the street, he said, and after taking supper in a restaurant, played faro for several hours in the Alhambra. After his faro game, he declared, he returned the horse to Dunbar's corral.

Holliday's story, if true, was a clear alibi, despite the fact that he failed to tell where he had gone on his trip out of town. Moreover, his alibi had apparent corroboration in a story told by a man named Fuller, who did a business hauling water from the Wells to Tombstone. Fuller declared that, just after he had left the Wells with a wagonload of water, about 4 o'clock on the afternoon of the stage hold-up, Holliday had joined him. Holliday, Fuller said, hitched his horse to the rear of the wagon and took his seat beside Fuller. Holliday, according to Fuller, had come back to Tombstone seated in Fuller's wagon. Wyatt Earp also corroborated Holliday's alibi.

"I received a wire message about 6:30 o'clock that evening direct from Bob Paul at Benson telling me that the stage had been held up," said Wyatt Earp. "Immediately after I had received the telegram, I found Doc Holliday playing faro, and it would have been impossible for him to have been at the scene of the attack on the stage. In identifying Holliday as the rider of Charlie Tribolett's blaze-face roan, John Slaughter simply made a mistake."

One point generally overlooked at the time stood out in Doc Holliday's favour. This was Luther King's statement that Leonard, Crane, and Head were alone in the attempted robbery. Despite the printed assertion of positive information that there were four robbers, it was never definitely settled there were more than three. It may be pointed out that there were stronger grounds for suspecting King as a possible fourth robber than for suspecting Holliday.

"Despite King's denials," said Wyatt Earp, "there was never any doubt in my mind that he was the fourth robber. I never took any stock in the fishy story he told when we captured him loaded down with guns and ammunition. If King had not escaped, I think his participation in the robbery would eventually have been proved."

Holliday was never arrested. If the authorities had any evidence against him, they never saw fit to bring it into court. Leonard, Head, and Crane were chased all over the map of southeastern Arizona, but Holliday lived unmolested in Tombstone. But from the time of the Benson stage affair, Holliday remained in a fourth dimensional vagueness of suspicion, his guilt never established and his innocence never proved. Which, it may be remarked in passing, worried the genial doctor not at all.

Gossip was still acute when this second statement, as astounding as the first, was printed in the newspapers:

> Evidence in the hands of the authorities implicates four robbers and five accomplices and arrests will follow as soon as everything is ready. Meanwhile it is certain that several men around Tombstone, among them one who was a participant in the preliminary pursuit, are under surveillance.

Identity of the five men under suspicion as accomplices was a more difficult riddle than the Holliday affair. Though the Clantons and McLowerys were mentioned it was generally assumed that the accomplices indicated were the Earps and Marshall Williams, and Williams was identified as the man who had "participated in the preliminary pursuit." There was no evidence against Williams, and he was suspected only because he was a friend of the Earps and was in a position to know when shipments of money and bullion went out on the stages. But the gossip had it that Williams had tipped off the treasure cargo to the Earps and the Earps had assigned Holliday as their personal representative to assist in the robbery and see the spoils were evenly divided. But these innuendos were circulated only in the most discreet whispers. None of the promised arrests ever was made, and it is doubtful that at this time Wyatt Earp and his brothers realized that they were under suspicion. It was not until six months later that the first and only open charge against them was made.

Long before the Earp-Clanton feud reached its climax of battle in Tombstone's streets, the three highwaymen who had made the attack on the Benson stage and were the indirect cause of the vendetta were in their graves. Jim Crane died with Old Man Clanton in the fight with

Mexicans in Guadalupe Cañon. Leonard and Head were killed at Owl City, New Mexico, by Ike and Bill Haslett, whose ranch the two outlaws had coveted and whose lives they had threatened. When Bob Paul fired on the stage robbers, his aim had been better than he knew. Leonard said with his last breath that he was glad to die to escape the agony from a gaping wound in his groin left by the shotgun messenger's charge of buckshot.

CHAPTER XII

FLASHES OF STORM

THE Earp-Clanton feud has passed into the melting pot of tradition in which so much frontier history has been changed into myth. The Southwest has a nebulous idea that in some way or other it grew out of the attempted robbery of the Benson stage, but it may be ventured that not a half-dozen persons in Tombstone or in all Arizona have any definite knowledge of its origin.

But the bloodstained facts of the old story are still memories strangely surcharged with bitterness. The opinions of the fathers have become the convictions of the children, and the hatreds that were quick with flaming life nearly a half century ago stalk grimly today as the ghosts of hatreds. The Earps are gone, the Clantons are dust these many years, but a new generation that knew neither is ready to do sentimental battle for the causes championed by its forbears. The cold ashes of the dead feud, under chemical analysis, would still show traces of venom.

The Earp-Clanton feud was an evolution rather than a sudden flare of lethal violence. Its origin was complicated. Contributory causes linked in involved sequence, were: The attempted robbery of the Benson stage and the murder of Bud Philpot; the robbery of the Bisbee stage; a proposition whatever it was—and there were two conflicting stories concerning it—made

by Wyatt Earp to Ike Clanton; a tipsy remark made
by Marshall Williams; Doc Holliday's flaming resentment; Ike Clanton's drunken spree.

Bad blood grew between the Earps and the Clantons
and the Clantons' close friends and partners in outlawry, the McLowerys, in the very early days of Tombstone's history. Only a few days after Wyatt Earp
arrived in Tombstone, a horse was stolen from him.
For a long time, he lost all trace of the animal. Then he
heard it was in the possession of the Clantons. Wyatt
Earp and Doc Holliday went to Charleston to investigate. Sheriff Behan was in Charleston on that occasion
to serve Ike Clanton with a subpœna in some court case.

"I was told by a friend of mine," testified Wyatt
Earp later, "that the man who carried Sheriff Behan's
subpœna from Charleston to the Clanton ranch rode
my horse."

Wyatt Earp was over in the Huachuca Mountains
later, looking after some water rights, and on his way
back to Tombstone, Scar-Face McMasters met him on
the road and told him, if he rode fast enough, he would
find his horse in Charleston.

"As soon as I reached Charleston," said Wyatt
Earp, "I saw Billy Clanton ride my horse through the
street and put him up in a corral. It struck me as pretty
brazen for Billy Clanton to ride my stolen horse about
in this public fashion within nine miles of Tombstone.
But Charleston was a Clanton-McLowery stamping
ground and was filled with friends of these desperadoes.
I was alone, but I determined to get possession of my
horse legally and take him back home. As Justice Jim
Burnett was away in Sonora, I telegraphed to Tombstone to my brother James to have papers for the re-

covery of the animal made out before Justice Wallace and sent over to me at once. Billy Clanton learned of this telegram and went to the corral to ride the horse out of town. I followed him and, with my hand on my gun, told him he could not take the horse, as it was mine and I proposed to have it with or without process of law. Warren Earp, my youngest brother, brought the legal papers to Charleston a little later, and Billy Clanton gave up the horse without service.

"'Have you got any more good horses to lose, Earp?' Billy Clanton bantered me.

"'Yes,' I told him, 'but I'll keep them locked in the stable after this so you can't steal them.'"

A few months after this incident, Wyatt, Virgil and Morgan Earp, and Marshall Williams joined Captain Hurst and four soldiers in a search for six government mules that had been stolen from Camp Rucker. At Charleston, Dave Estes, a Curly Bill man, told Wyatt Earp he would find the mules at the McLowery ranch near Soldier Holes. Estes had seen the mules there the day before, he said, and the McLowerys were then changing the government brand of U S into D S. The posse rode to the McLowery ranch and found the D S branding iron and the six mules bearing the blotted brands.

"Frank Patterson, a member of the McLowery outfit," said Wyatt Earp, "made some sort of compromise with Captain Hurst and agreed to give up the mules if my brothers, Williams, and I went back to Tombstone. I argued with Captain Hurst not to listen to this proposition and cautioned him that it was only a trick to get us out of the way. But he insisted, and we returned to Tombstone. When I met Captain Hurst in Tombstone three weeks later, he told me that, after we left the ranch, the McLowerys refused to give up the mules and threatened to fight it out with the soldiers. Captain Hurst left the mules in possession of the McLowerys and never recovered them. Captain Hurst warned me to look out for those outlaws, saying that, while he was at the ranch, they had made their threats that they would kill me and my brothers at the first opportunity. When I met Frank and Tom McLowery in Charleston a short time afterward, they tried to pick a quarrel with me, but I refused to fall into the trap. They told me that, if I ever followed them again, my friends would find me lying dead in the mesquite some fine morning."

The attack on the Benson stage added in a peculiarly incidental but intricate way to the growing hatred between the Earps and the Clantons and McLowerys. The attempted stage robbery, it will be recalled, occurred in March, 1881, and the trail of Leonard, Head, and Crane had been lost in New Mexico. Efforts to trace the three highwaymen having failed, Wyatt Earp, according to his story, opened negotiations in the early part of June for the betrayal of the bandits.

"I knew that Leonard, Head, and Crane were friends and associates of the Clantons and McLowerys," said Wyatt Earp. "It was well known among all officers of the law in Tombstone that Ike Clanton was a sort of chief among the outlaws, and that the Clantons and McLowerys were cattle thieves and in the secrets of the stage robbers, and that the Clanton and McLowery ranches were meeting places and places of shelter for the robber gangs. There was no doubt in my mind that Ike Clanton knew where Leonard, Head, and Crane were hiding.

"I met Ike Clanton, Frank McLowery, and Joe Hill in Tombstone one day, and told them I had a business proposition to lay before them. They went with me into the back yard of the Oriental saloon, and there we sat for an hour or more and held our conference.

"'There is a reward of $1,200 each for the capture of Leonard, Head, and Crane,' I told them. 'I have an ambition to be sheriff of Cochise County. The murder of Bud Philpot and Peter Roerig in the stage hold-up has incensed the public, and if I can capture the highway-men, I believe it will mean my election as sheriff. Moreover, Johnny Behan's crowd has been trying to give Doc Holliday the worst of it and make it appear that he was mixed up in the attack on the stage and in Philpot's murder. Holliday had nothing to do with it, and you know that as well as I do. If I can catch the three road agents, I can prove out of their own mouths that Holliday is innocent. If you three boys will help me capture Leonard, Head, and Crane, I will give you the entire reward of $3,600 to be split among yourselves as you see fit. All I want is the glory of capturing them.'

"'I would like to see them captured,' said Ike Clan-ton. 'Leonard claims a ranch that I also claim, and if I could get him out of the way, I'd have no further trouble over the land.'

"'I'd like that money,' said Frank McLowery, 'but if it ever came out that we had turned up these fellows, our lives wouldn't be worth a nickel.'

"'I'll give you my word that I will never reveal my source of information,' I answered. 'I'll organize a posse and go out and get the men and you boys need never be known in the matter at all.'

"'You'll have a fight on your hands if you ever run on them,' said Clanton.

"'I'll take care of all the fighting that has to be done,' I replied.

"'They'll never be taken alive.'

"'Then I'll take them dead,' I told him.

"'But in case you have to kill them, does the reward still go? Does the reward for them say "dead or alive"?'

"I wasn't sure on this point. So I told him I'd see Marshall Williams of the Wells-Fargo Company and learn definitely.

"I told Marshall Williams that same day to telegraph to the Wells-Fargo offices in San Francisco and settle this matter officially. He received an immediate answer by wire that the reward would be paid for the bandits dead or alive. Next day, I met Ike Clanton and Joe Hill on Allen Street in front of the little cigar store next door to the Alhambra and told them the telegram had come and they would get the reward even if Leonard, Head, and Crane were killed. They didn't take my word for it, but demanded to see the telegram. I got the message from Williams and showed it to them, and later showed it to Frank McLowery.

"I held another conference with the three outlaws in the back yard of the Oriental and it was arranged that Joe Hill should go to Eureka, New Mexico, near which they said Leonard, Head, and Crane were hiding, and lure them to the McLowery ranch at Soldier Holes where I would be on hand with a posse and capture them.

"'But how are you going to get them to the McLowery ranch?' I asked.

"'We have already talked that over and agreed on a plan,' replied Ike Clanton. 'Hill is to tell them there will be a paymaster going from Tombstone to Bisbee soon with a big swag of pay-roll money for the Copper Queen mine and we plan to stick up the paymaster and want them to come in and help us. We are leaving it to Hill to play this robbery up as an easy game that will make us all rich and, in view of the fact that Leonard, Head, and Crane missed $80,000 in the Benson stage hold-up and didn't get a cent, we figure it's a cinch they will jump at the chance to come in and help pull off a big robbery on the Bisbee road.'

"'How long,' I asked, 'will it take Hill to make the trip?'

"'I know right where to find the three boys,' Hill replied, 'and I believe I can ride over there, put over the deal, and get back in about ten days.'

"So far," Wyatt Earp continued, "my plan was working fine. Joe Hill set out for New Mexico on horseback next day, and before starting, as an evidence of good faith, he gave me his watch and chain and about three hundred dollars in money to hold for him until he got back. I said nothing to anyone about my plan. I didn't tell even Doc Holliday, who is about as close a friend as I had. I wanted to hear from Hill as to when Leonard, Crane and Head would be at the McLowery ranch before I organized my posse and laid my trap to capture them. Finally Hill returned with news that was bitterly disappointing.

"'I saw Bill Leonard and Harry Head in Owl City, New Mexico,' he said, 'but they were corpses in pine-board boxes and all ready to be buried. I arrived one day too late. They had been killed the day before by Ike and Bill Haslett.'

"This, I supposed, ended the matter but, as it turned

out, it was only the beginning. As bad luck would have it, Marshall Williams got drunk. I had not told Williams of my negotiations with Clanton, McLowery, and Hill, but he had got wind of the back-yard conferences I had been having with them at the Oriental, and in view of the telegram I had instructed him to send to San Francisco about the reward, he drew his own conclusions. While he was drunk, he met Ike Clanton and assumed a wise air, as a drunken man will, and pretended to know all about my plans.

"'I want you to know, Clanton,' he said, 'that Wyatt Earp is my friend, and anything you fix up with him will be all right with me, and you can count on me for any help you need.'

"Clanton flared up at this foolish remark.

"'I don't know what you're talking about,' he said. 'I have had no dealings of any kind with Wyatt Earp. You are drunk or you and I would have trouble right now. Wyatt Earp is no friend of mine, and if I ever hear of your connecting my name with him in any way, I'll kill you. Remember that and learn to keep your mouth shut.'

"Ike Clanton, mad as a hornet, hunted me up and told me I had blabbed the whole matter to Williams. I denied it, but my denial was useless, and he went away convinced that I had told Williams all about our transaction. A week or two later, Clanton came to me again and accused me of having told Doc Holliday. Again I denied it.

"Doc Holliday himself told me so,' Clanton said flatly.

"'I know Doc Holliday told you nothing of the kind,' I retorted. 'He could have told you nothing because he knows nothing. Doc Holliday is in Tucson now, but as soon as he comes back, I'll prove to you by him that I never have said a word to him about it.'

"When Doc Holliday returned from Tucson, I asked him about Ike Clanton's statement.

"'Ike Clanton is a liar,' declared Doc hotly, 'and I'll tell him so the first time I see him.'

"Ike Clanton filled Frank McLowery and Joe Hill up with the idea that I had told Williams and Holliday about our negotiations, and after that the three men shunned me like poison every time they came to town. This misunderstanding, which grew out of a drunken falsehood babbled by Marshall Williams, finally led to the battle in which three men were killed. The bitterness of these three outlaws was easy to understand. If, as they wrongly assumed, I had told of their plans to betray their old friends, it meant that they would be marked for death by all the desperate cutthroats of the Curly Bill confederacy. Unless they found some way to square themselves, they were doomed. The situation was serious for me. I was the one man who had full knowledge of their treacherous plot against their comrades, and I had it in my power to betray the plotters to the vengeance of their associates. As long as I remained alive, this danger of my betraying them would hang over their heads. Their safety depended on my death. From this time on, they and their outlaw friends were plotting and scheming to kill me. I heard every little while of their threats to put me out of the way."

This was the Earp side of the story of the origin of the Earp-Clanton feud as told by Wyatt Earp on the witness stand. Ike Clanton told the Clanton side in the same court.

"I met Leonard, Head, and Crane near Hereford on the San Pedro River five days after the attack on the Benson stage," said Ike Clanton. "Bill Leonard then told me that Holliday had taken part in the attempted stage robbery but was drunk at the time. Leonard said Holliday killed Bud Philpot, and if it had not been for this drunken blunder, the stage robbery might have been successful. I met Holliday next day in Jim Vogan's saloon in Tombstone and told him I had seen Leonard, Head, and Crane, and they were heading for the San José Mountains in Mexico. He asked me if Leonard had told me how Philpot happened to be killed. I told him no.

"'Bob Paul had the lines, and Philpot had the shotgun and tried to make a fight and got left,' Holliday said to me. 'I shot Philpot through the heart and saw him tumble off the cart.'

"Several times after that conversation, Holliday told me, if I ever saw Leonard, Head, and Crane again, to tell them he was all right and would not give them away.

"Ten or twelve days before the Benson stage hold-up, I had a talk with Morgan Earp in the Alhambra saloon. He told me he and Wyatt Earp had passed the tip to Bill Leonard and Doc Holliday that a large sum of money—I think he said $29,000—was going out on the stage.

"After Sheriff Behan's posse had abandoned the pursuit, I met Virgil Earp in one of the Allen Street saloons. He asked me to let Leonard know that the three Earp brothers had led the posse off the trail to give Leonard, Head, and Crane a chance to escape.

"'Tell Leonard,' said Virgil Earp, 'we were not trying to catch them. When the posse got to Helm's ranch at the foot of the Dragoons, Wyatt, Morgan, and myself saw that the trail led south toward the San Pedro Valley and the Mexican line, but we steered the posse on a false scent east across the Dragoons and on into New Mexico. Tell Leonard we did all we could for him and his pals and advise him to get Head and Crane out of the country, as we are afraid they may be captured and get us all into trouble. I want to get this word to Leonard to let him know we have not gone back on him.'

"Early in June," Ike Clanton continued, "I met Wyatt Earp in the Oriental saloon. He asked me to have a drink, and while our drinks were being mixed, he said he wanted to have a long private talk with me. After we had had our drinks, we stepped out on the sidewalk, and he said he could put it in my way to make $3,600. I asked him how and he said he would not tell me unless I promised either to do what he said or never to mention our conversation to anyone. I asked him if it was a legitimate transaction, and when he said it was, I promised never to tell. Then he told me he was afraid Leonard, Head, and Crane might be captured and confess to the connection of the Earps and Holliday with the stage hold-up, and he wanted them put out of the way as, he said, 'dead men tell no tales.' He said, if I would lure the boys into a trap where he and his brothers and Holliday could kill them, he would collect the $3,600 reward and turn it over to me. I told him I would have nothing to do with such a scheme, and turned on my heel and left him.

"All I ever knew about the connection of the Earps and Holliday with the Benson stage hold-up was what they themselves and Bill Leonard told me. Later, Leonard, Head, and Crane were all killed, and since their deaths I have been afraid the Earps would murder me because of my knowledge of their secrets."

Whether true or false, Ike Clanton's statement contained a number of discrepancies which, in the light of the evidence, were difficult to explain. Holliday's alleged confession of how he killed Philpot was contrary to the facts indubitably established by Bob Paul and other eye witnesses among the stage passengers. Philpot did not have the shotgun and try to make a fight, as Holliday was alleged to have said. Paul had the shotgun, as well as the reins, and he discharged both barrels of the weapon. If Holliday had taken part in the attack on the stage, it seemed improbable that, in his account of the affair, he would have made any such mistake.

Whether the killing of Philpot was a blunder, drunken or otherwise, was a question. It will be recalled that the first shot was fired at Bob Paul by one of the robbers afterward believed to have been Leonard himself. At this highwayman Paul emptied his shotgun and, as proved at the time of Leonard's death, struck Leonard in the groin. Paul was in the act of discharging his shotgun when Philpot was killed by a shot from a second robber at the opposite side of the road. This second robber, according to Ike Clanton, was Holliday. The first shot evidently was a more serious blunder in foiling the robbers' plans than the second. In view of the desperate fight Bob Paul made, this second shot seemed less a blunder than a logical detail of a murderous battle the first shot had precipitated.

Virgil Earp's alleged confession to Ike Clanton of having misled Sheriff Behan's posse seemed manifestly absurd. Wyatt, Virgil, and Morgan Earp were not the only experienced trailers in the posse. Buckskin Frank

Leslie was a veteran army scout who had trailed
Indians in a number of campaigns; Sheriff Behan himself had had experience in Indian wars; and Bob Paul
and Deputy Sheriff Breakenridge were no novices on a
man hunt. All these men were equally convinced with
the Earps that the trail of the three robbers led east
over the mountains and not south toward Mexico.
Moreover, Sheriff Behan was in command, and it was
reasonable to assume that he would not have followed
the trail into New Mexico unless he had believed it to
be the right one.

It seemed unbelievable also, if Wyatt, Virgil, and
Morgan Earp were accomplices in the stage hold-up,
that they would have taken part in the relentless pursuit of Leonard, Head, and Crane. There was no doubt
whatever that, at least in the early days of the chase,
when the trail led down the San Pedro River, west
around the Santa Catalina Mountains and back again
to the Dragoons, a distance of more than three hundred
miles, the posse was close on the heels of the highwaymen, so close that, on one occasion, a camp fire of the
robbers was found still smouldering. No one charged
that, in this part of the pursuit, the Earps attempted to
lead the posse off on any false scent. In these first days,
capture of the robbers seemed imminent at any time, and
if they had been captured, it is obvious that the Earps
would have been doomed to exposure and ruin.

Why Doc Holliday, Wyatt Earp, Virgil Earp, and
Morgan Earp should each one separately have confessed
guilt to Ike Clanton seemed past understanding. Who
was Ike Clanton that these four deeply sophisticated
men should have made him their father confessor? If
the Earps and Holliday were the criminals Ike Clanton

declared they were, for what reason would they have imparted to a notorious outlaw secrets that might have sent them to prison or the gallows? There is no evidence that they ever were concerned with Ike Clanton in any criminal enterprise but every evidence, on the other hand, that they were his enemies almost from the time of their arrival in Tombstone. In consequence, there was no logical reason apparent why they should have taken him, of all men, into their confidence.

Ike Clanton's story was utterly at variance with that of Wyatt Earp regarding Wyatt Earp's proposition relating to Leonard, Head, and Crane. Ike Clanton said there was but one conference, and it was between Wyatt Earp and himself alone. His statement was a tacit denial that Frank McLowery and Joe Hill had anything to do with the proposition, that Joe Hill made a trip to New Mexico to interview the three outlaws, or that any telegram was sent to San Francisco concerning the reward. These details gave a colour of truth to Wyatt Earp's statement and it was difficult to believe them the fanciful coinage of a liar.

From the day that Wyatt Earp and Ike Clanton told these two stories in court, the Southwest has argued as to which was true and which false. Whether true or false, Wyatt Earp's story was plausible, coherent, and logical. Ike Clanton's was filled with errors which it required no subtle lawyer's probe to lay bare. It may be added that Judge Wells Spicer, who heard both stories, believed Wyatt Earp's and based his decision on the assumption of its truthfulness. It may be added also that, at the time Ike Clanton told his story, he was in the shadow of a tragic defeat and tragic personal loss and was doing frankly everything in his power to discredit the Earps and Holliday and blacken their reputations.

As long as the Earps remained in Tombstone the statement by Ike Clanton was the only charge ever made openly that they at any time engaged in robbing stages. It was only after the Earps had shaken the dust of Tombstone from their feet that a thousand wild tales were set going about them. Then it was said they had had part in almost all the stage robbiers in the Tombstone country, and it became a part of the absurd legend that they had joined frequently with great gusto and exuberance in chasing themselves hither and yon over the landscape. These scandalous old tales have come down to to-day and are still given wide credence. But careful research has failed to bring to light any evidence except Ike Clanton's accusations that the Earps were ever involved directly or indirectly in any stage robberies. In the light of investigation, these old charges seem a farrago of suspicion and mendacities born of bitter personal and political hatreds.

The robbery of the Bisbee stage was one more milepost on the trail of hatred that led to tragedy. The stage pulled out of Tombstone at dusk on September 8, 1881. Levi McDaniels was driving, unaccompanied by a shotgun messenger and with four passengers aboard, three inside and one sitting on the box with the driver. The stage road between Tombstone and Bisbee in those days circled the Mule Mountains to the westward, kept to the level stretches of the San Pedro Valley through Charleston and Hereford, and came into Bisbee from the south. McDaniels' four-horse team was climbing a grade three miles beyond Hereford at 11 o'clock at night. A red moon was sinking behind the Huachucas. The Mule summits towered darkly close by on the east.

Old Mexico lay in a luminous haze across the line four miles to the south. The lead horses shied off the road as two highwaymen masked with handkerchiefs stepped out of the mesquite. One of the robbers had a shotgun; the other a six-shooter.

"Hold on!" commanded the bandit with the shotgun.

As McDaniels brought his team to a halt, the man with the six-shooter walked alongside the coach.

"Don't get excited, boys," he said. "Nobody's going to get hurt. It'll all be over in a minute."

He spoke in the manner of a doctor about to administer a dose of disagreeable medicine and encouraging his patients to be brave and keep cool. If the Benson stage robbers had been amateurs, these had the air of veterans.

"Throw out the Wells-Fargo box and the mail sack, driver," ordered the bandit with the six-shooter.

McDaniels obeyed.

"Now throw out everything in the boot."

McDaniels threw out everything except a roll of blankets.

"Never mind the blankets," said the robber. "We don't need them."

He peered in the window of the coach at the passengers.

"How are you all this evening, boys?" he said genially. "I'll have to ask you to climb out. On the other side of the road, if you please. And line up with your hands in the air. My partner will keep you covered till I join you."

S. W. Rae, Owen Gibney, and E. T. Hardy climbed out, and the robber walked around the coach and searched their pockets. He took $600 from Rae, a small sum of money and a gold watch from Hardy, and a diamond pin from Gibney.

"This stone," he said as he slipped the pin out of Gibney's necktie, "will look good on my gal in Tombstone. She likes diamonds."

Then the bandit told the passengers to get back in their seats and ordered McDaniels to drive on.

"Hold on a minute," called the robber with the shotgun as McDaniels started up the team. "You've overlooked that fellow sitting beside the driver."

"Sure enough, I have," said the polite robber with the six-shooter, and he climbed up on the front wheel.

"Excuse me, but I forgot you," he said to Matt Delehan, the fourth passenger. "You may have a little sugar."

Having extracted $50 from Delehan's pockets, he climbed down.

"I guess that's all," he said. "Now you can go ahead, driver. Good-night, boys."

The robbers obtained $2,500 from the Wells-Fargo box, according to express company officials. The mail sack, slashed open, was found at the scene. A Tombstone posse that took the trail next morning comprised Wyatt and Morgan Earp, Deputy Sheriffs Breakenridge and Nagle, Marshall Williams, Wells-Fargo agent, and Fred Dodge, Wells-Fargo detective. The tracks of the robbers led across the Mule Mountains into Bisbee.

Within a week, Frank Stilwell and Pete Spence were captured. Stilwell had been indiscreet enough after the robbery to take a pair of boots, almost new, to Shoemaker Dever of Bisbee with orders to take off a narrow pair of heels and put on a broad pair. The suspicious cobbler reported this to the authorities. The narrow

heels removed from Stilwell's boots fitted the tracks left
at the scene of the robbery by the polite bandit who had
ransacked the pockets of the stage passengers. Stilwell
was arrested by the posse in Bisbee. Wyatt and Morgan
Earp caught Spence in Charleston. Both prisoners
were taken to Tombstone, where they were released on
bond.

Stilwell and Spence, intimate friends of the Clantons
and McLowerys, had been suspected of many stage robberies, though until now they had escaped arrest. Spence
was ostensibly a gambler; Stilwell owned a livery business in Charleston. Stilwell was a handsome fellow,
twenty-seven years old, of engaging politeness and with
many friends. Though apparently retiring and rather
silent, he was given to gay amusements. He drank
moderately, played a dashing game of faro, and cut a
swath in Tombstone dance halls, where he achieved
distinction as a squire of dames, spending his money
recklessly, keeping champagne corks popping, and be-
stowing upon his favourites among red-light beauties
the diamonds, rings, necklaces, and watches he obtained
in his secret adventures on the highways. He was an
expert with a six-shooter and was regarded as a killer
among the desperadoes and outlaws who preferred his
friendship to his enmity. It was not definitely known,
however, that he had killed anyone, though he was suspected on logical grounds of having murdered one of
the many successive owners of the Brunckow mine, he
himself having been one of the numerous men who had
jumped that worthless old hole in the ground. He was a
native of Texas and had been in Arizona four years.
After working in the mines at Signal, he had lived for a
time in Tombstone and then moved to Charleston to

become a liveryman. He had been appointed a deputy
sheriff, and recently had been stationed in this official
capacity in Bisbee. His brother, Jack Stilwell, was a
famous army scout.

Pete Spence was a different type. He was about forty
years old, tall, gaunt, and taciturn. His real name was
said to be Lark Ferguson and he was a native of the
Big Bend country of Texas, on the Rio Grande, where he
was reputed to have killed in many robber adventures
fifteen or twenty Mexicans. He was, it was said, a peri-
patetic lead mine, carrying in his body many bullets
which he had acquired during his outlaw career. Spence
was nearly killed with a load of buckshot while robbing a
store in Corpus Christi, and was shot in the head in
another bandit exploit in New Mexico. After robbing a
bank at Goliad, he joined the Sixth Cavalry under the
name of Spence and took part in several Apache campaigns in Arizona, being finally discharged at Fort
Grant. He had dealt monte and faro in many tough
towns in Arizona and New Mexico, including Lordsburg, Silver City, Shakespeare, Galeyville, and Charleston, and at the time of the Bisbee stage robbery was
married to a Mexican woman and living in Tombstone.

The arrest of Spence and Stilwell arrayed them with
the Clantons and McLowerys against the Earps, and
the vengeance of these two outlaws became a part of the
romance of feud that stained Tombstone with blood.

"After we had arrested Stilwell and Spence," said
Wyatt Earp, "Ike Clanton and Frank McLowery came
to Tombstone evidently looking for trouble. With John
Ringo, Joe Hill, and Milt Hicks, they met Morgan Earp
on Allen Street in front of the Alhambra.

"'I'll never speak to Pete Spence or Frank Stilwell again,' Frank McLowery said, 'for allowing themselves to be arrested by the Earps. If ever you come after me, I'll promise you'll never take me.'

"Ike Clanton, Ringo, Hill, and Hicks stood by threateningly with their hands on their six-shooters. Morgan was alone.

"'If I ever have any occasion to come after you,' Morgan replied, 'I'll arrest you.'

"'I once threatened to kill you and your brothers,' said McLowery. 'Then, when I saw you were letting us boys alone, I decided not to do it and took back my threat. But now, since you are getting so busy in this part of the country, my threat still goes. You Earps and Doc Holliday are not as big as you think you are. You'd better look out, or we'll get you yet.'

"Morgan made no reply but walked away. During the next few days, Marshall Williams, Farmer Daly, Big Ed Byrnes, Old Man Winter, Charlie Smith, and three or four others came to me and told me to be on guard, as they had heard Ike Clanton, Frank and Tom Mc-Lowery, John Ringo, and Joe Hill all threaten to kill my brothers, myself, and Doc Holliday. I took their advice and kept my eyes open. I did not intend that any of these outlaws should get the drop on me if I could help it."

The situation as far as the Earps and Doc Holliday were concerned had grown suddenly desperate. War to the death had been declared against them. They were four men standing alone, hemmed in by deadly foes. Weaker men would have fled from Tombstone and sought safety over the horizon. Only men of iron courage would have stayed to take a chance and fight it out. Ike Clanton and Frank McLowery were only mouthpieces of outlaw hatred. Back of them was a murderous criminal organization, the boldest and most powerful in the history of the Southwest.

CHAPTER XIII

THE SHOW—DOWN

DARK and high the war clouds were piling. Forked hatreds snaked flamingly across the blind gloom, and vengeance threatened in rumbling thunder growls. The red deluge was about to burst. Nothing now could hold back the storm.

Swashbuckling Ike Clanton, unable to read the signs and portents of impending tragedy, drove alone into Tombstone on the afternoon of October 25th. Rash, blundering fellow, thus to venture single-handed into the stronghold of his enemies. But he believed in his soul the Earps were secretly afraid of him, would not dare to molest him, stood in awe of the banded outlaw strength that for years had been at his back. How quickly and cruelly was this proud freebooter to be stripped of his foolish illusions. So confident of his own safety was he that, as a law-abiding gesture, he left his Winchester rifle and six-shooter behind the bar at the Grand Hotel and sallied forth to tipple and take his pleasure in the saloons and gambling halls.

An hour past midnight, Ike Clanton was eating a light repast in the lunch room in the rear of the Alhambra saloon when Doc Holliday strolled in. Holliday's face went dark.

"You've been lying about me to Wyatt Earp," he flared.

"I never said anything to Wyatt Earp about you," returned Clanton in weak denial.

"You're a liar!" snapped Holliday with an oath. "You've been saying a lot of other things about me lately. Don't deny it. I've got the goods on you."

Holliday was in a cold fury. He called Clanton a drunken blatherskite, a yellow cur, a braggart, a coward. The doctor had a scurrilous and blackguard tongue when his dander was up, and he exhausted upon Clanton a full and rich vocabulary of opprobrium.

"Moreover," said Holliday, "you've been making your threats to kill me. Now's a good time to do it. We are all alone, man to man. Get out your gun and get to work."

Out flashed the doctor's own six-shooter.

"I've got no gun on me," cried Clanton.

"Don't tell me that, you lying whelp," said Holliday. "You've got a gun. You wouldn't have the nerve to be knocking around Tombstone at midnight without one. Go to fighting."

"No," responded Clanton, "I'm unarmed."

"Then, if you are not heeled," shot back the doctor, "go and heel yourself. And when you come back, come a-smoking."

Morgan Earp walked into the restaurant.

"Leave him alone, Doc," said Morgan, and he took Holliday by the arm and led him outside. Clanton followed him out on the sidewalk. There Clanton attempted vain explanations, while Holliday, still boiling with wrath, continued to abuse him. While the heated colloquy was in progress, Wyatt and Virgil Earp walked up, and Virgil ended the argument by threatening to put both men in jail.

"Don't shoot me in the back, Holliday," said Clanton as he walked away.

"You heel yourself," warned Holliday, "and stay heeled. Don't have any excuses the next time I see you."

Clanton found Wyatt Earp in the Oriental saloon a half-hour later.

"I wasn't heeled when Doc Holliday was abusing me," said Clanton. "No man can abuse me like that and get away with it. I've got my gun on now, and you can tell Holliday I'm going to kill him the first time I meet him."

"You're excited and about half drunk," said Wyatt Earp. "I'd advise you to go to bed."

"Don't get the idea in your head I'm drunk," said Clanton. "This fight talk has been going on long enough, and it's time to fetch it to a close."

"I'll fight nobody unless I have to," replied Wyatt Earp. "There's no money in fighting."

For a little longer, Clanton talked war and Wyatt Earp peace. Then Clanton went away. He returned in a little while and ordered a drink at the bar. He evidently had been nursing his resentment.

"You fellows had the best of me to-night," he said. "You were four to one. But I'll be fixed for you to-morrow. I'll have my friends here then, and we'll fight it out, man to man."

He paused as he passed out the door.

"I'll be after you fellows to-morrow," he flung back. "Don't forget it. I'll be ready for all of you then."

Wyatt Earp went home to bed, his customary calm in no way ruffled by the night's excitement, and suspecting that Clanton's belligerent talk was mere drunken bluster which would be forgotten next day. Ned Boyle, bartender at the Oriental, awoke him at noon.

"Ike Clanton's on a drunk," said Boyle. "He was flourishing his six-shooter in the saloon this morning. 'As soon as the Earps show up,' he said, 'the ball is going to open. I'll have my people with me, and we'll make a fight.'"

While Wyatt Earp was dressing, Harry Jones rushed in.

"What does all this mean, Wyatt?" he asked breathlessly.

"What does what mean?"

"Ike Clanton is on the warpath. He is armed with a Winchester and a six-shooter and is looking all over town for you Earp boys and Doc Holliday. He is threatening to kill the first man among you who appears on the street."

"Tut-tut," said Wyatt Earp. "I guess I'll have to look up Ike Clanton and see what's the matter with him."

Marshal Virgil Earp remained on duty all night and went to bed at sunrise. He had been asleep only a few hours when his brother Warren aroused him to inform him that Ike Clanton was huntng him to kill him.

"Don't bother me," said Virgil Earp, and he turned over and went to sleep again.

Morgan Earp again awoke him.

"Ike Clanton is threatening to make a clean sweep of the Earps and Doc Holliday," said Morgan. "Billy Clanton and Tom and Frank McLowery have arrived in town, all heavily armed. Better get up."

Morgan Earp met Doc Holliday in the Alhambra. The

doctor had finished a late breakfast and was lounging immaculately at the bar.

"Ike Clanton's going to kill you as soon as he finds you," warned Morgan.

"So I hear," returned the doctor with polite interest.

In addition to his six-shooter, the doctor had a sawed-off shotgun strapped to his shoulder beneath his coat. The shotgun was a detail of costume reserved by the doctor for state occasions. He had put it on just after adjusting his tie before his morning mirror.

Wyatt and Virgil Earp met in the Oriental saloon.

"With Billy Clanton and the two McLowerys in town, the thing begins to look interesting," said Wyatt Earp. "We'd better disarm Ike Clanton before he starts trouble. We'll hunt him up. You go round the block by Fremont Street. I'll take Allen Street."

Virgil Earp saw Ike Clanton talking with William Stilwell on Fourth Street between Fremont and Allen.

"I hear you are looking for me," said Virgil.

Clanton threw his rifle around threateningly. Virgil grabbed the barrel and clouted Clanton over the head with a six-shooter, knocking him down.

Wyatt and Morgan Earp came hurrying up. They disarmed Clanton and marched him to Justice Wallace's court. Virgil Earp went to find Justice Wallace. Wyatt and Morgan Earp remained to guard the prisoner. Clanton was wild with drink and anger. His hair was matted with blood that dripped upon his shoulder.

"If I had my six-shooter," Clanton shouted, "I'd fight all you Earps."

Morgan Earp was standing in front of him, Clanton's rifle in his left hand, the butt resting on the floor, and in his right hand, Clanton's six-shooter.

"If you want to fight right bad," Morgan sneered, "I'll give you this."

He extended the six-shooter butt foremost to Clanton. Clanton started from his chair to grasp it, but Deputy Sheriff Campbell pushed him down in his seat again.

"I'll get even with you for this, Wyatt Earp," shrilled Clanton.

Wyatt's graven-image face for a moment contorted with rage.

"You dirty, low-down cow thief," Wyatt Earp rumbled savagely. "I'm tired of being threatened by you and your gang of cutthroats. You intend to assassinate me and my brothers the first chance you get, and I know it, and I would be justified in shooting you down like a dog anywhere I met you. If you are game to fight, I'll fight you anywhere."

"Just wait till I get out of here," yelled Clanton. "I'll fight you then."

Wyatt Earp walked out of the courtroom. On the street just outside the door, he almost collided with Tom McLowery.

"If you're looking for a fight, just say so," said McLowery, his face going white with instant fury. "I'll fight you any place, any time."

"All right," flashed Wyatt Earp, "fight right here."

Full in the face Wyatt Earp slapped McLowery with his left hand, and with his right pulled his own six-shooter from its holster. McLowery had a gun stuffed down his trousers on his right hip, the butt in sight. But he made no move to draw it. Nor did he say a word.

"Jerk your gun and use it," roared Wyatt Earp, and at the same time he bludgeoned McLowery over the

head with his six-shooter. McLowery reeled under the
blow across the sidewalk and measured his length in
the gutter, blood gushing from his wound. Wyatt Earp
walked away.

Soon afterward, as Wyatt Earp stood smoking a cigar
in front of Hafford's saloon at Fourth and Allen streets,
Billy Clanton and Tom and Frank McLowery passed
him. All three had their six-shooters buckled around
them. They glared silently at Wyatt Earp, and Wyatt
Earp glared silently at them. The three men entered a
gunsmith's shop half a block away on Fourth Street.
Frank McLowery's horse was standing on the sidewalk
in front of the shop. This was a violation of a city
ordinance. Also it was an opportunity for Wyatt Earp
to confront these three armed enemies. If they wanted
a fight, he would fight them all single-handed. He
marched boldly to the shop and took hold of the horse's
bridle. Billy Clanton and Tom McLowery clutched the
handles of their six-shooters. Frank McLowery stepped
out and also took hold of the horse's bridle.

"Get this horse off the sidewalk," ordered Wyatt Earp.

Without a word, Frank McLowery backed the
animal into the street. Ike Clanton, who had had his
hearing before Justice Wallace and been fined $25,
walked up at this juncture. He was unarmed. He averted
his eyes as he passed Wyatt Earp close enough to touch
him and went into the gunsmith's shop. Wyatt Earp
supposed, and had reason to suppose, that Ike Clanton,
whose rifle and revolver had not been restored to him,
went into the shop to re-arm himself. Ike Clanton admitted later that this was his purpose. As it happened,
however, the gunsmith did not let him have a gun.

At this time, beyond any question, Billy Clanton and

Tom and Frank McLowery were all armed. And this was the last time Wyatt Earp saw any of the men until he met them in battle. But before the fight opened, Tom McLowery, all belligerency knocked out of him, perhaps, when Wyatt Earp clubbed him over the head with a gun, deposited his six-shooter in Moses & Mehan's saloon. None of the Earps knew this. In fairness to them, it may be added, they had reason to believe that all four of their enemies were armed.

Sheriff Behan was getting shaved in an Allen Street barber shop when he heard of trouble brewing. He ordered the barber to hurry.

"I must stop this fight," he said.

As the sheriff stepped out the door, his face smooth and rosy from the barbering, he spied Virgil Earp across the street and went over to him. Wyatt and Morgan Earp and Doc Holliday were standing in a group near by on the corner.

"What's the excitement, Marshal Earp?" the sheriff asked.

"Some scoundrels are in town looking for a fight," replied Virgil Earp.

"You must disarm them," declared the sheriff. "It is your duty."

"They have been threatening our lives," said Virgil, "and we are going to give them a chance to make their fight."

The dangerous situation was at a crisis. Sheriff Behan realized that, to avert tragedy, he must act quickly. He proposed himself to disarm the Clantons and McLowerys.

Sheriff Behan found the Clantons and McLowerys standing in a vacant lot near the O. K. corral on Fremont Street between Third and Fourth. Billy Claiborne, a tough young fellow from the San Pedro and a close friend of the Clantons, was with them. Frank McLowery and Billy Clanton had their horses. Hanging from the pommel of each saddle, according to Ike Clanton's own account, was a Winchester rifle in a leather scabbard.

"Boys," said Sheriff Behan, "I'm going to arrest and disarm you."

"What for?" asked Ike Clanton.

"To preserve the peace."

"I am unarmed," said Ike Clanton. "The Earps still have my rifle and six-shooter."

"Let me see," said the sheriff, and he put his arm around Ike Clanton's waist feeling for a gun, but found none.

"I've got no gun on me," said Tom McLowery, and he threw back both flaps of his coat to prove his assertion.

"I didn't come to town to make a fight," said Billy Clanton who had a six-shooter on his hip. "I came to get Ike to come home. No use in my giving up my arms. We are getting ready to leave town right now."

"That's so," cut in Ike Clanton. "My spring wagon is in the West End corral, and I've just left word there to have my team hitched up."

"I've got a six-shooter and my rifle is hanging there on my horse," said Frank McLowery, "but I won't give them up unless you disarm the Earps. Wyatt Earp beat my brother Tom over the head with a gun an hour or so ago, and there's no telling what the Earps will try next. But if you don't disarm the Earps, I'll promise to leave town as soon as I have attended to a little business."

Billy Claiborne said he was unarmed and was not of

the Clanton party, a statement corroborated by Ike Clanton. As the battle opened, it may be added, Claiborne threw up his hands and ran into Fly's photograph gallery where he hid until the firing ceased.

"You know where my office is," said Sheriff Behan to Frank McLowery. "I want you and Billy Clanton to go there and leave your weapons."

"Well, Sheriff," said McLowery, "we won't do it. We don't know what's in the wind, and we might need our weapons at any moment."

So it was established by Sheriff Behan that Ike Clanton and Tom McLowery were unarmed and only Billy Clanton and Frank McLowery had weapons. But there were four weapons in the crowd. If they had cared to do so, Ike Clanton and Tom McLowery could have armed themselves quickly with the rifles of Billy Clanton and Frank McLowery hanging on the saddles of the two horses.

Fremont Street in this block between Third and Fourth was a wide avenue at the edges of the business district with wooden sidewalks and a roadbed of packed red desert sand. On the west side, at the corner of Third, stood a small dwelling. To the south, between the dwelling and Fly's two-story frame photograph gallery, was the open lot perhaps thirty feet wide in which the sheriff's talk with the Clantons and McLowerys took place. Beyond a small adobe lodging house next door to Fly's, was the rear gate of the O. K. corral, which was, in fact, a livery stable running through to a frontage on Allen Street, roofed in front, but at the Fremont Street end flanked by rows of open-air horse stalls. Next to the corral was Bauer's butcher shop, with a striped awning over the sidewalk, and between Bauer's and Fourth Street a fenced-in lot with no houses on it. On the opposite side of Fremont at the Fourth Street corner was a large adobe building filled with stores, with business offices upstairs, among them that of Dr. George Goodfellow. Next door was the one-story frame in which the *Epitaph* was printed, then an assay office, the home of Sandy Bob, owner of the Charleston stage line, and on the corner of Third, Dunbar's corral in which Sheriff Behan owned an interest. Looking out Fremont, one saw the Whetstone Mountains, softly blue across the rolling mesquite land, while the Third Street vista to the east was closed by the massive yellow ramparts of Cochise's old stronghold in the Dragoons, nine miles away.

While Wyatt, Virgil, and Morgan Earp, and Doc Holliday stood on the corner of Fourth and Allen streets, R. F. Coleman rushed up to them excitedly.

"I met the Clantons and McLowerys a little while ago, down by the O. K. corral," said Coleman. "They are all armed and talking fight. You boys had better look out."

For a little longer, the Earps and Holliday stood in silence. Then they looked into one another's eyes and each one understood.

"Come on, boys," said Wyatt Earp.

Sheriff Behan, still in the vacant lot urging peace and disarmament on the Clantons and McLowerys, saw the Earps and Holliday turn the corner of Fourth Street and come walking with businesslike strides along the sidewalk on the west side of Fremont. Holliday was on the outside, Morgan next to him, Wyatt third, and Virgil on the inside. Their faces were cold and set, and they kept their eyes fixed steadily ahead on their enemies. All wore dark clothes except Holliday, and Wyatt

Earp looked almost funereal in a long black overcoat that hung below his knees. Holliday never appeared more neatly groomed as he swung along with an air of cool unconcern in a gray suit and an overcoat of rough gray material which hid his six-shooter in its holster at his hip and his sawed-off shotgun strapped to his shoulder. Yellow leather gun scabbards showed beneath the coats of Virgil and Morgan Earp. Wyatt's hand grasped a six-shooter in his overcoat pocket. The street was silent. The boots of the four men clicked noisily on the sidewalk planking.

"Here they come," said Sheriff Behan. "You boys wait here. I'll go and stop them."

As the sheriff started off, the Clantons and McLowerys were ranged in the vacant lot along the side of the corner dwelling. Frank McLowery stood a foot or two off the inner edge of the sidewalk, and to his right in order were Tom McLowery, Billy Clanton, and Ike Clanton. Fine-looking fellows, all of them, tall, lean, vigorous, with sun-tanned faces, having the appearance of cowboys in off the range, white sombreros, flannel shirts, pants stuffed in their fancy-leather half-boots. Billy Clanton was a blue-eyed, fresh-faced, handsome boy only eighteen years old but, for all his boyishness, an outlaw of experience and a dare-devil fighter. Frank McLowery, who had on mouse-coloured pants almost skin tight, rested his hand on the bridle of his horse which stood out broadside across the sidewalk. Billy Clanton's horse, unhitched, was nipping at weeds. It was 2:30 o'clock of a crisply cool, sunshiny afternoon.

Sheriff Behan confronted the Earps under the awning in front of Bauer's butcher shop and raised his hand to halt them.

"Go back," he said. "As sheriff of this county, I command you not to go any farther. I am here to disarm and arrest the Clantons and McLowerys. I won't allow any fighting."

The Earps and Holliday paid no attention but brushed on past the sheriff without a word. Sheriff Behan as peacemaker had done his best, but he had failed at both ends of the line—failed to disarm the Clantons, failed to stop the Earps. Now he followed behind with vain expostulations.

"I don't want any trouble," he kept saying. "There must be no fight."

The sheriff stopped at Fly's front door. If bullets began to fly, he could step at one stride to safety.

Keeping their alignment, almost shoulder to shoulder, the Earps and Holliday came on with lethal momentum. As they drew near, they pulled their guns. Holding their weapons at a level before them, they halted within five feet of the Clantons and McLowerys, so close that if the foemen had stretched out their arms their finger-tips would almost have touched. They could look into the pupils of one another's eyes. The whisper of an Earp would have been audible to a Clanton.

"You fellows have been looking for a fight," said Wyatt Earp, "and now you can have it."

"Throw up your hands!" commanded Virgil Earp.

What happened now in the smoke of flaring guns happened while the clock ticked twenty seconds— twenty seconds packed with murderous hatred and flaming death.

Ike Clanton asserted that all the Clantons and Mc-Lowerys threw up their hands "as high as their shoulders," at Virgil Earp's command, and that Tom Mc-

Lowery threw back his coat, saying, "I am unarmed." He declared, too, that Billy Clanton, as he held his hands in the air, said, "Don't shoot me. I don't want to fight." But according to Wyatt Earp, Billy Clanton and Frank McLowery jerked out their six-shooters and started shooting on the instant. Whatever the truth, two guns blazed almost simultaneously with Virgil's command. These two first shots, it was believed, were fired by Wyatt Earp and Morgan Earp.

"Billy Clanton levelled his pistol at me," said Wyatt Earp, "but I did not aim at him. I knew that Frank McLowery was a good shot and a dangerous man, and I aimed at him. Billy Clanton and I fired almost at the same time, he at me and I at Frank McLowery. My shot struck Frank McLowery in the belly. He fired back at me as he staggered out across the sidewalk into the street."

Morgan Earp's first shot struck Billy Clanton, who fell against the wall of the dwelling behind him and slid to the ground on his back. Dangerously hurt, the boy drew himself up on one knee, and grasping his six-shooter in both hands—a heroic figure of dauntless courage worthy of deathless bronze—kept on gamely fighting, his gun coughing swift spurts of fire.

Tom McLowery sprang toward his brother's horse, probably with intent to get Frank McLowery's rifle out of its saddle scabbard. The coolly alert Doc Holliday suspected such purpose. Throwing open his overcoat, Holliday seized his sawed-off shotgun hanging in its loop to his right shoulder and fired both barrels quickly with unerring accuracy. Tom McLowery, lifted off his feet by the heavy double charge of buckshot, crashed sidewise to the earth in a lifeless, limp huddle, his head between the horse's hind heels. As McLowery fell, Holliday allowed his shotgun to swing back on its shoulder band beneath his coat and fought from now on with his six-shooter. Terrified by the sudden rattle of battle and the acrid, drifting swirls of powder smoke, the two horses belonging to Frank McLowery and Billy Clanton dashed pell-mell from the lot and went careering off through the street in wild, clattering flight.

Ike Clanton, the pot-valiant one, whose drunken, braggart threats had brought on this tragedy, rushed upon Wyatt Earp and caught him by the left arm, hung on tenaciously for a moment, doing what he could do to distract him and spoil his marksmanship and make him an easy target for his foes. Wyatt Earp could have killed Ike Clanton. Nine out of ten men under the same circumstances would have killed him. But lionlike in his magnanimity as in his courage, Wyatt Earp only flung him aside.

"The fight has begun," said Wyatt Earp. "Go to fighting or get away."

Ike Clanton darted into Fly's photograph gallery into which Sheriff Behan already had disappeared, ran through a hall, and out the back door across a lot to Allen Street, where he hid in a Mexican dance hall. But if Wyatt Earp was merciful, no such quixotic chivalry actuated Doc Holliday, "the coldest blooded killer in Tombstone." As Ike Clanton fled across the lot, Holliday turned for a second from the fighting and sent two bullets after him which missed him by inches and thudded into the walls of an adobe outhouse.

Pitiful, chicken-hearted Ike Clanton. No hero soul in him. No knightly gallantry or warrior devotion that might have prompted him to stay and die with his brave brother and equally brave comrades. The panic fear of death was upon him, and he ran like a frightened rabbit to save his worthless hide. One almost feels a twinge of regret that this craven fellow escaped, but there is a certain pagan consolation in the knowledge that he preserved his paltry life only to lose it ingloriously in later years while again running from his enemies.

Billy Clanton, still down on one knee and handling his six-shooter with both hands, was resting his elbow on the crook of the other knee and taking deliberate aim at every shot. Virgil Earp fired at him, the bullet boring a hole through the flap of the boy's hat. Billy's blue eyes flashed and his face twisted into a murderous snarl as he threw the muzzle of his gun around upon the marshal and pulled the trigger. The ball cut through the calf of Virgil Earp's right leg and brought him to the ground. He, too, rose on one knee and continued firing. Now there were two wounded men fighting on their knees.

Frank McLowery was wavering and weaving about in the middle of the street, clasping his left hand now and again to his body where Wyatt Earp's bullet had torn into him. He was plainly in agony. Doc Holliday ran toward him, firing once as he ran and halted within a distance of ten paces of him.

"You are the man I want," cried McLowery. "I've got you now."

"Got me to get," flung back Holliday with a poisonous smile.

McLowery rested his six-shooter across his left arm and drew a careful bead. Just as he pulled the trigger Holliday suddenly turned sideways to him. This cool trick in the thick of the furious tumult of battle was characteristic of this cheerful desperado, whose poise no desperate circumstance could shake. The stratagem saved the doctor's life. With his side turned to his antagonist Holliday, who was only skin and bones offered the merest sliver of a target. McLowery's bullet crashed through Holliday's pistol scabbard and burned a deep crease across his thigh.

At that instant, Billy Clanton shot Morgan Earp through the shoulder.

"That one clipped me good," shouted Morgan, as the impact of the forty-five calibre ball bowled him over flat on his back.

Frank McLowery, staggering about blindly, had drawn close to Morgan Earp. Wyatt Earp saw his brother's danger.

"Look out for Frank McLowery, Morg," Wyatt called.

Morgan flung himself over on his side, snapped his pistol down on Frank McLowery, and let fly on a quick chance. Doc Holliday fired at the same moment. McLowery fell dead with a bullet through his brain. Whether Holliday or Morgan Earp killed him has been a subject of conjecture to this day.

Ike Clanton evaporated in shameless flight, Tom and Frank McLowery dead, Billy Clanton, in the last few seconds of the battle, was left on a lost field to fight alone. Wounded to the death, without hope or a single chance for his life, but still undaunted, the boy faced his remorseless foes.

"God damn you!" He hurled the curse at them as he crouched upon his knees. "I've got to kill one of you before I die."

He straightened up his lithe young body, his tortured face flamed defiance, and the sunlight sparkled on the long, nickelled barrel of his heavy revolver as he brought the weapon to a level for his last shot. A bullet fired, it was believed, by Virgil Earp, struck him full in the breast, and he toppled over upon his back. But the fearless youth was still not ready to die or give up the battle.

"Just one more shot," he murmured as if in prayer. "God! Just one more shot."

He was too weak to roll over, too weak to raise himself to shooting position. He managed to prop his head against the foundation stones of the house at his rear. Lying at full length on his back, he raised his gun and pointed it blindly toward his enemies. For a second, the weapon wavered weakly in the air. His finger fumbled on the trigger. Then his hand fell limply at his side. The six-shooter rolled upon the ground. A shiver shook him from head to foot. He collapsed and lay still. The battle was over.

Citizens carried Billy Clanton across the street into Dr. George Goodfellow's upstairs office.

"Pull off my boots," whispered the dying boy. "I promised my mother I'd never die with my boots on."

As he breathed his last, the promise to his dead mother was fulfilled. The bullet that had killed him passed through a letter from his sweetheart which he had carried in his pocket.

As the Earps started back up town, Virgil limping as he leaned on Doc Holliday's arm, and Morgan supported by Wyatt, Sheriff Behan bustled out of Fly's photograph gallery.

"I will have to arrest you, Wyatt," he said.

"I will not allow you to arrest me to-day, Johnny," Wyatt replied. "Maybe I'll let you arrest me to-morrow. I'm not going to run away."

At the inquest held by Coroner H. M. Matthews, eyewitnesses estimated that twenty-five or thirty shots had been fired during the third of a minute the battle lasted. Billy Clanton had been struck twice, once below the midriff, and a second time within an inch of the heart. Frank McLowery's body showed two wounds. The first, made by Wyatt Earp's first shot, was a straight, penetrating wound in the abdomen; the second was in the head, just below the right ear. Twelve buckshot from Holliday's gun had torn a hole in Tom McLowery's right side six inches below the armpit and between the third and fifth ribs. Coroner Matthews said the wound could have been covered by the palm of a man's hand. A report was circulated that Tom McLowery had been killed while holding his hands in the air. Coroner Matthews set this rumour at rest by testifying that the charge of buckshot had also left a torn wound in the fleshy rear portion of the right upper arm. Such a wound obviously could not have been made if McLowery's arms had been elevated.

The Earps were tried before Judge Wells Spicer late in November. The most important witnesses were Sheriff Behan, Ike Clanton, and Wyatt Earp. It was on this occasion that Ike Clanton told his story of the attack on the Benson stage in which he attempted to implicate Holliday and the Earps. Though some of the witnesses said that the two shots that opened the battle were fired by Morgan Earp and Doc Holliday, Wyatt Earp testified that the first two shots were fired by himself and Billy Clanton simultaneously.

"No shots were fired," Wyatt Earp said on the witness stand, "until Billy Clanton and Frank McLowery drew their guns. If Tom McLowery was unarmed, I did not know it. His six-shooter was in plain view when he and I had had our encounter an hour or so before in front of Justice Wallace's courtroom and I had no reason to believe that he had later laid aside his weapon. Though no evidence has been introduced to sustain me, I still believe he was armed and fired two shots at our party before Holliday killed him.

"Because of Ike Clanton's repeated threats against my life, I believe I had a perfect right to kill him when I easily could have done so but I did not do it because I thought he was unarmed. I believed before the battle that Ike Clanton and Frank and Tom McLowery had formed a conspiracy to murder my brothers, Doc Holliday, and myself, and I would have been legally and morally justified in killing any of them on sight. I had several chances to kill Ike Clanton in the twenty-four hours before the battle, and when I met Tom McLowery I could have killed him instead of hitting him with my gun. But I sought no advantage, and I did not intend to fight unless it became necessary in self-defense. When Billy Clanton and Frank McLowery drew their pistols, I knew it was to be a fight, and I fired in defense of my own life and the lives of my brothers and Doc Holliday."

The Earps were acquitted. Judge Spicer reviewed the evidence in a long written opinion and justified the battle, holding that the Earps and Holliday had acted in performance of official duty as officers of the law.

CHAPTER XIV

THE RED ROAD OF VENGEANCE

PLAY was slow that night at the Oriental. Too soon after Christmas, perhaps. Holiday gifts had told on purses. Only thin groups were at the faro and roulette tables, and only stragglers at the bar. Wyatt and Virgil Earp and Doc Holliday sat against the wall in desultory talk.

"Among the Christmas gifts from my many friends in Tombstone," remarked Doc Holliday with a whimsical smile, "was a neat little box wrapped in tissue paper and tied with pink ribbon. 'Ah-ha,' thinks I, 'here's a present from my sweetheart.'"

"Big Nose Kate probably," laughed Wyatt.

"All bundled up in soft white cotton," continued the doctor, "was a forty-five calibre bullet. A little card enclosed was signed 'Well Wisher' and said, 'I've got another one just like this that I'm going to give you some day—in the neck.'"

"All old Santa Claus dropped in my Christmas socks," observed Wyatt, "was some threats. From Ike Clanton's gang, I suppose. Those fellows are not through with us. I hear our friend, Mayor Clum, is being threatened. And Judge Wells Spicer for deciding in our favour. And Marshall Williams. The Lord knows what they're threatening Williams for."

"For being our friend," cut in Virgil. "Ain't that crime enough?"

"Johnny Behan probably thinks so," said Wyatt. "Except for Ike Clanton, the sheriff was the strongest witness the prosecution had. It wasn't Johnny's fault we weren't sent over the road."

"Harmless cuss," commented Holliday.

"Not so harmless as you think," returned Wyatt. "If it hadn't been for a bodyguard of citizens, we'd never have lived to get to Contention after our second arrest."

The Earps and Holliday had been rearrested on warrants after their discharge by Judge Wells Spicer at the preliminary hearing and taken by Sheriff Behan and a posse to Contention for trial. Fifty friends of the Earps accompanied them. The prisoners were released on writs of habeas corpus, and the trial never took place because the grand jury refused to return indictments.

"I think myself we'd have been assassinated on the road by Ike Clanton, Frank Stilwell, Pete Spence, and their friends," said Virgil. "But I don't think Johnny Behan knew anything about it. I'll give him credit for that."

"Maybe not," replied Wyatt. "But we'd have been killed just the same, if it hadn't been for our friends who went along."

"That certainly was a funny yarn Ike Clanton told on the stand," declared Virgil, "about meeting Leonard, Head, and Crane at Hereford after the Benson stage hold-up, and how Leonard told him Doc murdered Philpot. Those three fellows at that time were streaking through the mesquite two good jackrabbit jumps ahead of the posse, and they must have had to talk pretty fast to drop that piece of information into Ike's ear."

"Ike," replied Holliday, "overplayed his hand on the

stand. Judge Spicer thought his testimony too good to be true."

"I've heard," said Virgil, "that Johnny Behan contributed money to help prosecute us."

"Yes, that story's been going around," responded Wyatt, "but Johnny denied the charge on the witness stand."

"I'll never forgive you for not killing Ike Clanton when he grabbed you, Wyatt," said Holliday. "I wish he'd grabbed me instead of you. I'd have cooked his goose so quick he'd never have known what hit him. I did the best I could as it was, but he was running too fast, and I had to shoot too quick. Ike ought to turn professional sprinter. He'd make money as a foot-runner at county fairs."

"There's been talk," remarked Virgil, "that Ike had a gun on him but was too big a coward to use it. While he was on the witness stand, you remember, one of the lawyers said to him, 'Is it not the truth, Mr. Clanton, that as you were running from the fight, you threw away a large-calibre pistol?' There was a hunt made for that gun but none was found."

"I heard a story," said Wyatt, "that Ike, Finn, and Billy Clanton, a few weeks before the fight, pretended to have killed Curly Bill and tried to collect a reward from Old Man Hooker of the Sierra Bonita ranch. They say Hooker got tired of Curly's stealing his cattle and his monthly pay rolls and offered a reward of $1,000 for Curly's head. For his head, mind you. The Clantons took a dead man's head in a burlap sack to the Sierra Bonita, so the story goes, and said it was Curly Bill's and they had killed him at Monkey Springs. And Hooker, they say, paid the Clantons the $1,000.

Hooker, however, denied emphatically that he paid them a cent. But I wonder whose head that was?"

"Some Mexican's the Clantons had murdered in the San Pedro, probably," suggested Holliday. "They say they killed half a dozen greasers over there right after Mexicans got their daddy in Guadalupe Cañon."

The latest stage robbery came up for discussion. When the stage, on its way from Tombstone to Bisbee, passed Lewis Springs near the Clanton ranch, W. S. Waite, driver, and Charles Bartholomew, shotgun messenger, grew suspicious when they saw five men armed with rifles riding ahead off at the side of the trail. At Hereford, Bartholomew added a Winchester to his armament. While the stage was in the hills eight miles from Bisbee in the afternoon, five men in the road ahead opened fire at a distance of seventy-five yards. Two shots hit one of the wheel horses. Driver Waite turned the team around and went galloping away on the back trail. The robbers on horseback pursued the stage for five miles, keeping up a fusillade to which Bartholomew replied with shotgun and Winchester. The wounded horse grew weak, and, as the stage slowed down, two of the nine passengers jumped out. The driver stopped to pick them up. This halt gave the robbers their chance. They circled the stage out of gunshot range and blocked the road ahead. Then they sent a note to Driver Waite by a Mexican woodhauler saying that all aboard the stage would be killed unless the money box was tossed out. Waite and Bartholomew deemed it advisable to comply, and the box, containing $6,500 of Copper Queen pay-roll money, was thrown to the ground. Three of the robbers with handkerchiefs over their faces rode up and took possession of the treasure box. One of the bandits liked the looks of one of the lead horses and unhooked the animal and took it with him. The highwaymen ordered the stage to turn round again and head for Bisbee. But when Waite said he couldn't make the mountain grade with only two horses, they allowed him to drive back to Hereford.

"I suspect Ike Clanton of that job," said Wyatt Earp. "When I made the proposition to him to betray Leonard, Head, and Crane, he said he would lure them into a trap by inviting them to help in the robbery of a Copper Queen pay roll."

"If he did it," added Virgil, "I'd be willing to bet Frank Stilwell and Pete Spence were in with him."

"Stilwell and Spence are not playing Tombstone very hard these days," interposed Holliday. "But I hear they've been making threats against us."

"Yes," replied Wyatt, "I've heard they are planning to murder us. They're bad fellows. They may bushwhack us or shoot us in the back. But they'll never make a fight in the open. And, by the way, John Ringo, who used to make a habit of parading up and down Allen Street looking for trouble with us, hasn't been in town since the big fight."

"Ringo knows when to play safe, just like all the rest of these bold, bad outlaws," sneered Holliday.

"Ringo sent me a message the other day by Briggs Goodrich," went on Wyatt. "Goodrich met him in Charleston. 'Tell Wyatt Earp,' said Ringo, 'that, if any more fighting comes up, I'll have nothing to do with it. I'm looking out only for myself from now on.' Sounded as if Ringo wasn't as anxious for our game as he used to be. Maybe he's acquired the idea we're a little harder than he thought we were."

Virgil Earp arose.

"What time is it, Wyatt?" he asked.

"Lacks fifteen minutes till midnight," replied Wyatt. looking at his watch.

"Guess I'll take a look around town and see what's doing," said the marshal.

The front door of the saloon had hardly closed upon Virgil when Wyatt Earp and Holliday heard a roar of guns outside. They rushed out and found Virgil lying bleeding and unconscious in the middle of Fifth Street between the Oriental and the Crystal Palace. He had been fired upon with shotguns loaded with buckshot by five men in ambush in an unfinished building at the southwest corner of Fifth and Allen streets where the Tourist Hotel stands to-day. The would-be assassins escaped across a deep ravine at the edge of town and disappeared in the darkness through the hills in the direction of Charleston. They were never apprehended, it may be added, and their identity was never learned,

Virgil Earp had been wounded in two places. One bullet had entered his back above the left hip and passed through his body. Another had fractured the upper bone of the left arm and surgeons removed a section of the bone. It was thought at first his injuries would prove fatal. News went out from Tombstone that the marshal had been killed. He lingered between life and death for several weeks. Then he began to mend. But his arm remained helpless, and he suffered from the wound in his back to the end of his life. He was a cripple on crutches when the lurking enemies of the Earps, secretly plotting vengeance, struck a second time from the dark.

Mrs. Marietta Spence and Mrs. Francisco Castro, her

mother, sat on the porch of their cottage in the outskirts of Tombstone in quiet enjoyment of an evening in early spring.

"That star hanging over the Dragoons," remarked Mrs. Spence, "looks like a diamond as big as an orange."

Three men slinking through the street with furtive, noiseless tread materialized out of the night like ghosts.

"Why, hello, Pete," said Mrs. Spence. "I didn't hear you coming. You startled me."

"Cook us some supper," ordered Pete Spence brusquely, as he and his companions hurried inside.

Pete Spence was not one of the world's great lovers. This was his greeting to his Mexican wife after a month's absence from home.

The two men with Spence were Frank Stilwell and Florentino Cruz, an Indian-Mexican half-breed otherwise known as Indian Charlie. After eating their meal in silence, they retired into a locked room and talked in low tones until long past midnight. Stilwell and Cruz slept at the Spence home. At noon next day, which was Saturday, Spence and Indian Charlie went up town. Stilwell remained hidden in the house.

Spence and Indian Charlie ensconced themselves inside the door of an Allen Street saloon. For an hour they watched the passers-by on the sidewalk. No word was exchanged between them. Spence appeared nervous. The half-breed stood motionless, with stolid, inscrutable face. Morgan Earp chanced to saunter by.

"That's him," exclaimed Spence excitedly in a whispered shout. "That's him."

Indian Charlie became instantly transformed. He awoke from his seeming lethargy to tense, tingling

The robbers on horseback pursued the stage for five miles, keeping up a fusillade to which Bartholomew replied with shotgun and Winchester.

interest. It was as if a bronze statue suddenly had come
to life. He shot through the door like a bloodhound on a
trail. He hurried after Morgan Earp, passed him,
stopped, pretended to look in a shop window for a
moment, and then faced about. Morgan Earp apparently did not see him. But the keen black eyes of
Indian Charlie scrutinized Morgan Earp narrowly
from head to foot. On Indian Charlie's brain was pic-
tured indelibly, as by a flashlight camera, Morgan
Earp's strong young fighter's face, bold blue-gray eyes,
yellow hair, straight, stalwart figure. No danger that
the half-breed ever would forget this man. Indian
Charlie would know Morgan Earp henceforth anywhere
he saw him.

It was perhaps 10 o'clock that night that Spence,
Stilwell, and Indian Charlie left Spence's house. Stilwell and the half-breed had six-shooters buckled around
them and carried magazine carbines. No arms were visible on Spence, though he had a revolver in his hip
pocket. The night was cloudy and very dark. The
sinister trio slipped through the streets like phantoms.
At the edge of the lighted business section they separated. Stilwell and the half-breed slunk away toward
some clandestine destination. Spence mingled with the
throngs on Allen Street. He strolled along with a casual
air, idled on a corner, lounged in a doorway. But never
on bandit raid or Indian campaign did Pete Spence
scout more vigilantly than he was scouting this night on
Tombstone's crowded street. Somewhere off in the darkness, in their secret hiding place, Stilwell and Indian
Charlie were awaiting his directions.

Morgan Earp was leaning against the bar in Campbell
& Hatch's saloon and billiard hall on Allen Street be-

tween Fourth and Fifth when Bob Hatch, one of the
proprietors, returned at 11 o'clock from a performance
at the Bird Cage Opera House.

"You've been making your boasts for a long time,
Bob," said Morgan banteringly, "that you can beat
me playing pool. I'll play you now, and if I beat you,
I never want to hear another cheep out of you."

"All right, Morg," laughed Hatch, "I'll go you once,
if I lose. Come on."

The pool table on which they elected to play stood
at the end of the long hall close to the rear wall. At
the north side of this rear wall and opening into an
alley was a door, the upper portion of which was like a
window set with four panes. The two lower panes were
painted white, the two upper were clear glass. Morgan
and Hatch laid aside their coats, and the game began.
Sherman McMasters, Dan Tipton, and Pat Holland
seated in chairs against the side walls, looked on.

"This is for the championship," said Morgan jok-
ingly.

"You bet," returned Hatch.

While the game was in progress, Pete Spence wandered in off Allen Street, took a drink at the bar in the
front of the house, sent a momentary lazy glance across
the long intervening row of billiard tables at the players in the rear end, and sauntered out again. But as
soon as he stepped out on the sidewalk, his seeming
listlessness fell from him. Walking rapidly, he turned a
corner and faded into darkness.

Morgan's eighth ball clicked into a pocket. He had
won. Laughing uproariously, he gave Hatch a resound-
ing clap on the shoulder.

"Knew I could beat you," he bumbled jovially.

"Don't crow yet awhile," flashed back Hatch. "Wait till I get warmed up."

Just at that moment, Frank Stilwell and Indian Charlie arrived at the alley door. From the black darkness, they peered silently in through the upper clearglass panes. Pete Spence's scouting expedition had worked to climax. From the brightly lighted interior of the hall, the two upper panes in the door had the appearance of dark mirrors glimmering with dim reflections. No one saw the two cold faces looking in out of the night with burning, basilisk eyes upon the merry scene. No one suspected that just beyond the door lurked murder.

The second game had begun. Hatch was bending over the table making a studied shot. Morgan stood chalking his cue a few feet from the door and with his back to it.

Came in the momentary stillness a sudden deafening crash. Then quickly a second.

Morgan spun round toward the door. His cue flew from his hand and clattered against the wall. His arms shot above his head and, lunging in a stumbling fall, he crumpled upon his face among a myriad glittering splinters of broken glass. A gust of wind whisked through two shattered jagged panes in the door. Hatch, McMasters, Tipton, and Holland, stunned for an instant by the quick tragedy, rushed into the alley. Only empty darkness there. A staccato clamour of boots thudding on packed earth came to them out of the black distance.

Morgan Earp, still conscious, was laid upon a lounge in a card room. Wyatt, Virgil, and Warren Earp gathered round him.

"Bend down to me, Wyatt," Morgan murmured. "I'm dying."

Bending over him, Wyatt nodded his head grimly as the mortally wounded men whispered some secret in his ear.

Morgan lingered for a half hour. He smiled faintly as the clock on the wall marked midnight.

"The game's over," he said in a clear voice.

The game of life and the game of pool both over. Life for him had been in truth a game, and he had played it with the spirit of a cavalier adventurer, gaily, carelessly, recklessly, bravely—above all, bravely. He had cashed in his chips, shoved back his chair, and gone out with a smile into the eternal silence.

Of the two shots fired by the assassins through the door, one had passed through a lower opaque pane and the other through an upper pane of clear glass. The second bullet bored into the wall above Sherman McMaster's head. The first struck Morgan Earp in the small of the back, shattered his spine, and passing through his body, lodged in the thigh of George Berry standing by a stove at the front of the hall. Berry's wound caused his death.

"Berry's injury," said Dr. George Goodfellow, "was inconsequential and hardly more than an abrasion. Technically, he died from shock. The simple fact was the man was scared to death."

Bells of Tombstone tolled all day Sunday while Morgan Earp lay in state blanketed by flowers in the Cosmopolitan Hotel. The body was taken to Benson Monday, and, accompanied by Mr. and Mrs. Virgil Earp, Mr. and Mrs. James Earp, Wyatt Earp, and Doc Holliday, started by train to its last resting place in

Colton, California, home of the parents of the Earps. Virgil and James Earp were saying farewell to Arizona. Neither ever returned. Thus passed from the Tombstone scene Virgil and Morgan Earp, two of the fighting Earp triumvirate, one dead, the other broken in health and disabled by wounds, both victims of assassins who had tracked them relentlessly in skulking secrecy and whose cowardly vengeance had blazed out or the darkness of night. Of the three warrior brothers, Wyatt Earp alone was left—one, but a lion.

Stilwell, Spence, and Indian Charlie arrived at the Spence home while Morgan Earp was dying. Spence was white and trembling, according to his wife, and his teeth were chattering. Stilwell left almost immediately, and Indian Charlie an hour or so later. Spence arose from bed at 6 o'clock Sunday morning and ordered breakfast. He and his wife quarrelled and he slapped her. Possibly it was this slap in the face that caused his wife, at the coroner's inquest, to reveal the secrets of the murderous plot. After a hurried breakfast, she said, Spence left on horseback for Sonora. A wise trip it proved to be. Spence's sojourn in old Mexico doubtless saved him from the vengeance of Wyatt Earp, aroused now to the depths of his soul and filled with a raging lust for the blood of his brother's murderers.

Bright and early Sunday morning, Frank Stilwell was in Tucson. The distance between Tombstone and Tucson, even as the crow flies, is hardly less than seventy-five miles. Across the San Pedro Valley through gaps between the mountain groups, this veteran robber of stages, who knew every secret trail and cow path of the mesas and deserts, had made the journey on horseback between midnight and daybreak and here he was in Tucson, dropping into saloons along Myer and Church streets and greeting old friends and acquaintances with smiling insouciance. His swift, secret flight by night had given him an alibi sufficiently plausible, it might have seemed, to convince any jury of twelve men of his innocence of Morgan Earp's murder. But even the most cunning alibis, like other schemes of mice and men, gang aft agley. No jury of twelve men was to weigh the evidence of Stilwell's crime. No eloquent lawyers, wise in the technicalities and subterfuges of the law, were to argue subtly in his defense. To only one man was he to answer for his midnight deed of blood, and that one man was Wyatt Earp.

Before Wyatt Earp left Tombstone with Morgan Earp's body, he knew the identity of his brother's assassins. What the secret was that was whispered into Wyatt Earp's ear by Morgan Earp as he lay dying on the card-room lounge has remained a secret, as far as the public is concerned, to this day. Morgan Earp, it was believed, had caught no fleeting glimpse of the murderers who fired upon him through the glass of the alley door. But, according to Dan Tipton, Morgan Earp had received some mysterious warning a few hours before his death to be on his guard against assassination. This, it was thought, was Morgan Earp's dying secret, and it may have been accompanied by definite knowledge of the identity of the men in the plot. Whatever the source of the information, this much is certain: Wyatt Earp knew.

Ike Clanton was in Tucson when Stilwell arrived. Since Billy Clanton and the two McLowerys had died beneath the guns of the Earps and Doc Holliday, Ike Clanton had been threatening vengeance, and the Earps suspected that, in alliance with Stilwell and Spence, he had been at the bottom of the plots that had resulted in the wounding of Virgil and the death of Morgan Earp. It would have fared ill with Ike Clanton if, after these tragic affairs, he had chanced to encounter any of the Earps or Holliday. Armed or unarmed, he would have been killed without mercy. In Wyatt Earp's hatred, no magnanimity was mingled now.

Ike Clanton received several telegrams from Tombstone on Monday warning him that Wyatt Earp and Holliday were with the escort accompanying Morgan Earp's remains and would pass through Tucson late Monday afternoon. Ike Clanton showed these telegrams to Stilwell. The situation had a tinge of danger. What was to be done?

"You stay away from the depot," Stilwell advised Clanton. "Wyatt Earp and Holliday know you are here. They will be on the lookout for you. They haven't an inkling that I'm within fifty miles of Tucson. I'll give them a little surprise."

The train with the Earp party aboard drew into the station at Tucson. It was dusk. The town seemed a great dark blur with a few lights winking here and there in the houses. Deep shadows hung over the desert that swept away from the tracks. The mountains were darkly purple against the fading colours in the sky. Wyatt Earp and Doc Holliday stepped from a coach. They would get a breath of fresh air and take a turn for exercise up and down the long depot platform. But they were not to be caught napping by lurking foes. Wyatt Earp carried a rifle, Holliday a shotgun. The train was to stop ten minutes.

From the end of a street, Ike Clanton watched them

furtively. He would have liked to kill these two men. But they were rough-looking customers. They knew how to use those guns that rested lightly in the crook of their arms. Their deaths could wait a while. So, through the street back into town faded this apostle of personal safety.

Back and forth Wyatt Earp and Doc Holliday strolled leisurely. A man walking beside the track ahead of the train caught Wyatt Earp's eye. A diffused glow from the long ray of the locomotive headlight faintly illuminated the distant figure, and something about it seemed vaguely familiar.

"There, Doc," said Wyatt Earp in a tense voice hardly above a whisper, "look there. That's Frank Stilwell."

"By God, it is!" answered Holliday.

Stilwell was moving toward a string of box cars standing on a siding. His purpose, it was believed, was to take a position alongside the track and assassinate Wyatt Earp as the train went past. Possibly Wyatt Earp would be standing on a platform. If not, he might be killed by a bullet fired through a window. A shot in the dark was Stilwell's favourite form of murder.

Going on tiptoe as noiselessly as possible but almost at a run, Wyatt Earp and Holliday hurried after him. Stilwell passed along one side of the box cars as Wyatt Earp and Holliday sped along the other. At the far end of the string of cars, the three men met.

Two short whistles sounded from the locomotive. With vast, smoky puffs and a hissing of steam, the giant machine slid forward. Half drowned in the thunderous rumble of the train, a sudden explosive report boomed upon the fireman's ears as he leaned out the window of the engine pilot house. Then another. Four more in quick succession. Six in all.

"Sounded like shots," yelled the fireman across the cab to the engineer sitting at the throttle.

"Some drunk celebratin', I guess," the engineer shouted back.

The coaches began to flash by, their windows brilliantly lighted. Two men seized the step-rails and swung aboard. From his cushioned seat, Virgil Earp, his crutches leaning beside him, glanced up to see Wyatt Earp and Doc Holliday coming toward him through the aisle. Both were smiling. After they had taken seats, something Wyatt Earp said caused Virgil's eyes to grow suddenly bright and his face to glow. Virgil shot out his hand. Wyatt Earp, then Holliday, shook it with solemn fervour. A passenger reading a magazine across the aisle looked over his spectacles with a touch of surprise. Strange. Why should these three men who had been travelling together for hours be shaking hands in such crazy fashion? Well, the world was full of funny people. The man across the aisle fell to his magazine again.

A railroad trackman carrying a lantern saw at dawn next morning some undefined, dark object on the ground at the end of the string of box cars. He stopped curiously and swung his light toward it to see what it was.

"Humph!"

A dead man lay on his face in the shine of the lantern. The dark, packed cinders about him were stained moistly red. The trackman lifted the edge of the coat gingerly to learn the cause of a sharp bulge above the hip. The heavy handle of a six-shooter was projecting from the pocket. Whoever this poor devil was, he had died without a chance to draw his weapon.

At the inquest, the coroner discovered six wounds on the body, four made by rifle balls and two by buckshot. The rifle balls had passed entirely through. One charge of buckshot had shattered the left thigh and tearing through the abdominal region, had splintered the spinal column. The other had entered the breast over the heart, leaving a gaping hole, above which a great burned spot showed in the coat.

Wyatt Earp's vengeance had been swift. Morgan Earp had died at midnight Saturday. A little after sundown the following Monday, Frank Stilwell had paid for the murder with his blood.

An eastbound train was flagged to a stop after midnight at the little station of Rillito, nine miles west of Tucson. Wyatt Earp and Doc Holliday evidently had changed their minds about going to California. They boarded the train and returned to Benson. Before next morning's sun was high above the Dragoons, they were back in Tombstone.

But Tombstone no longer was stronghold or refuge for them. The power of the Earps had been broken and their day was over. Of the old fighting oligarchy of four men that had ruled supreme in the town for more than two years, only two were left, and with enemies closing in, the position of these two was precarious if not desperate. Though in the retrospect, the fall of the Earps from power gives an impression of crashing suddenness, it was rather a process of gradual disintegration. Victories and defeats had alike contributed to their overthrow. Beset by political and personal foes, by secret machinations and murderous violence, the wonder is not that their power was so brief but that it endured so long.

The Benson stage affair was the beginning of the end. Doc Holliday's innocence of participation in that crime had never been satisfactorily established and his friendship with Bill Leonard, leader of the bandits, had tended to confirm belief in his guilt. At the same time the whispered suspicions against the Earps had had their effect upon the public mind and had been strengthened by the testimony of Ike Clanton in court. The battle against the Clantons and McLowerys had been for the Earps a Pyrrhic victory with the effect of a defeat. Nothing had done more to swing public sentiment against them. Billy Clanton's heroic fight against hopeless odds and the fact that Ike Clanton and Tom McLowery were unarmed had engendered general sympathy for the three outlaws who had gone with splendid courage to their death and, while kindling to flaming intensity the hatred of the enemies of the Earps, had alienated not a few friends. Apologists found the tragedy difficult to defend and foes openly proclaimed it cold-blooded murder.

Morgan Earp's assassination had left a serious gap in the Earps' fighting strength and the departure of Virgil Earp disabled by wounds had meant the loss to the faction of police power. Finally the killing of Stilwell—an Earp victory, if one chooses to call it that—was disastrous in that it placed Wyatt Earp and Doc Holliday outside the pale of law. If it could be considered justifiable under the unwritten law, the written statutes would hold the slayers to strict account. The two avengers of Morgan Earp's death stood at the forks of the road. They must stand trial for murder or leave the country. A trial might mean acquittal but it might also mean the penitentiary or the gallows. They determined not to stake their lives and liberty on the dubious chance of a jury's verdict and made preparations to seek safe harbour beyond the boundaries of Arizona.

With Tombstone swarming with their enemies and with Sheriff Behan fully informed concerning the killing of Stilwell, their arrangements for departure were made without hurry and with no pretense of secrecy. For four days they remained in town busy in winding up their affairs. They shipped their effects out of the country, they told their friends good-bye. Warren Earp, Sherman McMasters, Texas Jack Vermillion, and Jack Johnson, minor satellites in days of power, decided to accompany them.

On the morning of March 25, 1882, Wyatt Earp assembled his five followers for a stirrup cup at the Oriental bar. All were armed with six-shooters and rifles. Their horses, with blanket rolls strapped on their saddles, were hitched in Allen Street.

"Tombstone," said Wyatt Earp, pouring out his liquor, "is a good old town, after all. I'm leaving a lot of friends behind me, and as the fellow says, a host of enemies. I'll keep my friends warm in my heart. As for my enemies, they can go to hell. The old town has been good to me and it's been bad to me. But good and bad luck are all one now. My job is finished. I've played a man's part. I regret nothing. I am ashamed of nothing. I'll never forget Tombstone, and Tombstone will remember me to its last day."

Wyatt Earp raised his glass.

"Here's happy days, boys," he said. "And good-bye to Tombstone."

As the men at the bar were turning down their fare-well bumpers, Sheriff Behan came bustling in. His customary smile was absent. He vouchsafed no word of greeting. This was not Johnny Behan but the Sheriff of Cochise County clothed in august authority.

"I have warrants here," he said austerely, drawing the two official documents from the inner pocket of his coat, "sworn out in Tucson and charging Wyatt Earp and J. D. Holliday with the murder of Frank Stilwell. I have come to arrest these two men."

Wyatt Earp set down his glass on the bar and with frigid eye looked the sheriff slowly up and down from head to foot.

"Johnny Behan," he said, "you have been my enemy from the time you set foot in Tombstone. You have lied about me. You have played every underhanded trick you knew how to play against me. I have never made a move that I have not heard your rattles in the grass. A man had only to be my enemy to be your friend. You have hated me. You have tried to put me in the penitentiary. You have done your best to ruin me. I have known every under-cover play you have made. But I have conducted myself like a gentleman toward you. I have treated you with a civility you did not deserve. But now I am sick of you, sick of your treacher-ies, sick of the gang behind you. I despise you. You can't arrest me." Wyatt Earp snapped his fingers under the sheriff's nose. "I'd see you in hell before I'd allow my-self to be taken a prisoner by you."

Wyatt Earp and his companions walked out the door past the sheriff, unhitched their horses, and swung into the saddles. With Wyatt Earp and Doc Holliday side by side in advance of the others who followed four abreast, the little calvalcade moved northward out Allen Street, the horses reined to a walk in a last gesture of defiance. Crowds lined the curbs to watch them go. Many a man was in those two lines of people who hated Wyatt Earp and Doc Holliday with a deep and bitter hatred. Many a curse was muttered. Many a glance surcharged with deadly malevolence was bent upon the two leaders. Hatred's last chance was passing by. Here were targets impossible to miss. But no one made a hostile move. Sitting calmly in their saddles, their faces of the stillness of marble, their rifles resting across their laps, Wyatt Earp and Doc Holliday rode through a lane of silence. With cool, steady eyes, Wyatt Earp watched the banked faces along one side of the street, Holliday those along the other. Only after they had arrived at the edge of town did the horsemen increase their pace. Then, at an easy gallop, they passed over a hill and were lost to view.

Old-timers, hostile, of course, will sometimes tell to-day in careless phrase how the Earps were "run out of Tombstone." This is how they were run out. In such deliberate manner did they take their "flight." They fled at a walk.

So Wyatt Earp and Doc Holliday turned their backs upon the past with its drama and romance and tragedy, and riding on over the deserts and the purple mountains, disappeared from Tombstone forever.

CHAPTER XV

THE OUT TRAIL

RAMON ACOSTA was tired and hot. He sat down to rest on a log and, getting out a sack of tobacco, rolled a yellow-paper cigarette. Near the ramshackle log cabin, Ted Judah was busy stacking firewood to be marketed in Tombstone.

"Sam Williams," remarked Acosta, letting a luxurious puff of smoke trickle from his nostrils, "has been gone a long time. Those mules must be hard to find."

The two young workmen were camped with other wood-choppers at Pete Spence's wood ranch on the western slopes of the Dragoons. The tawny, precipitous ramparts of the mountains rose straight above them. Far across the rolling green mesquite mesa they could see Tombstone at the edge of its silver hills.

"I wonder who those fellows are?" said Acosta, as six horsemen appeared over a rise in the mesa and rode toward them.

"How many men working in this camp?" asked a tall, blond man as the six horsemen drew rein.

"Five," replied Acosta.

"Who are they?"

"I'm Ramon Acosta. This man here is Ted Judah. Jose Ortiz is chopping wood higher up on the mountain. Sam Williams is out trying to find some mules that strayed from camp. There's one other fellow. I forget his name. What's his name, Ted?"

"Florentino Cruz," answered Judah.

The blond man nodded thoughtfully.

"Seems to me I know Florentino Cruz," he said. "Don't they sometimes call him Indian Charlie?"

"Yes, that's him," replied Acosta. "And Indian Charlie is a good wood-chopper."

"I've heard he was," said the blond man. "I'm looking for him. Right now I need a good wood-chopper like him in my business."

"But," protested the Mexican, "I don't believe you can hire Indian Charlie. He's working for Pete Spence."

"I'll get Indian Charlie," declared the blond man, making his jaws click upon the name. "Where is he?"

"See that hill over there," replied Acosta, pointing. "You'll find him there chopping wood."

Acosta and Judah saw the six horsemen halt at the foot of the distant hill. Three dismounted and tossing their bridles to the others to hold, began to climb the slopes and were quickly lost to view in the timber.

Indian Charlie did not put in an appearance at camp that evening at supper. He was still absent when the others rolled in their blankets for the night.

"Funny Florentino hasn't showed up," said Acosta, as he pulled the covers up to his eyes. "That half-breed must have got lost."

Next morning, as the sun was lifting over the mountains, Acosta and Judah went on a hunt for Indian Charlie. They found him near the top of the hill to which the six horsemen had been directed. He lay under a tree on his breast with his face resting on his arm.

"Sound asleep," laughed Acosta. "What do you think of this lazy fellow? Hey, *muchacho*, it's time to go to work. Wake up."

He stooped over and shook Indian Charlie by the shoulder. Then, suddenly, Acosta straightened up, a frightened look on his face.

"He's dead," he said.

Sam Williams, out looking for mules, had not returned to the wood-choppers' camp either. He had caught sight of the six horsemen and, recognizing the tall, blond leader, had hurried into Tombstone as fast as he could go, the fear of death upon him.

"I have heard," said Acosta at the inquest held in Tombstone, "that Sam Williams is a brother of Pete Spence."

Florentino Cruz or Indian Charlie was killed on the afternoon of the day Wyatt Earp and his five companions left Tombstone.

"I found four wounds on the body," said Dr. George Goodfellow. "Any one of three would have caused death. The fourth, on the hip, must have been made while the man was running."

Wyatt Earp, Doc Holliday, Warren Earp, Sherman McMasters, Texas Jack, and John Johnson were riding slowly westward from the Dragoons toward the Whetstones.

"I hope," said Wyatt Earp cheerfully to Doc Holliday as they jogged across San Pedro Valley, "that Frank Stilwell and Indian Charlie burn together in the same pit in hell. I am convinced that Curly Bill, John Ringo, and Hank Snelling also had part in plotting Morgan Earp's death. I'd like to send those three fellows after Stilwell and the half-breed. But we haven't time to hunt them all down now. But if I ever meet any of them anywhere on earth, ten years from now, or twenty-five, I'll kill them."

It chanced that, late in the afternoon on the day after Indian Charlie had gone to his death, Curly Bill and eight of his followers were resting at Iron Springs in the narrow valley between the Whetstone and Mustang mountains. It chanced also that Wyatt Earp and his five companions were heading for this same Iron Springs, which was thirty-five miles north by west of Tombstone. The water from the spring formed a pool about which was a copse of cottonwoods and willows, and at the south side of the pool was an embankment. a sort of natural breastworks, behind which Curly Bill and his men were taking their ease, their horses with the saddles on grazing in the thick willow brush.

Curly Bill sat with his back against the embankment. His men sprawled on the grass around him.

"I've been thinkin'," said the outlaw leader, "about gittin' out o' this here country. The old gang's goin' fast. Joe Hill cashed out jest recent. Hoss steps in a badger hole up around Clifton and breaks Joe's neck. After bein' shot at a million times, more or less, Joe goes and gits killed by a hoss. Then, jest before I leave Galeyville, Jake Gauss stretches hemp on account of another hoss. Jake's hoss don't seem to be able to run fast enough, and the bunch of stranglers ketches him. A feller's got to be a jedge of hossflesh if he aims to be a hoss thief. A lot of the other boys have went over the divide the past six months or so. Before they git me, too, I'm liable purty soon to git on my pony and jest keep on ridin'.

"It ain't that my nerves is on the break. I'm jest kind o' tired o' hittin' the high spots with bullets knockin' up dirt around me. What do I git out o' rustlin'? Fun for a week in Galeyville—that's about all. An' sick as a dog fer a week afterwards. They shore sell rot-gut licker in that burg.

"Whar'm I goin'? I'll tell you whar. Down in Chihuahua. I sneaked down there a few weeks back. No, didn't have no business. Jest wanted to take a looksee. Them Mexicans would have shot me up, I reckon, ef they'd knowed about all the greasers I've laid low in my day. But these here caballeros gits imbued with the idee I'm a cattle buyer. Might ha' took me fer a Mex fer all I know; I'm black enough and sling their lingo purty good. Well, I met a gal down thar, and her dad owns more cows than're in all Arizony.

"'Curly,' says I to myself when I sizes up this layout, 'this is jest the place fer an old cow hand like you.' So I'm aiming to head back fer Chihuahua and hook up with this here Mex gal and end my days thar peaceful. She's got the blackest eyes and the reddest lips you ever seen, and she's as white as me. Whiter, maybe. And as soon as the old man cashes in his chips, she gits all them cows."

One of the outlaws arose and took a look over the embankment southward across the level reaches of the valley.

"Say, Curly," he said abruptly, crouching down again, "what'd you do ef you met Wyatt Earp?"

"Kill him," answered Curly Bill in a matter-of-fact voice. "He bent a gun over my head in Tombstone once, and I've been layin' to git even with him ever sence."

"Well, you've got your chance to git even right now," retorted the outlaw. "Wyatt Earp, with five fellers with him, are right out yonder, ridin' straight fer this here water hole."

"You're a liar," said Curly Bill as he and all the

other outlaws grabbed their rifles and scrambled to their feet.

The story of what happened at the Iron Springs water hole was told by Wyatt Earp himself

"We had been riding in the hot sun since early morning," said Wyatt Earp, "and we were glad when we saw those shady trees ahead of us. We were going along slowly, taking it easy. I may have been a little ahead of the five other fellows, but we were all nearly abreast. I had two six-shooters at my belt, a double-barrelled shotgun, looped to my pommel, hung under my left leg, and a Winchester was hanging in a scabbard on the right side of my horse. Not a soul was in sight. There wasn't a sign of danger. But as we approached the water hole I had a queer feeling that I couldn't explain even to myself—a sort of hunch that something was wrong, and I unslung the shotgun from the pommel and held it across my lap.

"This green spot in the desert valley looked as peaceful as any place I ever saw. The tall cottonwoods stood as still as if there'd never been such a thing in the world as a breeze, and through gaps between the willows I could see the pool of water as smooth as a piece of glass and glistening white in the sun. I was thinking what a fine place this would be to camp for the night with good grass and plenty of water for the horses when, from behind a bank, up rose nine men. Every man had a rifle at his shoulder, and every rifle blazed. Those fellows wasted no time. They meant business.

"I may have been crazy with excitement and scared half to death as I saw that line of guns burst into flame within thirty feet of me. But somehow I seemed to myself to be as calm as I ever was in my life. I knew there

were nine men. How I knew I have no idea. I couldn't
have had time to count them. The mysterious way in
which they rose out of the ground like nine devils
clothed in fire brought back to me as clear as a flash the
stories of witchcraft and magic I had heard in my child-
hood. When I saw Curly Bill, only half of his body
showing above the bank, I seemed to hear myself saying, 'Well, there's Curly Bill. I'm a little surprised to
run on to him out here on the desert. He looks natural.
Hasn't changed a bit since that night in Tombstone
when Marshal White was killed. I wonder what old
Curly's been doing all this while.' Then it occurred to
me that it would be best for me to dismount. My horse
might jump and spoil my aim. I probably could shoot
better from the ground.

"I climbed down off my horse. I slipped one arm
through a bridle rein. My horse couldn't run off now
and leave me there. As I stood there by my horse's
head, cocking my gun, I looked the nine men over.
They struck me as pretty busy fellows, all with their
heads down on their rifles and all firing away. I noted
with surprise that every rifle seemed aimed at me. I
rather resented that. I wanted to kill Curly Bill. I believed he had been in both plots that had resulted in the
wounding of my brother Virgil and the death of my
brother Morgan. I felt that, if any one of those nine
men killed me before I killed Curly Bill, he would rob
me of my one chance for vengeance, and I'd never have
another. I seemed suddenly to be praying, and my
prayer was that I wouldn't be killed before I had killed
Curly Bill. So I raised my shotgun to my shoulder and
drew a careful bead on Curly Bill. As I sighted at Curly
Bill, he was sighting at me. I could see the deep wrinkles

about one of his eyes that was squinted shut. His other eye, held down close to his gun, was wide open. I noticed with curious interest that this one eye, blazing murder at me over his rifle barrel, was blacker than I remembered his eyes to have been when I saw him last. Then I pulled both triggers.

"Curly Bill threw up his hands. His rifle flew high in the air. He gave a yell that could have been heard a mile as he went down. I saw him no more. I knew he was lying dead behind the bank. Each one of my shotgun shells was loaded with nine buckshot. Both charges struck him full in the breast.

"Three seconds possibly had elapsed from the moment the outlaws rose from behind the bank till Curly Bill was killed. I had thought out my plans, arranged the sequence of my actions, argued with myself, and solved several grave problems, all in the wink of an eye. A psychologist might be able to make something out of that. I never could. It's always remained a mystery to me."

"Bullets," Wyatt Earp resumed, "were now singing songs all around me, soprano bullets, tenor bullets, bass bullets, a regular hallelujah chorus of bullets. My shotgun was empty. I reached across my saddle to get my rifle, hanging on the other side of my horse. But my horse, trembling and wet with the sweat of terror, began to rear and plunge, and I was unable to draw the gun from its long scabbard. I jerked out one of my six-shooters and, shielding myself as well as I could behind my horse, fired under the animal's neck.

"So far, I had paid no attention to the five men with me. I was busy with my own affairs. I supposed they had jumped from their horses at the same time I had and gone to fighting. I felt—I knew—that these brave comrades, a little too far back, perhaps, for me to see them, were putting up the battle of their lives, dropping on the sand to fire from one knee or standing boldly upright and, with undaunted courage, exchanging bullet for bullet with these murderous outlaws. The thought of these fearless and heroic friends fighting desperately at my back cheered and inspired me. I emptied one six-shooter and drew another.

"But my comrades' guns were not roaring in my ears, and I saw none of the outlaws fall except Curly Bill. This struck me as strange. Could it be possible that all my companions had been shot down at the first flaming blast from the outlaws' guns and were now lying silent in death? The idea almost unnerved me. Sheltered behind my horse, I shot a quick glance to my rear. Not one of my bold companions was in sight. Every mother's son, including my old pal Doc Holliday, one of the bravest men I ever knew, had turned tail at the first volley and gone scampering into the distance as fast as their horses could run. I had been fighting out there alone. No wonder the bullets were shouting a hallelujah chorus around me. The whole outlaw bunch was shooting at me. There was nobody else to shoot at.

"I realized right then that this was no place for a man of stainless soul and unimpeachable moral reputation and resolved to remove myself as speedily and as far as possible from the contaminating neighbourhood of these degraded outlaws. Keeping my horse between me and the enemy, I began to back away. It was slow, dangerous work: my maddened horse was almost unmanageable, and the outlaws kept popping away at me. When I had retreated a hundred yards or so, I attempted to mount. But my cartridge belt, which I had loosened two or three holes earlier in the day because of the heat, had slipped down below my hips, and I couldn't swing my right leg across my saddle. It cost time to remedy this. As I settled myself at last in the saddle, my pommel was shot away. I pulled my horse's head around, and sinking my spurs in the animal's flanks up to the rowel heads, I rode as if I were trying to break all the world's speed records.

"Far beyond the range of outlaw rifles, I met my five game companions. As they had fled from the battle-field, Texas Jack's horse had been shot dead under him. Holliday had halted and taken Texas Jack up behind him. That was a brave thing for Holliday to do. Char-acteristic of him, too. But this chivalrous knight of the six-shooter had left me out there by myself among the bullets. However, Doc had now regained his courage.

"'One grand little fight you made, Wyatt,' he said, riding to my side. 'Let's go back in and finish the job. Come on.'

"All the others were also ready to renew the battle. Their courage and high resolve almost brought tears to my eyes.

"'You fellows go back in,' I said. 'I've had a belly-ful.'

"My hat," added Wyatt Earp in conclusion, "had five bullet holes in it, two in the crown, and three in the brim. Bullets had ripped ragged rents up and down the legs of my pants. The bottom of my coat on both sides, where it had been held out by the holsters and the handles of my six-shooters, had been torn into strings and shreds. But, as by a miracle, I had not received a scratch."

Now came the great enigma in the story of Curly Bill. Did Wyatt Earp kill Curly Bill? Or did the outlaw captain climb on his cow pony and "jest keep on ridin'," marry his Mexican sweetheart in Chihuahua and live happily there ever after? The Tombstone country divided on the problem of the outlaw's death, and the argument blazed from the Pelloncillos to the Huachucas. The question assumed the importance of a public issue.

Wyatt Earp and the five men with him had known Curly Bill and could hardly have mistaken any other man for him. There was no doubt in the minds of any of them that Wyatt Earp had killed Curly Bill. Tell Wyatt Earp to-day that he did not kill Curly Bill and he will laugh at you. He is as sure that he killed him as that his name is Wyatt Earp.

But the outlaws in the fight at the water hole denied that Curly Bill met death. They admitted the battle took place. They said that Wyatt Earp stood his ground and did all the fighting and the others ran away. But they declared that none of the outlaws had been killed and none wounded. It may be remarked, parenthetically, that the outlaws who hated Wyatt Earp may have been actuated in this denial by a desire to rob him of the credit of killing the outlaw chieftain.

No search for Curly Bill's body was ever made. No corpus delicti to prove the tragedy was ever produced. A story became current in Tombstone that the outlaws had taken Curly Bill's body to Charleston and buried it secretly by night. But no man, except possibly the outlaws who officiated at the clandestine funeral rites, ever knew the location of Curly Bill's grave.

An account of the death of Curly Bill was printed in the Tombstone *Epitaph* the day after the fight took place. It was based, the paper said, on the story of an eyewitness whose identity was not revealed. It agreed in all particulars with Wyatt Earp's version. Brighton Springs in the San Pedro Valley a few miles southwest of Tombstone was given as the scene of the battle. But in its next day's issue, the paper said the statement that the fight occurred at Brighton Springs was intentionally wrong and had been made in a spirit of good sportsmanship to give the Earp party its chance to depart unmolested from Arizona. The *Epitaph* was friendly toward the Earps. Iron Springs is given here as the scene of the fight on the authority of Wyatt Earp himself.

The *Nugget*, taking the side of the outlaws, ridiculed the story that Curly Bill had been killed. A heated controversy developed between the *Nugget* and the *Epitaph*. The *Nugget* offered a reward of $1,000 for proof that Curly Bill was dead. The *Epitaph* answered this challenge by offering $2,000 for proof that Curly Bill was alive.

The story that Curly Bill settled down to peaceful pursuits in old Mexico persists to the present time. Old-timers will tell you that, ten years after his supposed death, Curly Bill was a prosperous cattleman "somewhere in Chihuahua," with a Mexican wife and a flock of little Curly Bills playing about the patio of his comfortable hacienda. And, these old codgers will add, Curly Bill may be living to-day.

Soft shadows of legend fell about Curly Bill. Purple mists of romance enfolded him. But after the fight at the water hole, the outlaw rode no more on his raids across the Mexican border. No more did his stolen herds storm thunderously through the valleys of the San Pedro and the San Simon. Mexican smuggler trains with aparejos bursting with gold and silver threaded the mountain defiles in safety. Vanished utterly was Curly Bill. Never again was he seen in Arizona.

Criticism burst about Sheriff Behan's ears because of the personnel of his posse of sixteen men organized for pursuit of Wyatt Earp and his followers. The posse included Ike and Finn Clanton, John Ringo, Hank Snelling, the two Tyle brothers, and a number of other hard characters, termed by the sheriff "cowboys," but by persons of less euphemistic phrase denominated outlaws. These men had all been friends of Billy Clanton and the two McLowery boys and were bitter enemies of Wyatt Earp and Doc Holliday. Ike and Finn Clanton had a brother's death to avenge, and John Ringo the death of three friends. The presence of these outlaws in the sheriff's posse held a hint of ugly possibilities. It suggested that the purpose of the pursuit was as much to pay off personal animosities as to comply with the demands of law and justice, and at the outset, it seemed more than likely that the chase would end in a battle of hatred and vengeance rather than in the capture of the fugitives.

In defense of his men, Sheriff Behan, in an impassioned but unguarded moment, referred to this "sharked up list of landless resolutes" as his "posse of honest ranchmen." Whereupon Tombstone burst into uproarious laughter. Even the sheriff's faithful friends had to join in the mirth. John Ringo and Ike Clanton as "honest ranchmen" certainly were immoderately funny. Tombstone papers, on the opposite side of the political fence, seized upon the expression and harped upon it with merry vindictiveness. The "posse of honest ranchmen" became one of Tombstone's immortal jests, and beneath the relentless jibes, Sheriff Behan quickly must have repented his rhetorical flourish in agony of soul. The sheriff's pursuit of the Earps added nothing to his laurels. His expedition missed by a hair's breadth being turned by an unhappy phrase into a joke.

An electric hush settled upon Tombstone. In feverish suspense the town awaited news. Sheriff Behan and his posse had gone out on the trail. For days the desert that had swallowed them gave back no word. What had happened out there in the vast silence? Had a battle been fought? Had the Earps been captured? Were the victors bringing the prisoners home in triumph? Then, suddenly, were the heavens opened and bulletins and communiqués from the sheriff came in a cloudburst over the telegraph wires: . . . The scent is growing hot. . . . The sheriff is close on the heels of the Earps . . . . Capture of the desperate criminals is imminent. . . . The Earps are trapped. . . . They must surrender or be killed. . . . There is no chance for their escape. . . . And so on. These messages from the front kept Tombstone for a time on tiptoe with excitement. But, strangely, the imminent big event never happened. Something went wrong with all the traps. The Earps were not captured. Neither were they killed. Tombstone began to lose interest. Portentous bulletins were greeted with a smile.

The Earp party, after the fight with Curly Bill at the Iron Springs water hole, rounded the Whetstone Mountains on the north, and rode east across the San Pedro and on through Dragoon Gap to Willcox. A letter from

I jerked out one of my six-shooters and, shielding myself as well as I could behind my horse, fired under the animal's neck.

Wyatt Earp dated April 4th and mailed at Willcox was printed in the *Epitaph*.

Deputy Sheriff Frank Hereford [the letter read] was hiding in a corncrib at Henderson's ranch when we arrived. He decamped, fearing violence. His fears were groundless. He would not have been injured. . . . We rested for a day at Hooker's Sierra Bonita ranch. Hooker did not, as has been reported, outfit us with fresh horses and supplies. We are all riding the same horses on which we left Tombstone except Texas Jack. His horse was killed in the Curly Bill fight. He purchased another animal. . . . Hooker did not pay me the reward of $1,000 offered by the Arizona Stock Association for the death of Curly Bill. No reward was asked for or tendered. . . . Leaving Hooker's, we went north within five miles of Eureka Springs. . . . We have kept careful track of the movements of Sheriff Behan and his posse of honest ranchmen. If they possessed even average trailing ability, we might have had trouble with them, which we are not seeking. Neither are we avoiding these honest farmer boys. We thoroughly understand their intentions.

Sheriff Behan and his posse arrived at Hooker's ranch the morning after the Earp party had departed. Henry C. Hooker, rich and influential, was famous among the pioneer cattlemen of Arizona. Concerning the sheriff's visit at the Sierra Bonita ranch, the *Epitaph* printed, in substance, this story:

Sheriff Behan asked Hooker the direction the Earp party had gone. Hooker said he did not know and would not tell if he did.

"If you will not tell me," said Sheriff Behan, "you are upholding murderers and outlaws."

"No," replied Hooker. "I know the Earps and I know you. The Earps have always treated me like a gentleman. Damn you and your posse. Your men are a set of horse thieves and outlaws."

One of Sheriff Behan's honest farmers spoke up.

"Damn the old son of a gun," he said. "Let's make him tell."

Hooker's hostler went out and got a rifle and, when he came back, he made the posseman skin back the name he had called Hooker.

When Hooker again criticized the posse, repeating that they were a lot of horse thieves and cutthroats, Sheriff Behan and Deputy Sheriff Woods told him these fellows were not their associates. "They are only with us," said the sheriff.

"Well," replied Hooker, "if they are not your associates, I will set an extra breakfast table for you and set them at a table by themselves." Which he did.

Sheriff Behan went from the Sierra Bonita to Fort Grant, where he offered $500 to Colonel Bidwell for some Indian trailers. "Hooker," remarked Sheriff Behan to the Colonel, "said he did not know which way the Earp party had gone and would not tell me if he did." Colonel Bidwell stroked his beard. "Did Hooker tell you that?" he said. "Well, then, you can't get any scouts here."

Sheriff Behan's pursuit ended in failure at the Arizona line. Wyatt Earp and his men passed into New Mexico, sold their horses at Silver City, and at Deming, took a train for Denver. The Colorado capital was their final destination. Efforts made to bring Wyatt Earp and Doc Holliday back to Tombstone for trial failed when Governor Pitkin of Colorado refused to honour the requisition issued by Governor Tritle of Arizona.

No man in Tombstone's history has been more bitterly maligned than Wyatt Earp. On the field from which he withdrew, his enemies were left in inglorious triumph, and what his enemies had failed to do to the man himself they did to his reputation. No charge was too black to be made against him, no slander too atrocious to be believed. Obloquy held an orgy. Political spite and malevolence born of vendetta revenged themselves upon him in a war dance of calumny and hatred. One hears to-day echoes of these old revilings.

If Wyatt Earp impressed himself upon Tombstone, Tombstone left its indelible mark upon him. When he took his departure he was not the same man he was when he came. The tragic experience of two years had wrought an immeasurable change. The difference was that between a mountain silent and peaceful in the sunshine and the same mountain bursting with volcanic fires and red with streaming lava.

When Tombstone first knew Wyatt Earp, he was an imperturbably calm man, not unkindly, not without humour and a certain geniality, magnanimous to his enemies, generous and loyal to his friends. His rise to a position of authority was a gradual, businesslike climb, unmarked by violence or bloodshed. He was at the peak of his power before he ever had a fight. Long after he had become the acknowledged six-shooter boss of the town, his guns remained silent, and he ruled only by the fear of the unpressed trigger. He nursed no petty grudges and harboured no murder in his heart. He wanted no quarrel with any man. His anger was a cerebral process rather than a passion; he grew wrathful only when he deliberately believed he had just cause for wrath. He was forced into feud warfare by a strange concatenation of circumstances, to a large extent accidental. But when he had to fight, he fought.

But neither the tumultuous developments that led to battle, nor the battle itself, shook him out of his old imperturbable calm. It was not until his enemies had assassinated one of his brothers and left another brother crippled for life that the slumbering whirlwind deep in the soul of him was unleashed. Then the coldly balanced man, apparently devoid of emotions, blazed into inextinguishable fury. Then he became suddenly transformed into an avenger, terrible, implacable, merciless. Up and down through the deserts he raged like a lion ravenous for blood. He tracked down the assassins. He killed them cruelly without pity. There was no flinching in what he did, and no alibis or apologies afterward. He became his own law in a lawless land and atoned for the blood of his brother with the blood of his brother's murderers. Right or wrong, he believed with absolute faith in the righteousness of the justice he administered at the muzzle of a gun. For the men he slew in vengeance, Wyatt Earp had no regrets. No remorseful memories troubled him. No ghosts came back to haunt him.

So hail and farewell to the lion of Tombstone. Strong, bold, forceful, picturesque was this fighter of the old frontier. Something epic in him. Fashioned in Homeric mould. In his way, a hero. Whatever else he may have been, he was brave. Not even his enemies have sought to deny his splendid courage. The problems of his dangerous and difficult situation, he solved, whether wisely or foolishly, with largeness of soul and utter fearlessness. No halo is for this rugged, storm-beaten head. He was a hard man among hard men in a hard environment. What he did, he did. The record stands. But, weighed in the balance, he will not be found wanting. Judged by all the circumstances of his career, the verdict in his case is clear—Wyatt Earp was a man.

Doc Holliday, as picturesque a desperado as the West ever produced, and as witty and companionable a fellow as ever smiled over the barrel of a murderous six-shooter, died of tuberculosis at Cottonwood Springs, Colorado, fifteen years after his Tombstone career ended. The "coldest blooded killer in Tombstone" had wasted to a corpse-like fragility, and death seemed merely an incidental and completing detail in the tragedy of his long illness. As the curtain rolled down upon the drama of his stormy career, Holliday looked death in the face, as he had looked life in the face, with his old calm courage and humorous cynicism.

"I used to offer odds of eight to five," he said, "that in spite of consumption, I'd cash out some day at the end of a six-shooter when I happened to run foul of a man an eighth of a second quicker on the draw. It seems almost like tough luck to lose that bet."

Holliday's last words were, "This is funny." The friends watching at his bedside thought his mind wandering. But, with his sense of humour strong to the last, the doctor doubtless considered it a choice joke that, after all his desperate adventures and narrow escapes, he should be dying in bed with his boots off.

Virgil Earp was for many years chief of police of Colton, California. He died in Goldfield, Nevada, in 1905, of pneumonia, and was buried in Portland, where he had a daughter living. He was sixty-three years old. His widow, who was his second wife, lives in Los Angeles. James Earp died in January, 1926, in Los Angeles.

Warren Earp, youngest of the five Earp brothers, returned to Arizona and was killed in Willcox in 1900 by Johnny Boyet, a cowboy, in a quarrel that grew out of a card game. Though the circumstances of the killing indicated that it was premeditated and deliberate murder, there were no eyewitnesses, it is said, and Boyet was acquitted. Warren Earp had been driving stage between Willcox and Globe, but at the time of his death was a sanitary inspector for the Arizona Cattlemen's Association and made his headquarters at Hooker's Sierra Bonita ranch. Morgan and Warren Earp were the only ones of the Earp brothers to die by violence.

Wyatt Earp, after leaving Arizona, spent some time in Denver and the Gunnison country. He kept a saloon in Nome, Alaska, in the flush days of the Klondike gold excitement. He was later in Goldfield and Tonopah, towns that sprang from the Nevada desert overnight in the last great Western gold stampede, and for a brief while gave back to this modern day a vivid picture of the wild boom camps of the old frontier.

Now, at the age of seventy-eight, with a wife at his side, Wyatt Earp is enjoying his declining years in peace, comfort, and prosperity. He owns a gold-mining property in the Mojave country and oil wells near Bakersfield. His home is in Oakland, but to be near his business interests, he lives the greater part of his time in Vidal, near San Bernardino, and in Los Angeles.

CHAPTER XVI

JOHN RINGO was drunk. For ten days he had been morosely, broodingly, tragically drunk. As straight as an Indian, he stalked about Tombstone streets, a tall, silent, sombre figure, looking a little more like Hamlet than ever, his hollow black eyes clouded and melancholy. As a toper, he was not hilarious. No antic impulse moved him to shoot out the lights or indulge in whooping cowboy deviltries. The intellectual outlaw took his pleasures quietly. He played a little faro and a little poker and of an evening dropped in at the Bird Cage Opera House. But chiefly he mellowed the acerbity of life by steeping himself in great quantities of pleasant liquors. He was in Tombstone frequently in these piping summer days of 1882. The Earps had been gone for months, and the old town gave him friendly welcome.

Ringo's boon companions on this ten-day drinking bout were Buckskin Frank Leslie and Billy Claibourne. Buckskin Frank still tended bar at the Oriental. Like Ringo, he went on sprees which sometimes lasted a week or two. Clairbourne was himself a fairly stiff tippler, but he had the elasticity of youth in his favour. Ringo was now thirty-eight and Leslie forty. Hard drinking had begun to tell on both. Ringo's periods of hopeless despondency had grown upon him, and he frequently threatened suicide. Leslie was the same light-hearted desperado he had been in earlier days, but liquor now brought the devil in him close to the surface, and his drunken mood was murderous.

On a blazing hot day in the latter part of July, John Ringo, with two bottles of whisky in his pockets, rode out of Tombstone on a drunken trail to mysterious death. Buckskin Frank Leslie and Billy Claibourne followed him. The three met again at Antelope Springs, nine miles from Tombstone, and continued their spree for three days in the saloon of Jack McCann, who formerly had kept the Last Chance, between Tombstone and Charleston, and had saved Johnny Behind-the-Deuce from the lynchers. Next, the three pottle companions went to Soldier Holes and then to Myers Cienega in Sulphur Springs Valley, where, in the Widow Patterson's boozing ken, they wound up their long orgy.

"Ringo drank like a crazy man the two days he was at my place," said Mrs. Patterson. "He was blind drunk both nights when he went to bed. Leslie was tapering off. He slyly threw much of his liquor on the floor, and I don't think he was so drunk as he pretended to be. Late on the last night of their stay, I heard a noise in the kitchen. I found Ringo in his underclothes rummaging through the pantry shelves. 'Looking for whisky,' he muttered. 'Must have whisky.' He was twitching and shaking and there was a wild look in his eyes. I thought he was on the verge of delirium tremens. After a few drinks next morning, he seemed better and rode off alone, saying he was going to Galeyville."

Later in the morning, Bill Sanders passed Ringo near a chain of water holes known as the Tanks, or the Last Water. Ringo looked at Sanders out of unseeing

eyes and rode on in silence. Three miles west, Sanders
met Frank Leslie, also riding alone and, in Sanders's
judgment, showing no signs of intoxication. Claibourne
was nowhere in sight. Leslie asked if Sanders had seen
Ringo, and when Sanders replied that Ringo was only
a few miles ahead, Leslie hurried on as if to overtake
him. Sanders wondered at the time why this murderous desperado, whose reputation credited him with
being able to kill a man to see him fall, should be following Ringo's trail.

Where West Turkey Creek Cañon, sometimes known
as Morse's Cañon, opens out into Sulphur Springs Valley, Coyote Smith's ranch house stood in open timber.
On a steep bank twenty feet high that rose from the
creek on the opposite side at some distance below the
house grew a giant live oak of peculiar formation.
From a short, stump-like central stem rose slantingly
five trunks, each of the thickness of an ordinary forest
tree and green with leaves the year around. Close to
the ground and held in position by the five boles, a flat
rock formed a seat in the cool, deep shade. Near by ran
the freight road between Tombstone and Morse's sawmill ten miles farther up the cañon in the Chiricahuas.
This tree was known to all the lumber haulers on the
trail. Beneath it they were accustomed to eat their
lunch at the noonday halts.

Between 12 and 1 o'clock on the day that Bill Sanders
met Ringo, Coyote Smith's wife heard a shot.

"Will must have killed a deer," Mrs. Smith remarked
to her son Henry.

Will Smith, her brother-in-law, working at a coal pit
in the hills, had heard a deer blow in the woods the
evening before and had taken his rifle with him when he

went to his work that morning. But Will Smith had not fired the shot. He came running to the house in alarm.

"Thought it might be Indians," he said. "Maybe it was one of the Mormon Smith boys shootin' into that covey of quail that's been usin' down the creek."

That evening at milking time, Henry Smith drove the cows through the bottom land below the big live oak. Whistling a little tune, the youth had no suspicion that, on the bank over his head, the red sunset was shimmering on the face of a dead man.

Jim Morgan, a teamster, passing by on the trail with a load of lumber near noon next day, found John Ringo dead. The outlaw was sitting on the flat rock in the forks of the live oak, his body leaning back against one of the five trunks of the tree, his head sunk on his breast. His six-shooter, held in his right hand, had fallen into his lap and caught in his watch chain. Five chambers of the cylinder were loaded; the hammer rested on the single empty shell. His rifle stood propped against the tree. His white felt hat, stained with blood, was on the ground at his feet. The silver watch in the breast pocket of his blue flannel shirt was still ticking. In his right temple was a bullet hole, and at the top of his head a great shattered wound where the ball had passed out. Brains were scattered over the tree trunks.

Ringo's coat and boots were missing. Bound about his feet were portions of his undershirt which he had torn into strips. Around his waist were two belts, one for cartridges for his rifle and the other for cartridges for his six-shooter. The latter was buckled on upside down, and all but two shells had fallen out of it. What had become of his horse was not apparent.

All the circumstances seemed to indicate conclusively

that, as he so often had threatened, Ringo had ended his troubled life while sunk in the despairing gloom of the nerve-shattered insanity that had followed his debauch. Jim Morgan, Theodore White, and Bill Knott, acting as a coroner's jury, decided his death was suicide, and a few hours after the body was found, Ringo was buried near the foot of the live oak.

Ringo's horse, still saddled and with a broken piece of picket rope about its neck, was found a week later at Robert's Cienega in Sulphur Springs Valley, six miles from the mouth of West Turkey Creek Cañon. Ringo's coat was tied in a roll at the back of the saddle, and on the pommel the bridle was hanging. Not far from the horse, one of Ringo's boots was discovered; the other was never found. In the inner breast pocket of the coat was a group photograph of four persons believed to be Ringo's father, mother, sister, and the sister's child. Coyote Smith's widow, who at the age of eighty-three still lives in the old homestead in the cañon, retains this photograph to-day. Ringo's watch and horse were turned over to Sheriff Behan in Tombstone. The watch was sent to Col. Coleman Younger, Ringo's grandfather, at San Jose, California. Sheriff Behan learned that the horse had been stolen from a Mexican living in the Dragoons and restored it to its owner. It was reported, several years later, that one of Ringo's sisters had the body exhumed and shipped to California. This, according to the Coyote Smith family, is untrue. Ringo, they declare, still lies in his grave under the oak tree.

Faith in an old superstition regarding the effects of delirium tremens led the mountain folks to believe Ringo had taken off his boots under the hallucination

that there were snakes in them. It seemed more prob-
able that, sick and exhausted, he had removed his boots
and tied them to his saddle before stretching out on the
ground for a nap. While he slept, his horse doubtless
had been frightened, broken its rope, and galloped
away. Awaking to find horse and boots gone and forced
now to travel on foot, Ringo evidently had used the
torn pieces of his undershirt to protect his feet against
stones and cactus. The cartridge belt on upside down
was evidence of Ringo's distracted state of mind.

Soon after Ringo's death, a rumour became rife in
Tombstone that Frank Leslie had murdered him. The
story may have had its origin merely in Leslie's reputation as a heartless killer. Or in the fact that Leslie followed Ringo out of town. Or in a statement credited
to Billy Claibourne. But it was believed that Leslie
had boasted of the deed. Such braggadocio would have
been very dangerous; confessed murderers were going
over the road to Yuma even in those lawless times.
Old-timers can remember no such boasts. If Leslie ever
said he killed Ringo, he must have made the statement
in whispered confidence only to his closest friends. Leslie
had no cause to kill Ringo, as far as anyone knew. No
one had ever heard of any quarrel between them. To
all appearances, the two men were friends. The manner
of Ringo's death seemed to preclude the possibility of
Leslie's having killed him. It is certain Ringo met
death while sitting in the forks of the tree. The spat-
tered brains proved that beyond question. And the
single empty chamber in Ringo's six-shooter seemed to
prove that he had killed himself. But the story that
Leslie murdered him remained definite and insistent.

It passed into tradition, and most people in that country believe it implicitly to-day.

Despite the evidence of suicide, Henry Smith and his mother, who were the first to see Ringo's body after Jim Morgan had discovered it, recall two details of the tragedy that are difficult to explain.

"I found no traces of powder burns around the wound in Ringo's temple, though I looked carefully for them," said Henry Smith. "If Ringo had shot himself, holding the muzzle of his gun against his head, the flesh around the wound would have been flame-burned and black with powder. Then the pieces of undershirt wrapped about Ringo's feet were as clean as if he had just removed the shirt from his body. There was no mud—hardly any dirt—on them. There had been a hard early-morning thunderstorm in the cañon on the day we heard the shot that killed Ringo. It had left the ground very muddy. If Ringo had walked any distance to the oak tree, the foot bandages would have been soaked and coated with mud. Bill Knott, my brother-in-law, who was on the coroner's jury and is still living, also declares the foot wrappings were clean, and there were no powder burns around the wound. He says the verdict of suicide was returned as the easiest and quickest way out of the affair. The jurors didn't want to lose time in a long coroner's investigation."

Mrs. Smith corroborated her son's story.

"I have never believed Ringo committed suicide," said the venerable woman.

Bill Sanders's story seemed to lend colour to the theory that Leslie killed Ringo. The point in the trail where Sanders said he met Leslie riding hard to over-

take Ringo was only twelve miles or so from where
Ringo was found dead.

However, only by an involved ratiocination can it be
figured out how Leslie possibly could have killed Ringo.
Leslie might have encountered Ringo just as Ringo had
wrapped his feet in the fragments of undershirt. Leslie
might have taken Ringo behind him on horseback to
the oak tree. So the foot bandages would have remained free from mud or dirt. Once seated in the oak
tree, Ringo might have fallen into a drunken stupor.
Then Leslie might have killed him with Ringo's own
six-shooter without holding the weapon close enough
to leave powder burns.

It seems ridiculous to imagine the tragedy occurred
in this way. But before dismissing such a possible explanation as utterly absurd, it may be well to wait a
while. Crimes are not always to be solved by logical
deduction. Impossibilities have a queer way of changing
into facts.

"The Widow Patterson," said Henry Smith, "was
convinced that John Ringo's ghost haunted her home
at Myers Cienega. She got so she wouldn't go in a dark
room alone for fear of seeing Ringo. When she'd drive
over to spend the day with my mother, she'd tell how
she'd seen Ringo standing in some dark corner and looking at her out of his black eyes so sorrowfully she had
to weep. Almost every night she said she heard Ringo
rummaging among the shelves of her kitchen pantry,
still looking for whisky. When my mother would suggest rats, Widow Patterson would become indignant.
'Rats nothing,' she would say. 'It's John Ringo's ghost.'

"For years there have been stories in the cañon that
Ringo's ghost was often seen under the live-oak tree

where he was killed and where he lies buried. Some
people are still afraid to pass the spot at night. Several
lumber freighters driving for Morse's sawmill claimed
to have seen Ringo walking up and down under the
tree and shining like phosphorus in the dark. One said
he had seen the ghost sitting in the forks of the tree in
broad daylight. Bill Sanders owns the farm where
Ringo is buried, and his home is not more than fifty
yards from the grave. If the place were haunted, you'd
think some of Sanders's folks would have seen the
ghost, but they never have.

"Once, my father, driving home late at night, saw a
white figure moving near the live oak. 'That's Ringo,
sure,' he thought to himself, and his hair stood on end.
But the ghost turned out to be a teamster called Curly
looking for his bell horse that had pulled up its picket
pin and run off from camp. Curly was dressed in his
white cotton drawers and undershirt."

Coyote Smith once kept a saloon across West Turkey
Creek from his ranch house. Following the trail over
the Chiricahuas from Galeyville, Curly Bill and his
outlaws used to stop there on their way to Tombstone
and Charleston.

"When I was a boy," said Henry Smith, "I knew
Curly Bill and Ringo, Joe Hill, Bill Leonard, Jim Crane,
the Clantons, McLowerys, and all the rest. They used to
drink and gamble in my father's place for two or three
weeks at a time. I've seen Frank Leslie with them more
times than I can tell. As jolly a fellow as I ever saw was
Buckskin Frank, forever singing songs and keeping
everybody laughing with his funny stories. Shooting
at flies on the wall to show their marksmanship was a
favourite pastime with these fellows, and the lizard that

sunned itself on a window sill or the mouse that stuck
its nose out of a hole was taking long chances. The walls
looked like sieves, they were peppered so full of bullet
holes. A rough bunch but good-hearted, and they spent
their money free as water. Many a wild carouse John
Ringo had within a hundred yards of where he sleeps
to-day."

John Ringo's grave is within the circle of the deep
noonday shadow of the dark-leafed, giant live oak in
whose five-stemmed forks he died. Few travellers ever
see it now. Few people beyond a radius of a dozen miles
know where it is. The cañon trail, once crowded with
wagon trains creaking beneath loads of lumber, is almost obliterated. Morse's sawmill is gone. Only a chance
horseman rides over the mountains from the San Simon
on the old road the outlaws used to take from Galeyville. Far across the shimmering, sunny reaches of Sulphur Springs Valley the Dragoons are like a ribbon of
amethyst in the west. Against the eastern sky loom the
blue and shadowy Chiricahuas. The wide mouth of
West Turkey Creek Cañon is like a wooded grass-green
park. The air holds the sweetness of juniper and pine.
A woodpecker tapping on a dead sycamore by the creek
makes a hollow, booming sound in the deep silence.
Lonely and still and peaceful is the spot where the outlaw lies.

The flat-topped mound of large, loose rocks that
marks Ringo's grave is twelve feet long, four feet wide,
and as high as a man's thigh. The stones, obtained from
the creek that flows with a soft, plashing murmur at
the foot of the embankment, are water-worn and smooth
and in colour, brown and gray. No earth or cement
holds them in place; the least among them is of a weight

of four or five pounds, and a huge boulder unmarked by
inscription of any sort is built into the head of the
mound. Deeply impressive is this crude, lonely tomb
without name or epitaph. It suggests, in its immense
size, the cairn of some old giant of a lost, heroic age.
After all, that may be what he was, this strong man who
flung away his life but, through pillage and maraudings
and robber adventures, preserved something of the
honour of his youth; this outlaw fighter with the courage and chivalry of a knight of old, who here in his
sepulchre of iron rocks sleeps forgotten in the morning
shadows of the Chiricahuas.

Billy Claibourne was a Texas cowboy who had come
to the Tombstone country with John Slaughter when
that pioneer cattleman drove his first herd from the
Panhandle into the San Pedro Valley. In his early days
in Arizona, Billy was a rollicking, good-natured fellow
but a steady, hard-working, dependable ranch hand.
Unfortunately for him, John Slaughter's ranch was only
a short distance from Charleston, and Billy was soon
snared in the whirlpool of that wild town's fascinations.
Every pay day found him drinking and gambling in
Charleston saloons. There he fell in with the Clantons
and McLowerys, who were John Slaughter's neighbours,
and was soon hobnobbing with Curly Bill and all the
outlaws who rode with that redoubtable leader. One
of these—it may have been Curly Bill himself—began
to call him Billy the Kid. To be known by the name of
the famous New Mexican desperado was unction to
Billy Claibourne's soul, and he became ambitious to
justify the pseudonym and develop into a full-fledged
bad man. When he killed a man in Charleston over a
card game, he seemed on the high road to all the sinister

glories of a desperado's career. He had won a reputation
as a killer. He was looked upon thereafter as dangerous
and quick on the trigger and fraternized on terms of
equality with all the bad men of the country. Though,
as far as was known, he took no part in Curly Bill's
raids and robberies, he was a familiar figure in all the
outlaw haunts. John Ringo early won his admiration
and became his particular friend.

After Ringo's death, Claibourne went to Globe and
found work in a smelter.

"While knocking about Globe with some companions," said William Lutley, now one of Tombstone's
leading citizens, "we ran into Billy Claibourne and
asked him what he was doing there.

"'I'm working double-shift in the smelter,' he
answered, 'to get enough money to go to Tombstone
and kill Frank Leslie.'

"We were dumbfounded at this statement. We asked
him what Leslie had ever done to him and why he in-
tended killing him.

"'Never done nothin' to me personal,' Claibourne
responded. 'But I aim to kill him for murderin' John
Ringo.'

"The story that Leslie had killed Ringo was not
news to us. We had all heard it. But we felt a little like
laughing at Claibourne's seriousness. He was a pretty
tough young fellow, but the job he had picked out for
himself struck us as a pretty big one for him to tackle.
As bad men, Claibourne and Leslie were not in the same
class. Leslie was a professional, Claibourne an amateur.
We knew that, in a fair fight, Claibourne would have
no more show against Leslie than a puppy dog pitted
against a gray wolf.

"'Look here, Billy,' one of my companions said, 'you just quietly forget that little plan and keep on working in the smelter. Leslie's killed about a dozen men. He's a sure-enough desperado, a dead shot, and the quickest man with a gun in Tombstone. You leave him alone. If you go fooling around Leslie, you'll only get yourself killed.'

"But Claibourne wouldn't listen to us. He was bound he was going to kill Leslie, and that's all there was to it. He and Leslie had been drunk so often together that I suppose this familiarity had bred in Claibourne a contempt for Leslie. Claibourne evidently thought that, as a killer, Buckskin Frank was overrated."

Claibourne arrived in Tombstone on his mission of vengeance on November 19, 1882. The first thing he did was to get drunk. Foolish fellow. If ever he needed a clear brain and steady nerves he needed them now. A loaded man is hopeless against a loaded six-shooter. When Nemesis staggers, it is safe to copper vengeance and play the bet to lose.

Frank Leslie was standing on the outside of the bar in the Oriental saloon talking with a group of men when in reeled Billy Claibourne. Fingering their glasses idly, the men at the bar looked at him without interest. They did not know him. But Claibourne shouldered in among them and, with much profanity, began to spout blatant incoherencies. Leslie caught him by the arm and led him aside.

"Here, Billy, this won't do," said Leslie in friendly wise. "These people are friends among themselves and are having a quiet drink. You are a stranger to them, and you've got no business butting in like this. You go on down the street. You're drunk."

Claibourne went out but soon came wandering back.

"You insulted me a while ago, Frank Leslie," he shouted. "You can't treat me like that."

Leslie took him by the coat collar and hustled him into the street. In a little while, Claibourne, armed with a Winchester, was standing at the corner of Fifth and Allen streets, just outside the front door of the Oriental. A little crowd gathered. With drunken, noisy bluster, Claibourne was proclaiming that he would have Frank Leslie's life.

Leslie had gone on watch as bartender. He was drawing beer and mixing drinks. A friend rushed in excitedly and told him Claibourne was outside threatening to kill him. Leslie went on quietly serving customers. Another friend dashed in with the same information.

"Ho-hum," said Leslie in a tired sort of way. "Billy and I've always been good friends. I guess I'll have to go out and see what's the matter with the boy."

Leslie took a six-shooter from a drawer and stepped into Fifth Street through a side door. Claibourne stood swaying beside Nick Noble's fruit stand on the corner, his rifle across his arm. Leslie walked to within ten paces of him before Claibourne saw him.

"I don't want to kill you, Billy," said Leslie, his gun cocked in his hand.

Claibourne threw his rifle to his shoulder without a word. Both men fired at almost the same instant. Claibourne's bullet tore a hole in the board sidewalk at Leslie's feet. Leslie's struck Claibourne in the breast near the heart.

Leslie cocked his six-shooter again. But he did not fire a second time.

"Don't shoot any more," Claibourne called out as he fell across the fruit stand. "I'm killed."

Leslie went back into the Oriental, tied on his white bartender's apron, and again took his place behind the bar.

"What'll be yours?" he asked a customer cheerfully. "A dry Martini?"

He mixed the cocktail deftly, strained it off into a glass, and dropped an olive in.

Claibourne, mortally wounded, was removed to a hospital. Poor Billy Claibourne had made a mess of the tragedy he had so carefully planned, and had blundered stupidly from first to last. If he had had a sense of good theatre, he would have told Leslie why he purposed to kill him. Unless the victim knows why he is about to die, vengeance is robbed of its sweetness. By all rules of the stage, Claibourne should have thundered, "Frank Leslie, you murdered my friend, John Ringo, and I have come to avenge his death in your blood." Or something like that. But Leslie knew nothing of Clairbourne's true motive until afterward, and Tombstone was left to suppose the shooting was merely the result of a drunken row. Certainly, Billy Claibourne had no flair for play-acting. As an avenger, he was an unheroic and undramatic fiasco.

Some of his cowboy friends gathered about Claibourne's hospital cot to watch his last moments. For a half hour he screamed curses on Leslie. Exhausted, finally, he sank back upon the pillow and calmly awaited the end.

"Frank Leslie," he said quietly with his dying breath, "murdered John Ringo. I helped him carry Ringo in there and seen him do it."

Those were Claibourne's last words, according to his cowboy friends, who repeated them to Henry Smith. Their meaning was not entirely clear, but they threw a new light on the mystery of Ringo's death. When he made the statement, Claibourne, it may be added, fully realized that in the next minute he would be dead.

All the evidence in the Ringo case has now been heard. Physical facts, as the lawyers say, pointing conclusively to suicide. An eleventh-hour witness declaring with his dying breath he saw him murdered. One, of course, may suspect, if one cares to, that Claibourne's statement was a last desperate, revengeful effort to injure the man he had failed to kill. But one must remember also that men, consciously dying, rarely lie. So the matter awaits the verdict. How did John Ringo die? Suicide or murder—which?

Leslie was acquitted of the Claibourne killing and remained in Tombstone until 1890. Then he went to Yuma, where he lived in retirement—and stripes. The tragedy that ended his Tombstone career occurred at Leslie's ranch in the Swisshelms. Leslie, Jim Hughes, and Diamond Annie, Leslie's latest flame, a pretty woman of Tombstone's red lights, were drinking at the ranch when their supply of whisky ran out. Leaving Hughes and the woman alone, Leslie rode across country to the nearest groggery for more liquor. Upon his return, after nightfall, he flared into a jealous rage and killed Diamond Annie and shot Hughes through the breast. After lying hidden for several hours in deep saccaton grass, Hughes made his way to Bill Reynolds's ranch two miles distant. Next morning Leslie knocked at Reynolds's door. It was believed he meant to "kill the evidence" of the murder by killing Hughes. Rey-

nolds told him Hughes was not there. Behind the door
at that moment and within three feet of Leslie, Hughes
was standing with a double-barrelled shotgun. When
Leslie rode into Tombstone, he said Hughes had killed
Diamond Annie and escaped. After Hughes had told
the true story of the affair, Leslie confessed and was
sentenced to twenty-five years in Yuma penitentiary.
He was pardoned after serving four years.

J. H. Macia of Tombstone met him in Tucson and,
as Leslie was out of funds. Macia shared his room with
him.

"The old superstition that thirteen is an unlucky
number hasn't worked out in my case," Leslie remarked
to Macia. "I killed thirteen men and never once saw
the inside of a prison. It was my fourteenth that caused
all my trouble. But," he added with a whimsical shrug,
"my fourteenth was a woman."

Tombstone saw Buckskin Frank for the last time
when, soon after his release from prison, he passed
through town accompanied by Professor Dumble, geol-
ogist of the Southern Pacific Railroad, on the way to
coal mines being developed by the railroad company in
Mexico. A story came back that, while Leslie was employed as wagon boss at the mines, he killed three Mexicans whom he had caught stealing wood. He was next
heard of in San Francisco. There, it was reported, he
married a woman who had become interested in him
while he was in the penitentiary and who was credited
with being instrumental in obtaining his pardon. It is
known that he was in Alaska during the Klondike gold
excitement. Upon Leslie's return from the North, Jeff
Milton of Fairbank met him in San Francisco. Leslie
was prosperous then and was living at the Russ House.

The next twenty-five years are a blank in Buckskin Frank's story. Tombstone had no word of him. What devious roads he travelled, what adventures befell him during this last quarter of a century, remain secrets of the gods.

A little old man, looking as if he might have seen rough experience on the cross-ties, wrinkled, gray, and threadbare, walked into a billiard hall in Oakland one day in 1924 and asked in a quavering voice for some kind of light employment. His hard gray eyes were bright, his movements were touched with catlike furtiveness, and there was a suggestion of steel-wire toughness in his wizened body. But he was a pathetic figure of old age, hungry, penniless, homeless, and down and out. Out of pity, the proprietor gave him a job dusting off the tables and racking the pool balls and permitted him to sleep at night on a cot in a corner of the place. For several weeks the old codger went about his duties, and a sprightly, queer little elf he seemed to be, as gay and light-hearted as you please, full of wise cracks and drolleries and ready witticisms. Then, one morning, when the house was opened for business, he was gone. Gone, too, was a revolver stolen from a desk in the office, and the proprietor wondered with vague alarm what this ancient person, apparently well past eighty, might possibly have wanted with that gun. The old man, by his own admission, was all that was left of the famous Frank Leslie, once of Tombstone.

This was the last that was ever heard of him. Buckskin Frank, enigmatic man of many murders, had deteriorated into a shabby nobody and faded silently into the misty grayness of nowhere.

CHAPTER XVII

BURIED TREASURE

HO, FOR buried treasure! Throw the saddles on the ponies. Slap the blanket rolls and the grub and the old camp kit on the pack mule. Be sure of plenty of bacon and frijoles. And don't forget the picks and shovels. There before you runs the trail. Out yonder across the desert a fortune of three million dollars is waiting for you. All you have to do is find it.

Get your directions right and keep them dark. Don't confide them to your best friend. The danger is that your friend may smile in your face with great show of incredulity and then hurry off and dig up the treasure before you get there. That is sometimes the way with friends.

A dying outlaw who helped bury the treasure wrote out in detail the directions for finding it. That should mean smooth sailing for you. He certainly should have known all about it. He also drew a map, now faded and yellow with age. But never mind the map. The directions will do. And here they are:

Go first to Davis Mountain. Davis Mountain is the key to the whole secret of the treasure. Once there, the hidden riches will be yours. But if you miss Davis Mountain, you might just as well have stayed at home. That you may not, by any possible accident, mistake Davis Mountain for any other peak, keep your eyes open for a rounded, bald, granite dome visible for miles across rolling plains that run from it to the east. From the summit, with a good pair of field glasses, you can see over a good-sized slice of New Mexico. The old sugar-loaf stands boldly up against the sky, and you should be able to identify it at the first glance.

When you arrive at Davis Mountain, head west. A mile or a mile and a half due west, you will find a cañon. The east wall of this cañon is formed by wooded hills. The west wall is sheer rock precipice. A creek flowing through the cañon plunges over a ledge in a small cataract about ten feet high.

Bubbling from the bottom of the west wall is Silver Spring in the shade of a tall juniper tree. At the foot of this tree is a grave marked by slabs of stone at head and foot. This is the grave of an outlaw. Five hundred dollars in gold is buried in a tin can at the head of it. But let that go for the present.

Up the cañon and south of Silver Spring at a distance of exactly one mile and three tenths is Gum Spring. Between these two springs somewhere—and you may have trouble here, as the cañon floor is overgrown with brush—lie scattered in the grass the remains of a burned wagon. Probably all the charred woodwork has rotted away by now, but the rusty old iron felloe-rims, axles, springs, and hubs, slightly imbedded, perhaps, in the soil, should be there yet.

From Silver Spring to Gum Spring, the west wall of the cañon curves inward to form a shallow cove. At the deepest point of this concave space and a little out from the wall—three feet or such a matter—stands a slender stone which, as it will doubtless strike you at once, resembles a small obelisk. As a detail, it may be added that this stone is three feet high, squarely shaped, and one foot thick. On the east face of this rock pillar, carved deeply as with a chisel, are two crosses one above the other and standing out clearly to the eye. When you locate this rock of the two crosses, you may regard the three million as all but in your pocket.

Now, at this rock, face Davis Mountain and step twenty paces east. You will find yourself at a point on a straight north-and-south line between Silver Spring and Gum Spring. And you will notice the wreckage of the burned wagon just in front of you. Stop right here. This is the spot. You will be standing directly above the buried riches.

All, you see, just as clear as daylight.

Buried here in the Davis Mountain Cañon, according to the story, is the pillage of many robberies in old Mexico and the Southwest. A cigar box full of diamonds that were stolen from the vaults of a bank in Monterey and that once glittered on the dusky beauties of that rich old city beyond the Rio Grande. Two statuary figures of pure gold, one of the Saviour and the other of the Virgin Mary, that once occupied sanctuary niches in the great cathedral at Matamoras. Sacks of gold and silver money. Thirty-nine bars of solid gold bullion and several rawhide aparejos containing ninety thousand Mexican dollars captured in an attack on a smuggler train in Skeleton Cañon. The value of three million dollars placed on the treasure was the estimate of the dying outlaw who is supposed to have taken part in the robberies and the burial of the loot. It took a four-horse team, according to this freebooter, to haul the treasure to its secret hiding place.

Anyone who ever happens to unearth the treasure need not be surprised to find a few feet below the surface a skull and white, mouldering human bones. This will be the skeleton of a Mexican whom the outlaws hired, on promise of a rich share, to freight the treasure in, and who was murdered and buried with it when his labour was completed. In this, the robbers followed the best tradition of the old buccaneering sea rovers who buried their gold on lonely tropical islands, the dead man's lips being sealed upon the secret of the treasure and his ghost forever after keeping watch and ward above it.

Down in Sonora, a smuggler train was making ready to start for Tucson with what may have been the richest cargo ever to cross the international line. Great secrecy had been observed. Since Curly Bill's massacre of the smugglers in Skeleton Cañon, the Mexicans had grown wary. But while preparations for the journey were being made, a swarthy fellow fluent in Spanish, boisterously friendly and with money to spend, was busily hobnobbing and drinking with the smugglers. This was Jim Hughes. A veteran of Curly Bill's robber expeditions, Hughes was a sly, intriguing man, adept in treacheries, but as bold as he was cunning. A half-breed Mexican himself, his crossed blood made him particularly useful to Curly Bill in scouting out news of the smuggler trains coming north across the border. Acting now as a spy for the San Simon outlaws, Hughes was looked upon by these men of Sonora as a Mexican, an impression that he helped along by scathing denunciations of the whole breed of gringos. He was soon in the confidence of the smugglers and over the *tequila* in the *cantinas* had little difficulty in worming from them all their plans. The smugglers were to follow the old trail through Skeleton Cañon. They were to market gold bullion in Tucson. The pack sacks of their mules were to be loaded with dobe dollars on one side and an equal weight of bar gold on the other. This information set the spy's heart thumping. When the smuggler train set out on the trail, Jim Hughes, far ahead, was riding hard for the San Simon.

When Hughes arrived in Galeyville, Curly Bill was in Charleston. No time was left to report to the outlaw chieftain, and Hughes determined to enrich himself by a coup of his own. Hastily assembling a small band of outlaws, he headed for Skeleton Cañon. Where the cañon opens into the San Simon Valley, he placed his men in ambush in the mesquite along the low cañon wall. Who the men with Hughes were has been a matter of dispute. Milt Hicks and Jack McKenzie certainly; Zwing Hunt and Billy Grounds possibly; Ike and Billy Clanton probably. There was one other whose identity is not known. The question of the presence of Zwing Hunt and Billy Grounds had an important bearing on the story, later to evolve, of buried treasure at Davis Mountain.

Down through Skeleton Cañon over the Peloncillo Mountains came the Mexican smuggler train, mule bells jingling in the morning sunlight. A half mile from the mouth of the cañon and an equal distance below the Devil's Kitchen, the scene of Curly Bill's murderous exploit of a month before, the fifteen Mexicans halted for lunch. While their coffee simmered on a little camp fire and they sat eating on the grass, the cañon wall above them flamed with crashing rifles. Three Mexicans fell dead. Panic seized the others. They sprang on their ponies. Down the cañon they galloped in the midst of a mad welter of pack mules stampeding with wildly jangling bells. Three more Mexicans were killed, it is said, before the smugglers went racing out of the mouth of the cañon and escaped across the San Simon Valley.

Zwing Hunt, it is said, was struck in the shoulder and brought down by a bullet fired by the Mexicans in their flight. Also, it is said, Billy Grounds carried his wounded comrade to an oak tree at the cañon's mouth and laid him on the ground in the shade. There, it is said, Billy Grounds dressed the wound after bathing it with water fetched from the creek in his hat. It is a pretty story, and it gave the tree, which stands now in Ross Sloan's corral, the name of the Outlaw's Oak.

The Mexicans routed, Jim Hughes and his men mounted their ponies and went helter-skelter in pursuit of the pack mules to kill them and save the treasure. The terror-stricken mules had rushed out of the cañon and were running in every direction across the San Simon. Lumbering under their heavy loads of silver money and gold bullion, the animals, one by one, were soon overtaken and shot. Only one mule escaped.

What to do with the ponderous treasure that had fallen into their hands became the problem of the outlaws. It was plainly impossible for six or eight men to carry it away on their ponies. They decided to cache it, it is said, and leave it until such time as they could return for it with a wagon. The dead mules lay here and there over a wide area, some a mile apart. It was slow work to rifle the aparejos and carry the money and gold bars into the cañon. But the job was completed at last, and the spoils of the fight, it is declared, were buried under a group of three live oaks near the mouth of the cañon.

The value of the loot of this robbery has been variously estimated. The Mexican money stolen, according to one story, amounted to $90,000, and the gold bars numbered thirty-nine.

The treasure was lifted by the outlaws within the next few days, it is supposed, and under the guidance of Zwing Hunt and Billy Grounds hauled in a four-horse wagon, driven by a Mexican, to the Davis Mountain Cañon and reburied in a pit already half filled with robber loot brought by Zwing Hunt and Billy Grounds out of Mexico. The Mexican teamster, it is said, was murdered and the wagon burned.

Whatever may be confused or uncertain in this Skeleton Cañon story, it is a fact that skeletons of the dead mules lie about the San Simon Valley near the cañon's mouth even now, and the rawhide aparejos are still found here and there, rotted by the rains and suns of years. Certain, too, it is that, for many years after the fight, Mexican silver dollars, scattered broadcast by the runaway mules, were picked up all over the country. Cowboys at the San Simon ranch played poker all the next winter with the money they found in the Skeleton Cañon neighbourhood. Every now and then, even to-day, these tarnished old silver pieces are discovered, and only a little while ago, Mr. Joseph Wheeler, wealthy cattle man, whose ranch is within a few miles of the cañon, found six coins that are relics of the attack on the smuggler train nearly a half century ago.

A mysterious old German appeared in Skeleton Cañon early in the 'nineties. He built à little hut at the forks above the Devil's Kitchen and for two years lived alone in his wilderness hermitage. Who he was, or even his name, never was learned, and he is known in the buried treasure tradition only as the Old Dutchman. But the

Old Dutchman was a busy fellow, and he was forever digging holes. There was little travel through Skeleton in those days and few people ever saw him. But an occasional cowboy, combing the hills for cattle during a round-up, would stop and talk with the Old Dutchman smoking his pipe beside his cabin door. From stray hints dropped in these infrequent conversations with cowboys grew a story that the Old Dutchman had been with Jim Hughes in the attack on the smuggler train and since that day had served ten years in some penitentiary. Now, as it was supposed, having recently regained his freedom, he had come back to find the treasure buried by the outlaws.

If the Old Dutchman was with Hughes, he should have known, of course, the spot at which the plunder of the robbery had been cached. But evidently he did not know or he would not have spent two years hunting for it. But, at any rate, one day the Old Dutchman was gone. He had vanished into the mystery out of which he had come, and nothing more has been heard of him from that day to this.

But a half mile below the Devil's Kitchen under a group of three live oaks on the bank of the creek, he had left a deep hole—the deepest and largest of all the holes ever dug by treasure hunters in the cañon—and many believed that in this excavation he had at last found the treasure. The ruins of the Old Dutchman's cabin still stand at the forks of the cañon; the scars of his industry with pick and shovel still pit the ground, and the last hole he dug is still wide and deep. But whether he lifted any treasure is a riddle that remains unanswered.

Though it seems fairly certain that the outlaws them-

selves removed all their booty from Skeleton Cañon,
the story persisted that they had left at least part of
it behind. Wherefore, treasure hunters without end
swarmed for years to the cañon. Some were equipped
with divining rods. Some placed their faith in the
magic of willow wands. Some had taken counsel of
old Mexican crones who claimed the power of second
sight. Some had consulted Indian witch-doctors. Others
still had learned the exact spot at which the treasure
could be found from spirit mediums who declared they
had received the information direct from the ghosts
of the Mexicans murdered in the cañon by the outlaws. But if any of these industrious delvers ever came
away from Skeleton with anything more than sore
muscles from unwonted work with pick and shovel,
no one ever heard of it.

Porter McDonald, long chief of police of Tombstone, aided and abetted in the enterprise by James
T. Kingsbury, Tombstone lawyer, received from a
secret source several years ago information that he
deemed worth investigating. He was led to believe that
the treasure was buried on a ledge of the cañon wall
within sight of the great hole dug by the Old Dutchman. On his prospecting trip to the cañon, however, he
found no more than the others, but he was convinced
that a violent earthquake that shook all that part of
Arizona in 1886 had hopelessly entombed the hiding
place of the treasure under tons of rocks toppled from
the cañon wall.

Davis Mountain, far-off peak of purple mystery,
begins now to loom imposingly through the haze of this
buried treasure romance.

But before the story starts off on the trail for this

rounded, bald, granite sugar-loaf, a murdered man must rise from the dead. Zwing Hunt, dangerously shot in the Stockton ranch fight in which Billy Grounds was killed, escaped, it will be remembered, from a Tombstone hospital, and a little later, Hugh Hunt, his brother, reported his death by Indians. The body was identified by men who had known him, and some dead man is sleeping to-day in a lonely Arizona cañon with a juniper tree for headstone, on which is carved Zwing Hunt's name.

But Zwing Hunt, risen in marvellous resurrection, appeared in his proper person a few weeks afterward, according to his uncle, at his old home in San Antonio. He lived, it is said, only a short time after his return and died from the old wound he had received in the fight at the Stockton ranch. But he lived long enough, apparently, to set going the strange story of Davis Mountain and its buried outlaw gold.

When Zwing Hunt was about to die, he telegraphed, it is said, to his uncle, who lived in some other part of Texas, to come to him. His uncle, whose name has not survived in the tale, arrived.

"We came out of Mexico with two four-horse wagons loaded with plunder."—This is Zwing Hunt's deathbed story as related by his uncle.—"Our raid had lasted three months. We numbered twenty-nine men when we went in. Only eighteen of us got out alive. In Monterey, while Billy Grounds and I sat on our horses shooting up and down the street, our partners robbed the bank. They brought out two gunny sacks filled with money and a cigar box full of diamonds. We took possession of Matamoras and sacked the town. From the cathedral there we brought away statues of the

Virgin Mary and the Saviour. These figures are life-size
and of pure gold. When we got back on this side of
the Rio Grande, we got rid of some of our loot. The
rest we hauled to Davis Mountain.

"One of our men who had been shot in Mexico died
at Davis Mountain and we buried him by Silver Spring.
Five hundred dollars in gold had fallen to his share. He
had risked his life for that money, and at last he gave
his life for it. We decided to let him keep it forever,
and we buried the dead man's money in a tin can at
the head of the grave."

When he had finished his story, Hunt, it is said,
wrote out instructions as to how the treasure could be
found. Then he drew a map on a piece of writing paper,
and on this map he set down in their relative positions
Davis Mountain, Silver Spring, Gum Spring, the wreck
of the burned wagon, the rock of the two crosses, and
the spot at which the treasure was buried. This old
map is still in existence, and several copies of it are
owned in Arizona.

Hunt, as his uncle declared, added several casual
details to his story. He said that the outlaws bathed in
the waterfall in the cañon, that they played poker in
a cave on Davis Mountain, and that, from the mountain, with a pair of field glasses, they could see into
New Mexico. Of Davis Mountain, he said, according
to his uncle, "We called it Davis Mountain because a
man named Davis was killed and is buried there."

But Zwing Hunt failed to say where Davis Mountain
was.

He told, it might seem, everything worth knowing
about the treasure and how to find it except the one
big thing that was the key to all the rest. His uncle,

it seems, did not question him on this point. Why he didn't seems almost as puzzling an enigma as Davis Mountain itself. Except for the passing mention that from Davis Mountain one could see into New Mexico, there was nothing in the outlaw's alleged narrative that gave the slightest hint as to the location of this mystery peak. And, according to his uncle, when Zwing Hunt closed his eyes for the last long sleep, he left Davis Mountain the great sphinx riddle of the story of buried outlaw gold.

So you see the directions left by the dying outlaw are, after all, not quite so clear as you may at first have believed.

Virgil Boucher, an elder brother of Billy Grounds, whose real name was Billy Boucher, fell under the spell of the romantic tale Zwing Hunt is alleged to have told his uncle. Virgil Boucher came from Texas to Arizona for the first time to hunt the treasure in 1884, bringing with him what purported to be Zwing Hunt's original map and written directions. For more than thirty years, intermittently, he followed the trail of the treasure, making eighteen expeditions into the mountains of southeastern Arizona—the Chiricahuas, Stein's Pass, Peloncillo, Guadalupe, and Silver Creek ranges. Failure after failure did not discourage him, and when he died three years ago in Duncan, New Mexico, he still believed, with the unshaken faith of a religious zealot, that the tale of the Davis Mountain treasure was true.

Mrs. Maggie Clinger of San Antonio is Billy Grounds's sister, and she is troubled with no doubts whatever that the treasure is right where Zwing Hunt's uncle said Zwing Hunt said it was.

"I'm just as sure about that treasure as that my name

is Maggie Clinger," said Mrs. Maggie Clinger. "I can see Silver Spring, the rock of the two crosses, and all the rest of it just as plain as if I had been in the cañon myself. I know I could walk straight to the spot where the treasure is buried, if," said Mrs. Maggie Clinger, "I ever got to Davis Mountain."

Bill Sanders, of West Turkey Creek Cañon, has been one of the most inveterate as well as most optimistic searchers for the treasure. He has lived in southeastern Arizona since early times, and knows the mountains as few men know them. He went on several expeditions with Virgil Boucher. He has acted as guide for a dozen parties of treasure-hunters. He has seen the original Zwing Hunt map and studied the written directions. He, too, has implicit faith in the truth of the story.

"There are Davis Mountains in west Texas," said Bill Sanders. "But there is no Davis peak. I heard a few months ago that the wreck of a burned wagon had been found on top of a mountain in the Davis group. I went there and spent three weeks. The wreck of an old burned wagon was there, and I couldn't figure out how it ever got on top of the mountain, but there was nothing in the Davis range that answered in any way Zwing Hunt's description of the Davis Mountain country.

"But after twenty years of puzzling over Davis Mountain, I believe I have at last identified it. Harris Mountain, in my opinion, is Davis Mountain. I think Zwing Hunt got the two names twisted. Harris Mountain is the eastern gatepost of Turkey Creek Cañon, a few miles from the site of old Galeyville. It is a bald, rounded sugar-loaf. The plains of the San Simon Valley run off from it on the east. The state line of New Mexico is only twenty miles away, and you can see into

New Mexico with the naked eye. And there is a tunnel-like cave in Harris Mountain in which the outlaws could have played poker. The grave 'of a man named Davis' is not there, but the grave of a man named Harris is. Also the grave of Harris's wife and two children, all murdered by Apaches in 1873. The Indians carried off Harris's fifteen-year-old daughter, and she married a buck and had a papoose. She was rescued from the Indians in 1876 by a detachment of the Second Cavalry, and while she was being taken to Fort Bowie she pointed out the spot on the mountain where her family had been massacred. The soldiers found the skeletons and buried them. The peak has been known as Harris Mountain ever since.

"At the foot of Harris Mountain, to the west, is Turkey Creek Cañon, which is not in any feature like the Silver Spring Cañon described by Hunt. But 'a mile or a mile and a half due west' of Harris Mountain is a little cañon running up into Round Valley, and I have an idea this is the cañon of the treasure story. I am going to explore this Round Valley Cañon thoroughly, pretty soon, on a hunt for Silver Spring and Gum Spring and the rock of the two crosses."

Harken now to the words of Rube Hadden of Paradise.

"I knew all the fellows in the fight in Skeleton Cañon," said Rube. "There were only six. They were Jim Hughes, Milt Hicks, Jack McKenzie, Ike and Billy Clanton, and another fellow, whose name I've forgotten. Zwing Hunt and Billy Grounds were not within fifty miles of the fight. I heard all about the fight from Hughes, Hicks, and McKenzie a day or two afterward. They got only $4,000 out of the robbery. Of this,

$1,400 was in Mexican dollars. The rest was in gold
bullion, which they sold. Only three Mexicans were
killed. For a few days, Hughes, Hicks, and McKenzie
hid the gold bars in a log cabin at the mouth of Cave
Creek Cañon below Galeyville and left Al George to
watch them, while they hunted up a buyer. When they
had disposed of the bullion, the three of them went on a
big drunk in Tombstone. Hughes and his bunch buried
nothing in Skeleton.

"As for the story of the big treasure buried by Zwing
Hunt and Billy Grounds at Davis Mountain, it's pure
bunk. I told Virgil Boucher so when he was through
here. But he was a nut over this treasure, and God Al-
mighty couldn't have made him believe the yarn was
not true. All this about the cigar box full of diamonds
and the lifesize gold figures of the Virgin and Christ is
simply bosh. Zwing Hunt and Billy Grounds never
were in Mexico in their lives.

"As outlaws, they didn't amount to much. I knew
Zwing Hunt when he was driving a lumber wagon for
Morse's sawmill. He was a better mule-skinner than he
was a bandit. Billy Grounds, whom I knew also, was
only nineteen when he was killed. If these two boys
had had all the experience as bold freebooters in Mexico they are credited with in this fool story, they would
never have acted like scared amateurs when they tried
to stick up the stamp mill at Charleston.

"Zwing Hunt was killed by Apaches. There's no
doubt about that. Billy Breakenridge and Phil Montague and several others who had known Hunt well
identified the body. So, you can bet everything you've
got Zwing Hunt never got back to his old home in
San Antonio and never told any deathbed story. The

way I figure out this buried treasure romance is that
Zwing Hunt's uncle faked it. It sounds like a *marahuana*
pipe dream. There is no Davis Mountain. It is not on
any map, and nobody in this country ever heard of a
peak by that name. In my opinion, it never had any
existence except in the crazy imagination of Zwing
Hunt's uncle."

But don't be disheartened by any such talk as this.
Don't let a crabbed old pessimist like Rube Hadden
dampen your ardour or shatter your rainbow dreams.
Remember that the Cocos Island story, the world's
most gorgeous legend of buried treasure, rests on facts
just as nebulous as these, and though the Cocos Island
treasure never has been lifted, faith in it has burned
like a steady flame for a hundred years. The clear-strain
treasure hunter never loses faith or hope.

So, ho, for buried treasure once again! Saddle the
ponies and slap the blanket rolls and the grub and the
old camp kit on the pack mule. And don't forget the
picks and shovels. Out yonder across the desert a fortune of three million dollars is waiting for you—
maybe. All you have to do—perhaps—to make it yours
is first to find Davis Mountain.

CHAPTER XVIII

THE HONEYMOON CATTLE DRIVE

JOHN SLAUGHTER'S pearl-handled six-shooter shines out in opalescent beauty in Tombstone's history. But it is remembered not so much for its gleaming handle as for its flaming other end. Slaughter's four years as sheriff of Cochise County, 1887–1890, was a period of reconstruction and marked the dividing line between lawlessness and law in the Tombstone country. This pearl-handled forty-four was the tool with which Slaughter cemented a permanent fabric of law and order.

John Horton Slaughter was of a family that had been rooted in the soil and traditions of the South since the days of the thirteen colonies. He was born in Louisiana, October 2, 1841, according to an entry in the old family Bible, whose dilapidated, dog-eared pages give evidence of a line of churchgoing forbears. With slaves and household chattels, his parents moved to west Texas while he was a baby. The Texas war of independence, San Jacinto, and the Alamo, were still fresh in the memories of Texas people, and the news of the battles of Palo Alto and Resaca de la Palma at the beginning of the Mexican War of Polk's administration gave him his first-remembered thrills as a boy. He grew up on the Texas steppes when buffalo were still plentiful and settlers had to fight for their lives against Kiowas and Comanches. He enlisted as a soldier under

the Stars and Bars of the Confederacy at the outbreak
of the Civil War, but after brief service was invalided
home. Though little fighting against Yankees fell to
his experience, he saw hard fighting against Indians and
outlaws as a Texas Ranger under the noted Captain
Tom. In early manhood, he embarked in the cattle business on his own, married Miss Adeline Harris, and established his ranch in Atacosa County in the Panhandle.

Slaughter shared in the prosperity that came to the
Texas cattle industry when the first Western railroads
opened to the prairies the rich markets of the East, and
the price of steers went at a bound from one dollar to
twenty dollars a head. He not only raised cattle but
bought them all over west Texas, and he drove his herds
to market at Dodge City and the towns and army posts
west of the Pecos. In those boom times of the trails, he
acted as his own herd boss and took part in all the
dangers and hardships of the long drives—fighting
Indians, trail-cutters, and desperadoes and becoming
proficient, in a day of the strong arm, in protecting his
own and holding what was his against every form of
rapacity and lawless violence.

While Slaughter was buying cattle in the Devil's
River region of southwestern Texas, Bill Gallagher,
bad man and notorious trail-cutter, laid claim to several
hundred of Slaughter's steers. Gallagher had the reputation of having killed thirteen men in Wyoming, where
he was known as "the man from Bitter Creek." For
him, as for Buckskin Frank Leslie, thirteen had not
proved an unlucky number. It was fourteen that turned
out to be the numeral of disaster, as in the case of the
Tombstone desperado. Gallagher's reputation as a killer
might have frightened some men, but not Slaughter.

All bad men looked alike to this young Texas cow man. His courage was as desperate as theirs and his skill with firearms as finished. No man from Bitter Creek, though he came from the headwaters of that classic stream, could intimidate or bulldoze him. Gallagher's brain was perhaps not so quick as his trigger finger. He would not have attempted to raid Slaughter's herd if he had known Slaughter. When Gallagher started to cut out the brands he claimed as his own, Slaughter stopped him.

"Do you see that trail out yonder leading north?" said Slaughter. "That's your trail. Hit it."

Slaughter was a small man, and the giant from Bitter Creek bridled at this audacity.

"Do you know who I am?" he blurted ferociously.

"Hit that trail," said Slaughter, "and hit it quick."

For a moment Gallagher stared into Slaughter's hard black eyes. The bad man saw something in those eyes that convinced him that that trail over yonder leading north was, after all, his trail. Without a word, he hit it.

Driving his herd up the Pecos bound for market at Las Vegas, Slaughter went into camp near Fort Sumner at the old Bosque Grande ranch of John Chisum, cattle king of New Mexico. Bent on revenge, Gallagher, who lived in these parts, rode alone to Slaughter's camp. He was armed with a shotgun loaded with buckshot and two six-shooters. This armament, formidable under ordinary circumstances, again proved Gallagher's lack of perspicacity. He was plainly a blundering rank-and-file desperado who knew only how to pull a trigger. Slaughter, on the other hand, was a master strategist. He had not fought Comanches and outlaws all these years in the Panhandle for nothing. Gallagher's prospective fourteenth victim was different from all the other thirteen.

Gallagher saw Slaughter standing alone on an open hillside that sloped from the Pecos and rode toward him at a gallop. His idea was to get to close quarters as quickly as possible, where his double-barrelled shotgun would give him every advantage. None of his murders had ever looked easier. But, to Gallagher's amazement, Slaughter did not wait quietly to be massacred. With his long-range rifle, Slaughter shot Gallagher's pony from under him while the bad man was still out of shotgun range. Horse and rider went down in a smother of dust. This was disconcerting. But, having disentangled himself from his pony, Gallagher went charging forward on foot, opening fire with a six-shooter. Still he was badly handicapped. At the distance, his six-shooter was no match for Slaughter's rifle. One of Slaughter's bullets broke Gallagher's right arm. Gallagher drew his second six-shooter and still went forward firing. He staggered under the impact of a second bullet that struck him in the breast. Two more tore through his body and brought him down. Slaughter's cowboys carried the wounded man to the Bosque Grande ranch house. Slaughter stood at the side of the bed as Gallagher was dying.

"You done right, Slaughter," said Gallagher. "If you hadn't got me, I'd ha' got you. I don't mind much bein' killed. It would ha' served me right if I had been downed twenty years ago. But it kind o' pains me to be out-generalled that-a-way. Ef I'd had any sense, I'd fetched along a rifle. I didn't have no business with that shotgun. I'd oughter knowed better."

That was the whole trouble with Gallagher—lack

of generalship. He seems to have had courage. If he had mingled a little brains with it, the "man from Bitter Creek" might be living yet. He "oughter knowed better."

When he had sold his herd at Las Vegas, Slaughter discovered that he had lost many cattle on the drive up the Pecos. On his way back to Texas, he combed the herds of ranchmen in a hunt for his brand. This was his right under the law. But there was mighty little law on the Pecos in those days, and the effrontery of this stranger in demanding the return of his own property was deeply resented by the cattlemen of that wild country. But Slaughter's courage was clean strain and, painstakingly and patiently, he saw the dangerous job through to the end. From John Chisum's range, Slaughter gathered in sixty of his lost steers. Chisum produced a bill of sale to show he had purchased them. Slaughter smiled grimly in the old cattle king's face.

"And you got 'em at a fine bargain," Slaughter said as he ordered his cowboys to drive the cattle away.

From the herd of a man named Underwood, Slaughter reclaimed more than a hundred of his cows. Underwood swore he would have the cattle back or kill Slaughter. With two friends, Underwood rode to Slaughter's camp. When he saw the three heavily armed men approaching, Slaughter dismounted on the opposite side of his horse and levelled his rifle across the saddle.

"I bought and paid for them cattle," shouted Underwood as Slaughter covered him.

"Try to take them," answered Slaughter.

But Underwood thought it diplomatic to decline the invitation and, with his two companions, rode home.

Farther down the Pecos, two rustlers and two half-

breeds announced their intention of murdering Slaughter.
A Mexican vaquero with Slaughter became panic-
stricken as he saw the four bravos galloping toward
camp.

"Fight or git," ordered Slaughter.

The Mexican got. Before he went, Slaughter in a
jiffy paid him what money was coming to him, and
reached for his own rifle at the same moment. By the
time Slaughter had drawn the gun from the sheath,
the Mexican had faded to a speck in the distance and
was still going. Slaughter dropped a few long-distance
bullets among the four enemies who were lifting the
long yell as they came racing for him. The little leaden
greeting surprised them. They halted. Then, as the bullets continued to shower about them, they turned tail
and ran.

Guns and threats having failed to stop Slaughter in
the work of collecting his lost cattle, John Richardson,
whose herd also had come under levy, swore out a warrant. The deputy sheriff reported to Richardson that
he had been unable to serve the paper.

"Why not?" flared Richardson.

"Well," replied the deputy, "Slaughter wouldn't let
me. He drew a gun and told me to light out. Under the
circumstances, I thought it best to keep the warrant in
my pocket."

But after the deputy had gone, Slaughter rode for
Richardson's ranch. He proposed to discuss this matter
personally. Richardson met him on the road.

"I've made up my mind to withdraw that com-
plaint," said Richardson. "Sorry to have caused you
any trouble."

So, at last, having recovered most of the cattle he had

lost, Slaughter drove them home to his ranch in the Panhandle.

When Slaughter first visited Arizona, in 1877, there were not as many cattle in the territory as he himself came to own in later years. The small population was centred in the towns. The railroads had not yet arrived. The land still lay under the menace of Apache raids and ambuscades. But riches were waiting in this country for the cattle man with the courage to brave its dangers and the fortune to survive them. The great valleys that swept north out of Mexico and succeeded one another from east to west like the troughs of mighty waves whose crests were mountain ranges were ideal cattle country without cattle. Winters in this border region were like spring; occasional light snows quickly melted or evaporated. It was cool in the mountains in summer and pleasant in the valleys in winter, and in mountains and valleys were abundant grass and browse the year round. The San Simon, Sulphur Springs, and San Pedro valleys seemed calling aloud for cattle to come and grow fat in the belly-deep gramma of their wild pastures. For two years Slaughter wavered. Then the silver strike in the Tombstone hills with its consequent influx of thousands of people and the sudden rise of a city in the desert brought his determination to a focus. He pulled up stakes in the Panhandle and began the long trek to the San Pedro.

When the grass was turning green in the spring of 1879, Slaughter lined his cattle out on the trail. Guarded by cowboys, the herd wound across the Llano Estacado, down the western escarpments of those treeless plains, across the Pecos and the Peñasco in the neighbourhood of Seven Rivers and on through the Sacramento mountains. At Tularosa, Slaughter ordered a halt. There was need for rest. The journey had been hard, and it would grow harder farther on. Just beyond lay the White Sands, the volcanic desert of the Mal Pais, and the desolate strip known to the early Spaniards as the Jornado del Muerto. But something else besides rest prompted Slaughter to halt just here. At Tularosa, there was a girl. Oho, Mister Slaughter, a little romance, eh? Now the cowboys understood why he had taken this particular route, why he had relaxed a little his old-time iron discipline, how it happened they had caught him every once in a while smiling to himself. If they had had the brains of a yearling steer, they'd have suspected something like this. Well, the boss had been a widower for two years, and his heart was lonely. Now Viola Howell had quietly dropped her rope over his horns. That's the way such things happened. And Viola Howell was a beauty, if you please, as fresh and wholesome and sweet as an anemone on the spring mountains. So in Tularosa, Viola Howell and John Slaughter were married. The trample of hoofs and the clash of horns were their epithalamium and the cattle, pushing on through deserts and mountain valleys under dust clouds that went up to the skies, blazed a honeymoon trail into Arizona.

Mr. and Mrs. Amazon Howell, the bride's parents, threw in their herd with Slaughter's and, accompanied by Stonewall and James Howell, their sons, followed the fortunes of their new son-in-law.

They came at length to the Rio Grande. A week before, the river had been a placid stream whispering about innumerable dry sand banks and so shallow a man could wade it. Now the spring freshet caused by melting snows in the mountains had turned it into a wild torrent swirling and roaring between low mud banks. Driftwood tossed on its foaming yellow surface; occasional trees, undermined and uprooted, shot down the current like battering rams torn loose from their moorings.

Slaughter was confronted with a problem such as sometimes faced the pioneers of an earlier day on the Oregon and Overland trails. Fortunately, he knew the frontier technique of crossing swollen rivers. On cattle drives to the Kansas railroads, he frequently had had to swim his herd and float his wagons across the Red and Cimarron when those streams were on a rampage. He had three wagons loaded with household goods to ferry across the Rio Grande, one drawn by six horses, the other two by four. To both sides of his wagons he attached long logs projecting beyond the ends to float the wagons and steady them. Having repacked his cargoes and lashed everything tight, he was ready for the plunge

Slaughter and his bride, Mrs. Howell and her son James, took their places in the six-horse wagon. John Baptiste, a Negro known as Old Bat, for years a servant in the Slaughter family, and famous for his teamster skill, was in the driver's seat. Mr. Howell, the bride's father, an expert swimmer, grasped the bridle reins of the near-leader and led the team into the water. For a short distance, the horses staggered and slipped as the stream boiled around them. Then they were swept off their feet, sank until only their heads and shoulders showed above the surface, and struck out on the long swim. The wagon washed down stream; Old Bat pointed his horses at an up-stream angle.

They had reached midstream when the right-hand

horse of the two in the middle, known as the swingers, caught its foreleg in the crosstree of the leader ahead. The contretemps threw the animal off its swimming stride. It went under and came up snorting and plunging. Its mad antics confused and terrorized its team mates. Disaster threatened. But Old Bat, with four lives in his keeping, rose to the occasion. That off-swinger had to swim—that's all there was to it. About the unfortunate beast the old Negro made his black-snake snap and snarl. His deep bass voice roared threats and objurgations. "I'll larn you to swim, drat yo' bay hide. Buckle down thar. Git on 'cross dis rib-ber." Mr. Howell, swimming at the down-stream side of the near leader, one hand on the bridle, shouted encouragement to the team to stave off panic. "Whoa, boys!" "Steady, boys!" Mrs. Slaughter suddenly became hysterical. She began to scream wildly at the top of her voice. Her mother attempted to quiet her. No use. Her husband put his arms around her and tried to calm her. Equally vain. She had to scream, and she screamed in spite of hell and high water. With Old Bat roaring, Old Man Howell emitting soothing yells, the bride shrieking, and the off-swinger madly plunging, it was a wild time out there in the middle of the raging Rio Grande. But the leaders struck bottom at last. The other animals found their footing. Out of the eddying flood and up the steep bank they went in mighty lunges.

After the two other wagons had got safely over, the yelling cowboys sent the cattle into the river with a rush. In a moment, the broad stream was crowded with heads, streaking like horned meteors across a yellow sky, bumping into tangled masses, filling the air with mad bawlings and the hollow clashing of horns. Some went under. Calves swimming beside their mothers were crushed and drowned. Down stream dead bodies floated. But one by one the brutes struck the solid ground of the far shore. They shook the water like rain from their glistening hides and fell to grazing.

The herd was lined out upon the trail once more, and the wagons got under way. The big adventure over, everybody laughed—even the bride. From the other side, the Rio Grande had seemed a stream of turgid ugliness. From this side, it had a certain majestic beauty. When it comes to rivers, the bank you stand on sometimes makes all the difference in the world.

'See that range ahead?" Slaughter said to his bride one morning after the drive had left Silver City and Shakespeare behind and had come into the northern reaches of the Animas. "Arizona is on the other side of those mountains."

Mrs. Slaughter thrilled joyously. It was as if he had echoed the words of old schoolday essays—"Beyond the Alps lies Italy."

Through the Stein's Pass Mountains the cattle poured out into the San Simon Valley and, rounding the northern end of the Chiricahuas, passed into Sulphur Springs Valley. Here on the eastern slopes of the Dragoons, beyond which the new town of Tombstone was booming into life, Slaughter pitched camp for the summer. The drive begun in Texas in the latter part of March ended in Arizona May 10th.

In this Sulphur Springs Valley camp, Slaughter, standing at the gateway of the Promised Land, was

saved from death by Billy Claibourne, one of his cowboys, the same Billy Claibourne afterward killed by
Buckskin Frank Leslie. Attacked by an infuriated steer
and borne to the ground, Slaughter, in another moment,
would have been fatally gored if Claibourne had not
galloped up and flung himself from the saddle upon the
animal's horns. In as fine an exhibition of bull-dogging
as ever drew thunders of applause from crowded stands
at rodeos in Cheyenne, Pendleton, and Chicago, Claibourne fought and wrestled the mad brute to the earth,
pinioned it down, conquered it, and enabled his em-
ployer to scramble from his perilous predicament. Those
of to-day who look upon bull-dogging as mere cowboy
sport of no possible practical value doubtless would
place a more serious estimate upon it if they had witnessed Claibourne's life-saving feat.

"I figured," said Claibourne gallantly, as he laughed
over the incident, "that if I had been killed I'd not
have been leaving a young widow behind."

Slaughter, having scouted the country for a ranch
location, settled in August a little south of the old
Hereford stage station in the San Pedro Valley. Here he
built a two-room shack of poles, with dirt roof, dirt
floor, and a slab door without a lock, and here, in this
crude home at the end of honeymoon trail, he and his
bride set up housekeeping.

Prosperity came quickly. Markets were close at hand.
Meeting the demand for cattle became the big problem.
A second herd Slaughter had left behind in the Panhandle was brought out by John Roberts, his foreman.
Slaughter himself returned to Texas the following winter and drove out a third herd. He was awarded con-
tracts for supplying beef to the San Carlos reservation

and to the construction camps of the new railroad being built from Benson to Nogales. His growing business necessitated extensive cattle-buying in Mexico, which swarmed with cattle when Arizona had almost none. Carrying cash money to pay for his purchases, he made many trips across the line. Outlaws and Apaches lurked beside his trails. Many times they sought to trap him. Against white and red marauders he was at constant war, and braving death became a part of his daily routine. There was no fear in Slaughter, but his wife, in her lonely cabin, lived in the shadow of fear. Any day, Indians might butcher her and leave her body in the burned ruins of her home. Any day, a messenger might come with information that her husband had been ambushed and murdered.

"When Mr. Slaughter started for Texas to bring out the third herd," said Mrs. Slaughter in recalling their pioneer experiences, "his young daughter Addie and I accompanied him. He sent his cowboys ahead with orders to meet him in Deming. He and I and the little girl took the train at Benson over the Southern Pacific Railroad that had just been built. Deming, the future metropolis of western New Mexico, consisted then of several tents and two box cars. One of the box cars was a grocery store and the other the residence of a locomotive engineer and his wife. Our cowboys had failed to meet us; we had no place to sleep; it was the dead of winter and terribly cold. Mr. Slaughter asked the engineer's wife to allow Addie and me to pass the night in the box car but her husband was away on his run, and the poor woman, alone in that wild country, was afraid to take us in. Late that night, while we huddled about a camp fire, the train came in and the hospitable engineer, apologizing for his wife's conduct, took us to his strange little dwelling. As I sat warm and snug by the stove, I realized what a wonderful home a box car can be.

"Next night our cowboys had still not arrived. Again Mr. Slaughter asked the engineer's wife to take us in, and again, being alone, she refused. Once more, when the train rolled in, the engineer came for us. But Mr. Slaughter this time declined the invitation; he had had enough of that woman's foolishness, and we shivered by our camp fire till morning. Then we learned our cowboys, having misunderstood orders, were in camp twenty miles east. Mr. Slaughter paid a man with a team of horses twenty dollars to drive us there—a dollar a mile. When we found our cowboys, we felt a little bitter over the unnecessary hardships we had endured when, with better luck, we might have been enjoying the good cheer of a comfortable camp.

"On the trip back from Texas with the herd, we had a number of Indian scares. Victorio and his Apaches had been plundering and murdering through all that part of New Mexico for months, and every little while we would hear of the massacre of some ranchman and his family. The herd had been bucking snowdrifts for three days almost without a bite of food when in a blinding blizzard of wind and snow we went into camp ten miles from Fort Bayard. There was a foot of snow on the ground and still the snow came down in sheets that slanted sharply on the whistling, icy gale. And we could find no wood for a fire. A teamster passed with three logs on his wagon. Mr. Slaughter offered him ten dollars for a log. But, refusing money, the man gave us one. Soon we had a fire roaring. Darkness was falling when a stagecoach bound for Fort Bayard came along. The driver begged Addie and me to go with him to the fort. The officers would welcome us and make us comfortable, he said, and the next morning he would bring us back to camp on his return trip. But I could not think of leaving my husband. At the outset of the trip, I had made up my mind to share all dangers and hardships with him, and on this night of storm, I felt my place was by his side. There was no sleep for anyone. Addie and I froze by our fire; Mr. Slaughter and his men, numb with cold and white from head to foot with frozen snow, rode herd all night and had all they could do to prevent a stampede. We heard fifty miles farther along the trail that, the very next day after we had met the kind-hearted stage-driver, he was murdered by Apaches at the spot where we had camped."

Slaughter kissed his wife good-bye at the door of his San Pedro Valley ranch, and rode off for Mexico to buy cattle. With him were John Roberts and Old Bat, and $12,000 in Mexican silver jingled in the aparejo of his pack mule. Having gathered together a small herd, he made camp near Magdalena in Sonora. A troop of forty-five heavily armed Mexicans coming up from the south rode into the village.

"*Quienes son estos?*" Slaughter asked of one of half a dozen vaqueros he had hired.

"*Estos*," replied the vaquero in a frightened whisper, "*son bandidos.*"

All the country south of the line was then infested with these roving robber bands that pillaged and murdered with a free hand. As they drank in the cantina, the bandits had word of the gringo cattle buyer and his sack of money. By all the saints, they swore over their mescal, before next sunrise that treasure should be theirs.

One by one, Slaughter's Mexican vaqueros came to him and, with apologies and profound regrets, gave notice that they could no longer continue in his service.

"Be on your guard to-night, señor," said one, "but as for me, my mother has just died, and I must hasten home."

"It will be well, caballero," said another, "if you and your men sleep with your eyes open, but my brother lies at the point of death, and I must hurry to his bed-side."

So they departed, and Slaughter, Roberts, and Old Bat were left to fight it out alone, three against forty-five. Knowing it would be death to sleep in camp, Slaughter went from house to house in the little town seeking shelter for the night—the shelter of bullet-proof adobe walls. But the town people shook their heads. They could not afford to be hospitable. Fear of the bandits closed their doors. While the bandits still sat at their toddies, Slaughter and his two companions stole out of the village with their treasure-laden mule. In the mountains five miles away, they went into hiding in a carefully selected position on a ledge high against the wall of a narrow cañon. . . .

Mrs. Slaughter, in her cabin on the San Pedro, heard a pounding of horse's hoofs. A courier brought news that Slaughter had been murdered. The message she had so long dreaded had come at last. She hitched up her buckboard and set off alone for the Mexican line, her horses at a run. At the Elias ranch, where the customs officials made their headquarters, no one had any information. Slaughter and his men had crossed the border a week before and nothing more had been heard of them. Mrs. Slaughter drove hard for Magdalena. Far ahead, she saw a filmy speck on the horizon. It grew into what seemed smoke. It took on the appearance of a cloud. Then unmistakably it changed into a curtain of dust shaking against the sky. She whipped up her horses. The sun began to flash on the horns of cattle. She made out the herd winding toward her. A little later, she threw herself into her husband's arms. Roberts and Old Bat drew round her laughing.

When the Mexican bandits had drunk their fill of mescal, they mounted their horses and rode out of Magdalena to Slaughter's camp. It seemed a simple matter to massacre these three gringos and steal their money. But the camp was deserted. Off to the mountains the bandits galloped on the trail. They dashed into the cañon. As they rode at dusk through a narrow passage where the precipitous cliffs almost came together three rifles blazed from the shadows darkening the gorge. As the bullets whizzed among them, the Mexicans halted for one amazed moment and then fled for their lifes.

"And that," Slaughter used to say, "is the only time I remember ever having been murdered."

All this while, Slaughter was achieving a reputation as an Indian fighter. Adept in all the wiles and stratagems of the cunning war craft of the Apaches, he outfought them on their own ground and in their own way. The lore of the war trails he had learned from the savages themselves enabled him to avoid their hidden snares and ambuscades and surprise the trappers in the traps they had set for him. No band of Apaches invaded the San Pedro that Slaughter did not take its trail. He fought to protect his own, and in time he made the land safe wherever his cattle grazed. The Apaches came to fear this sleepless man who fought so desperately, and at last old Geronimo himself gave his warriors orders to leave Slaughter and his herds alone. His success as an Indian fighter made Slaughter in demand as a scout with the army, and he saw service under Generals Crook and Miles against Geronimo, Nana, Natchez, Juh, Chatto, Bonito, and Chihuahua. He took part in the last campaign against Geronimo, and was with General Miles when in 1886 the famous old chief surrendered at Skeleton Cañon.

John Slaughter had two singular but firmly rooted convictions. One was that he could not be killed. The other was that he lived under the care of a Guardian Angel that warned him against invisible and unsuspected danger and protected him in every desperate emergency.

When Mr. and Mrs. Slaughter left Charleston one day to drive to Santa Cruz, Ed Lyle, Cap Stilwell, and four other men, all outlaws and Slaughter's enemies, cut across country to intercept them. Passing through a wild region, Slaughter saw the six men spurring hard for a clump of willows far ahead beside the trail. He believed the outlaws meant to assassinate him from ambush. He gave the reins to his wife and sat with a shotgun across his lap.

"We'll both be killed at those willows," cried Mrs. Slaughter in a panic.

"Don't be afraid," returned Slaughter. "Neither of us will be killed. Those outlaws won't kill a woman and they can't kill me. If they fire on us, I'll jump out and do my fighting on foot. You wait for me out of range. I'll rejoin you."

Mrs. Slaughter lashed her horses. It was a race between her and the outlaws. She won. The six horsemen were still several hundred yards distant when her buggy swept past the clump of trees. The outlaws did not attempt pursuit.

"What did you mean by saying they couldn't kill you?" asked Mrs. Slaughter.

"Just that," answered her husband. "No man can kill me. I wasn't born to be killed. How I know that, I cannot explain. But I know it. When my time comes, I'll die in bed."

Slaughter met Lyle a few days later in Herrera's store in Charleston and drew his six-shooter.

"Lyle," he said, "that little affair the other day is the last trick you'll ever play on me."

"I'm unarmed, Slaughter," pleaded Lyle. "Don't kill me."

"I ought to kill you, but I'll give you your life," replied Slaughter. "But you get out of the country. I'll give you twenty-four hours. If I ever see you around here again, I'll kill you."

A horseman galloped out of Charleston on the Benson road early next morning. At Benson he kept on going. This was the well-known desperado, Ed Lyle, obeying orders. And the San Pedro country knew him no more.

Slaughter met Cap Stilwell in a week or so in a Charleston saloon. Both went for their guns and Slaughter got the drop. As he looked into the muzzle of Slaugher's six-shooter, Stilwell got his twenty-four-hour orders. Next day he followed Lyle.

Mounted on his gray horse that for several years was as familiar to Tombstone as Slaughter himself, Slaughter was riding toward Tubac, the ancient pueblo founded by the pioneer Spaniards south of Tucson. He was bound for Marsh & Driscoll's ranch to buy a bunch of cattle and had the money to pay for them in his pockets. He was in no hurry; he jogged along at a leisurely gait. The peaceful landscape was bathed in sunshine; no one was in sight in all the circle of the horizon. Suddenly something seemed to whisper into Slaughter's ear, "You are in danger. Ride fast and ride hard." He made no attempt to reason away the warning or to argue with his invisible guardian, but, putting spurs to his horse, rode at top speed into Tubac. There he talked a few moments with a storekeeper and rode toward his destination. But now he rode slowly. He no longer felt the urge for speed. Whatever the danger was, he knew it was past. An hour later, three Curly Bill outlaws galloped into Tubac, their horses lathered with sweat. They inquired of the storekeeper if Slaughter had passed that way. When they learned that Slaughter was an hour ahead of them, they cursed their luck and took the back trail. These three outlaws, as it was afterward established, had trailed Slaughter from the San Pedro Valley. The mysterious warning had saved Slaughter's money and probably his life.

Slaughter's ranch near Hereford was only a few miles south of that of the Clantons, and Slaughter's herds suffered from the depredations of these bold rustlers. Several times, Slaughter rode to the Clanton ranch with a band of cowboys at his back and forcibly took back his stolen stock. Once he met Ike Clanton on his land and, drawing his gun, ordered him off, telling him he would kill him if he ever again caught him on his range. This rankled with Ike Clanton. He boasted in Charleston saloons he would even matters with this cattle man who was attempting to lord it in the Clantons' own domain. Mr. and Mrs. Slaughter, in their buckboard, were driving from Tombstone to their ranch one night. It was a quiet night, and the valley was lighted by a full moon. Abruptly, Slaughter made a remark for which there seemed no reason.

"You drive the team," he said to his wife. "I want my gun in my hand."

"Why, what's the matter?" asked his wife in astonishment. "I see nothing to cause alarm."

"Neither do I," replied Slaughter. "But do as I say."

Mrs. Slaughter took the lines, and her husband drew his six-shooter and held it in his lap. They drove on for several miles. Nothing happened. The drawn revolver seemed so out of keeping with the peaceful night that Mrs. Slaughter began to laugh. Far ahead they suddenly heard the beat of a horse's hoofs. A horseman rode out of the misty distance. The moonlight glittered on a six-shooter in his hand. It was Ike Clanton. As the moonlight glittered on Slaughter's six-shooter also, the outlaw went by in silence. Slaughter had had no means of knowing he would encounter an enemy on the road. It was another one of his uncanny warnings.

On another occasion, the clairvoyance of Slaughter's gray horse seemed superior to that of its master. Riding alone at night on the trail of a criminal and fatigued by a hard day's journey, Slaughter picketed his horse and threw himself on the ground to sleep. The tired horse would neither rest nor graze. It nudged

Slaughter with its nozzle. Sleepy and annoyed, Slaughter pushed it away. But the animal persisted. Still
Slaughter refused to pay heed. Finally, the horse
pawed Slaughter gently on the head with its forefoot.
This was enough. The warning was clear. Slaughter
saddled and rode. After going ten miles or so, he again
threw himself down for sleep. This time the horse
grazed quietly. Slaughter always believed some unseen
danger threatened him that night, but he never learned
what it was.

So, in the fullness of time, John Slaughter rose to
riches and power on the frontier and became a cattle
king. Fighting fearlessly and ceaselessly for his life,
his home, his property, and the right to live in peace,
he developed those qualities of mind and body that
fitted him, when the hour came, to rule in Tombstone
as sheriff and establish order in a land that had been
the most lawless in the Southwest.

CHAPTER XIX

DEEP in the shaft of the Sulphuret mine a miner swung his pick. A loosened fragment of rock rolled against his boots. From the cavity oozed a few drops of water. They trickled down a stone slab in little dashes and zigzags and curlicues that were in very truth hieroglyphics of disaster. The cryptic message written by the water on the mine's dark wall spelled the doom of Tombstone.

The mines were at the high tide of prosperity. Immense quantities of silver were being taken out. The rich lodes seemed inexhaustible. Then, without warning, water was struck at a depth of five hundred feet. An initial trickle became a flood. A subterranean lake or river apparently had been tapped. It seemed to underlie the entire range of hills. All the mines were affected. Bailing was impossible. The water boiled into the shafts in geyser spouts as thick as a man's body.

The Grand Central and Contention mines, at an expense of $300,000, installed steam pumps. But the pumps drew water from all the mines. Their task, it was apparent from the beginning, was almost hopeless. When the surface pumping works were destroyed by fire in 1886, the water rose in the shafts all over the hill to a great depth within an hour, and all the Tombstone mines closed down. The water was like an impenetrable armour plate guarding vast silver treasure still unmined. Wealth with an estimated value of hundreds of millions of dollars remains in the Tombstone hills to-day. Probably it will remain untouched forever.

With the silver foundations on which it had been built suddenly washed away, Tombstone suffered a disaster comparable to that from an earthquake or a volcano in overwhelming eruption. Its boom collapsed. An army of miners departed. The exodus of citizens was like a flight. All the trails were crowded with wagons piled high with household goods rolling off over the horizon. From fifteen thousand to three thousand, the number of inhabitants dwindled so quickly the change seemed like black magic. Stores, saloons, and gambling places closed their doors. Allen Street, once noisy with traffic, showed only a dull spark of animation. Plate-glass windows of vacant business establishments stared blankly, like the eyeless sockets of death's heads, out into the empty thoroughfare. Grass grew in outlying streets lined, block on block, with tenantless dwellings. Spiders spun their webs in the cribs and dens and haunts of revelry of the old red-light district. All the old picturesque life vanished; yesterday it was here, to-day it was gone. With the coming of night, the silence of the mesquite mesa leaped upon the town, as if from ambush, and clutched it in deathly stillness. The shell of a metropolis housed the population of a village. The busiest, gayest, wildest, toughest little city in the Southwest faded into a ghost town. Tombstone, dying in the desert, was left to its tragedy.

This decadent period was notable for a lax administration of law and the absence of strong men at the helm of public affairs. Crime flourished as never before. Though the heroic era of Curly Bill was gone, and cattle raids across the border were out of style, and outlawry had lost its romance, the criminals were pestiferously active. It was an age of thieves rather than bandits. The country was overrun with a vermin of horse thieves and cattle thieves. Though they operated on a small scale, they kept eternally at it. No horse was safe in its stall, no milk cow in a stable lot or pasture. Burglars, practically unknown on the old frontier, made their appearance. Men were held up on dark streets. It became dangerous for a citizen to venture out of town, because of lurking highwaymen. Criminals were showing a disposition to organize. Their depredations became bolder and more extensive. Tombstone was their headquarters, and the town was gradually passing under their secret domination. Casting about for a man with the force and courage to handle a serious situation that every day was growing more sinister and menacing, Tombstone turned its eyes upon John Slaughter. He had no ambition for office. His cattle business kept him fully occupied. But his election as sheriff was a public call to the man for the hour and the job. Like a modern Cincinnatus, he turned his back upon his ranch and his personal interests to perform a public duty. For the next four years, the history of Sheriff Slaughter was virtually the history of Tombstone.

A memorable, wholly unique character was this John Slaughter. Of iron will, iron courage, iron determination —a man of iron. A remarkable combination of thinker and fighter, intellect and trigger finger. A grim, impressively silent man, isolated, wrapped about with loneliness, keeping his own counsels and his own secrets, taking advice from no one. No genius for words, almost inarticulate, but a man of quick judgments and decisive action. A cold exterior belied a fiery, restless, relentless personality. His spirit was like a flame burning in a casing of ice. An upright, honourable man, direct, businesslike. To his friends, friendly. To his enemies and the enemies of law embodied in himself, coldly, tragically, remorselessly merciless.

He was a small, powerful man; broad shoulders, thick neck, only five feet six inches in height, black hair, black moustache, black beard, coal-black eyes. A naturally fair skin had been burned by years of wind and sun to the tinge of tanned leather. He radiated alertness and energy. The snap and vim of him suggested an electric aura.

"No one on whom Slaughter bestowed the most casual glance ever forgot his eyes," said A. H. Gardner of Tombstone. "They were the blackest, brightest, most penetrating eyes I ever saw. I should think it would have been difficult to lie to Slaughter. When he looked at me, his eyes seemed to be burning a hole into my brain. I used to fancy he was taking an inventory of all my secrets. If someone had held a newspaper at the back of my head, it wouldn't have surprised me if Slaughter, looking straight through my skull, had read the want ads."

Slaughter not only saw everything in front of him with marvellously keen vision, but everything at both sides as well. He rarely turned his head. He turned his eyes instead, taking in all about him with constant sidelong glances. He talked with lips that hardly moved. His voice was low and of throaty quality, but he spoke distinctly. He rarely raised his voice, but everyone within sound of it listened. Those to whom he gave an order jumped to obey it. He did not stammer, but he had a way of beginning a remark with "I say, I say." One of his quaint maxims was: "I say, I say, always shoot first and holler 'Throw up your hands' afterwards."

Though not a dandy, he was fussy about his clothes, which were always of expensive material, tailored, and immaculate. His broad-brimmed white hat was creased along the centre in his sheriff's days, but in later years was tucked in around the top to give the appearance of a low crown. He took a Western man's pride in his boots—he never wore shoes—and had them made to measure by a special boot-maker. They were half-boots, after the cowboy fashion, high-heeled, with a touch of colour and fancy stitching at the tops, and of the finest, softest leather. His trousers were always tucked in them, and his heavy-rowelled spurs were never removed. Any one who failed to see Slaughter's face could identify him by his feet.

A black Mexican cigar clenched between his even white teeth seemed a part of him, and associated with him as indelibly in Tombstone's memory as his gray horse were a diamond ring on the little finger of his left hand and a pearl-handled six-shooter worn at his belt where his right hand could drop on it instantly.

Slaughter was rather free and easy with his intimates, but maintained an aloof dignity among strangers and resented familiarity. A man who had met him in Texas greeted him boisterously in a Kansas hotel with "Hello, Tex." "Good-morning, sir," responded Slaughter with cold courtesy. Next day, the irrepressible person again shouted "Hello, Tex." Slaughter fixed his glittering black eyes on the man. "My name is Slaughter," he said. "If you ever think it necessary to speak to me again, just remember my name is Slaughter."

With those sharp black eyes of his, Slaughter was able to see distant objects sometimes invisible to those of ordinary vision. Riding one day with his niece and another young woman, he pointed to a crack on a mountain wall.

"Do either of you girls see anything up there?" he asked.

Both scrutinized the cliff long and carefully. No, they saw nothing.

"But wait a moment, Uncle John," cried his niece. "Don't show us. We'll find it yet."

Again they scanned the bluff with meticulous glances.

"There's absolutely nothing there," they declared.

"Let's see," answered Slaughter.

He drew his six-shooter and, apparently without taking aim, fired. Something fell from the crack in the mountain wall. The astonished young ladies hurried to see what it might be. It was a buff-coloured owl of the exact shade of the rock against which it had been perched.

No one ever saw Slaughter that his pearl-handled six-shooter was not hanging at his side. He wore it in his home. It used to be suspected that he slept with it on. He doubtless would have felt undressed without it. Moreover, he could do some remarkably fine shooting with it. He was rated, in unprecise phrase, as a dead shot. Certainly he was a crack shot. Whenever he shot, something usually dropped. His gleaming gun handle might have borne a number of notches if he had cared to file them there. How many is still a matter of conjecture. Modern Tombstone's answer to inquiries on this subject is vague. "Slaughter killed plenty," is the usual reply. Estimates run from six to eight or twenty.

And all estimates are guesses. Slaughter never told how many men he had killed, and he alone knew. He cared nothing for fame as a man with a gun-handle record. The record itself was enough. He remained silent on his record to the end of his life. But hidden in his silence were many tragedies.

For his job as sheriff, all the experience of Slaughter's life had equipped him, all his past had been preparation. He was not an office sheriff. He did not sit at a mahogany desk and give orders to deputies. He was a hard-riding sheriff, forever in the saddle. Whatever hard or dangerous work there was to do, he did it himself or took an active part in it. Nor was it his wont to ride with a posse at his back. In pursuit of a criminal, he usually rode alone. He was a frontiersman who knew his frontier. He could follow a trail invisible to eyes less keen with the uncanny ability of an Apache. Deserts and mountains were like a printed page to him. A broken stalk of grass, a bent weed, an upturned pebble, guided him. He did not dash off at random to some town to which it might be logical to assume a fugitive would flee. It was his custom to track a man step by step, and sign by sign. And usually, at the end of the trails he followed, a man threw up his hands or died.

Slaughter was not troubled with hair-line distinctions, and in dealing with criminals he sometimes lost sight of the fact that he was only an officer of the law and became the law itself. He had little confidence in courts and juries but implicit faith in the justice of John Slaughter. Instead of arresting a man, he sometimes ordered him out of the country. There was, of course, no law in the statute books to sanction such a czarlike ukase. But, for the nonce, these orders became the law, and very effective law at that. Invariably, the man upon whom fell the edict of banishment folded his tents and disappeared. What is more, he never came back. He knew Slaughter would kill him if he did not go, and would kill him if he ventured to return. To him, the fierce little tiger man guarding the peace of Tombstone loomed like a heroic statue of certain death.

Horse-stealing was not punishable by death under Arizona law, but under Slaughter's personal code it was a capital offense. If a horse were stolen from a Tombstone stable, as not infrequently was the case, the citizens could always count upon seeing shortly Slaughter's strapping gray standing saddled at the hitching rack in front of the courthouse. Then down the steps the sheriff would come marching, mount, and ride out of town. He would say good-bye to no one. No one, not even his chief deputy, would know where he was going. For a week, perhaps, nothing would be heard of him. Then, some fine day, he would come riding back, the stolen horse jogging behind on a lead rope. No questions would be asked. Slaughter would vouchsafe no information. What had become of the horse thief remained Slaughter's secret.

"I was inspector of customs located at Tombstone for two years while Slaughter was sheriff," said Jeff Milton of Fairbank, a fighter himself. "He and I were good friends. He rode by my house one day going out after a horse thief.

"'I'll saddle up and go along and help you, John,' I said.

"'Never mind,' Slaughter answered. 'It's only one Mexican. I'll get him.'

"I guess he got him. Slaughter rode back with the

stolen horse. Every time he went out after a stolen horse, he always brought it back. But I don't remember ever seeing him bring back the horse thief.

"Slaughter would never allow any man to get behind him—not even a friend. I used to try it, just for fun. While I talked with him, I'd edge around a little to one side. Slaughter would turn and keep his face to me. I'd edge a little farther. Slaughter would turn again. If I kept up the joke, Slaughter would turn completely round before our conversation ended.

"When I was in Benson one day, I stepped up to a lunch wagon to buy a sandwich. Four nigger soldiers were standing at the counter, and one of them shoved me aside. I stuck a six-shooter in his belly and made him and his three buddies line up and keep their hands in the air until I'd finished my sandwich. As I walked off, I met Slaughter.

"'I say, I say,' said John, 'I don't know why those niggers didn't shoot you. I've been standing here with a cocked six-shooter trained on 'em all the time you were eating.'

"And," added Milton, "if those niggers had made a move, Slaughter would have turned that six-shooter loose. I don't believe Slaughter thought any more of killing a man, if it seemed to him the man deserved death, than he did of putting a bullet through a tin can."

Full of stories of the early days is Jim Wolf, past seventy now, who for more than thirty years has been living absolutely alone on a little cattle ranch in the San Pedro Valley a few miles south of Charleston.

"Many a time," said Jim Wolf, "when John Slaughter wuz out alone trailin' a criminal, he'd stop at my

ranch house. Sometimes I'd hear a halloo at my door
at night after I'd gone to bed, and it'd be old John
after a cup of coffee. 'I'll make it for you, John,' I'd
say. But he'd never let me. 'Go on back to bed,' he'd
tell me. 'I'll make it.' And he'd rustle up a fire, and soon
he'd have a pot of coffee boiling. When he had turned
off a good, hot cup, he'd walk out and git on his pony
and ride away. He never talked none. I had hard work
gittin' more'n 'Yes' and 'No' out o' him. And I never
had the least idee where he wuz bound on these trips.
Nobody else, I reckon, until he rides back to Tombstone.

"I remember I wuz workin' down by my corral one
day when a Mexican comes ridin' by on the purtiest
black pony I ever seen. He wuz goin' along at a right
smart gait, but I stops him.

"'Say, partner,' sez I, 'that's a right nice little hoss
you're straddlin'. I kinder think I'd like to trade you
out o' him.'

"'*Esta bueno, señor,*' sez the greaser. 'What have you
to trade?'

"I offered to trade him an old spavined mule I owns,
but he laughs at me and I sees that Mex knows some-
thin' 'bout hossflesh. Well, we dickers quite a time.

"'I'll tell you what I'll do,' sez I at last. 'I'll give
you them two hosses o' mine you see right over yonder
in that thar corral and,' sez I, 'twenty dollars to boot.'

"That sets this greaser thinkin', and he looks like
he's gittin' ready to trade when he seems to hear something back down the trail and he turns around in his
saddle and takes a long look. I don't see nothin', but
whatever it is, it seems to make him kinder nervous
and he sez he's in a sorter hurry jest then and has got

to be ridin', but he'll see me some other time. So he gallops on off.

"But as I wuz tellin' you that wuz jest about the purtiest black pony I ever seen, and as he was ridin' away I kept lookin' at that pony, and the more I looks at it the purtier it seems to git.

"'Now,' sez I to myself, drawin' my own conclusions about the greaser, 'that Mexican's done stole that animule and he ain't got no business with it nohow, and I'm jest goin' to have that black pony for myself, and that's all thar is to that.'

"So I steps in the house and gits my rifle. Ef I takes a short cut across my alfalfa pasture, I kin ketch that Mexican by a clump of alamosas along the road. I wuz just startin' when along comes John Slaughter.

"'Seen a Mexican ridin' a black pony passin' along here recent?' sez John.

"'Jest left here 'bout five minutes ago,' sez I.

"'Which-a-way did he go?' sez John.

"'That-a-way,' sez I, and I p'ints up the valley toward the Mule Mountains. 'I ain't busy, John,' sez I. 'Can I help you any?'

"'No,' sez old John, and he rides off.

"The next time I'm in Tombstone, they tells me Slaughter come ridin' back to town leading that black pony. Seems like the Mexican had stole it from Mrs. Amazon Howell, Slaughter's mother-in-law. I asked ef Slaughter had brung in the Mexican. No, he hadn't. 'Then how'd he git the pony back?' I asks. Well, nobody knowed. He'd brung the pony back, but he hadn't brung back no Mexican, and that's all they knowed about it. That struck me as kinder funny. I wondered whatever had become o' that Mexican hoss thief. Of course, I didn't ask John. That'd been a mistake. Nobody never asked Slaughter no questions. It never did no good to ask him none, and sometimes it wuz sorter dangerous.

"'Bout a week later, I reckon it wuz, I wuz ridin' over round the mouth of Bisbee Cañon lookin' for some cows when I notices a passel o' buzzards sailin' round over the mesquite, and I rides over to the spot. There lays this here Mexican that'd come ridin' past my ranch on the black pony. I knowed him as soon as I seen him. So I goes on lookin' fer my cows, which finally I rounds up and drives back home. And I never says nothin' to nobody about what I sees in the mouth of Bisbee Cañon.

"I reckon it wuz two or maybe three months later I wuz in Bisbee. They wuz big excitement in town. Some cow punchers had jest found the skeleton of a human bein' lyin' out in the mesquite in the mouth of Bisbee Cañon. They'd brung in the bones and a few pieces o' clothes they'd found at the spot, and the coroner wuz fixin' to hold an inquest. I wuz kind o' smilin' to myself when I runs into old John Slaughter.

"'They tells me,' sez old John, 'some punchers has found a human skeleton over in the mouth o' Bisbee Cañon,' sez he.

"'Yes,' sez I, slappin' him on the back and laughin', 'and,' sez I, 'I knows what greaser used to own that skeleton.'

"'Is that so?' sez old John. 'Well,' sez he, 'that Mexican won't never steal no more hosses.'"

Juan Soto's case illustrates Slaughter's methods as neatly as anything that happened during his two terms in office. Juan Soto was a Spaniard who had come originally from California and was prosperously settled in Contention. He handled his affairs so adroitly as the leader of a band of robbers that operated up and down the San Pedro, running off cattle, holding up travellers on the highway, and committing an occasional murder, that the citizens of Contention had no suspicions that he was a criminal but held him in great respect. Slaughter himself was in the dark for a long time as to Soto's connection with the thieves, though he often wondered where all the money came from that the Spaniard spent in lordly wise across Tombstone bars.

Sheriff Slaughter had a deputy working for him named Burt Alvord, in whom he had great confidence and who rewarded that confidence by shrewd, faithful service, though in after years he himself turned outlaw and engineered a number of daring train robberies. Alvord was a roistering good fellow who drank and gambled and made many friends in the shady walks of life. These friendships he cultivated assiduously for business reasons, being a good detective and having a good detective's faith in the value of stool pigeons. It was one of these secret informers who first directed Alvord's suspicions toward Juan Soto.

But suspicion was one thing and evidence another, and Slaughter found it extremely difficult to fasten guilt definitely upon the crafty Spaniard. The sheriff learned that Soto was frequently away from his home in Contention all night on mysterious missions and returned at dawn. He learned also that, before coming to Arizona, Soto had been a member of a desperate band of criminals in California. While Slaughter was busy with his investigations, two cattle buyers were robbed and murdered near the Mexican line. Information he received left no doubt in the sheriff's mind that this atrocity was the work of Soto's band and that Soto himself had taken a personal part in it. Slaughter rode over to Contention and brought Soto back a prisoner.

Soto was acquitted at his trial in Tombstone. As he left the courtroom a free man, he smiled a sly smile of triumph in Slaughter's face. Which, it may be remarked, was a tactical error. It was whispered that the jury had been bribed. That may or may not have been true. The evidence was strong, but there were certain missing links, and the jury had given Soto the benefit of what it deemed a reasonable doubt. But, knowing what he did about Soto's clandestine affairs, Slaughter looked upon the verdict as an outrageous miscarriage of justice. Soto's guilt had not been proved to the satisfaction of the jury. Slaughter knew he was guilty. The jury of twelve men had brought in a verdict of innocence; the jury of one man returned a verdict of guilt. When, a few days later, Soto rode to his home in Contention at dawn after one of his nocturnal adventures, Slaughter stepped from a doorway with his pearl-handled six-shooter at a level.

"Soto," said the sheriff, "I'll give you ten days to get out of the country."

But the amazed Spaniard had other plans. He argued the matter.

"The jury acquitted me," he objected. "My business is here in Contention. You've no right to order me out of the country."

"The jury failed to put you in the penitentiary where you belong," replied Slaughter. "But I'll kill you if I catch you in this country after ten days. That's your time limit. Remember—ten days."

Slaughter's peremptory order struck Soto as pretty

high-handed. Unjust, also, in view of his acquittal, and, moreover, unlawful. The sheriff had no right to order him out of the country. Absolutely no right of any kind. Soto voiced his indignant resentment in Contention saloons.

"I am Juan Soto," he said to his Mexican admirers, tapping himself upon the breast. "That fellow Slaughter thinks he is dealing with a baby. But I will show him."

The ninth day arrived. Soto was tippling among sympathetic comrades.

"Well, Juan," said one of his friends, "what are you going to do about it?"

"Do?" flared Soto with a defiant laugh. "I am going to stay right here in Contention. I've just as good a right to stay in this country as Slaughter himself. He can't run me out."

The sun of the tenth day shone brightly over Contention. Soto's Mexican comrades gathered in a saloon. They would have a social glass with Juan. He was in trouble. A drink or two would cheer him up. But Soto did not appear. His friends looked at one another with faint, dubious smiles. Juan had talked so big and brave the night before. It was unbelievable that, after all, he had obeyed the order of this fellow, Slaughter. Ah, there down the street, Señora Juan Soto was sweeping off her front steps. The Mexicans would inquire.

"*Buenas dias, señora. Adonde esta Juan?*"

The woman, leaning on her broom handle, gave a shrug.

"*Se fue,*" she replied. "*Este es todo. Yo no se por adonde.*"

That was all. Juan Soto had vanished.

It was a year later that a number of robberies were

committed in Sulphur Springs Valley around Pierce.
Juan Soto recently had settled in the valley. As that
was not the San Pedro, he thought perhaps Slaughter
would leave him alone. Then, doubtless, Slaughter had
forgotten all about him. Twelve months is a long time.

Slaughter rode out of Tombstone alone one day, bound
east. A few days later, he rode back. He had been over in
Sulphur Springs Valley on a little business. That was all
anyone ever learned from Slaughter. But Juan Soto
suddenly and mysteriously disappeared. He never was
heard of again in Sulphur Springs Valley nor in Arizona,
nor, as far as anyone knows, anywhere else. A rumour
of unidentified origin spread abroad that Juan Soto was
dead.

Then there was Van Wyck Coster at Willcox. Slaughter gathered much evidence against Coster, who was a
business man of comfortable means and good reputation
among unsuspecting citizens. Slaughter's evidence was
enough, it was said, to send any ordinary person to the
penitentiary. But Slaughter had had enough of courts
and juries. His experience in the Soto case had taught
him a lesson. He would take no more chances on a
corrupt or misguided verdict. Then, why put the country to the unnecessary expense of a trial? Having tried
and convicted Van Wyck Coster in his own mind,
Slaughter rode over to Willcox to pass sentence.

"But, what the hell?" said Coster. "You can't run
me out of this country. I've done nothing."

"I'll run you out or kill you," replied Slaughter.
"I've got the goods on you and have had 'em for a long
time."

Coster wriggled and squirmed. When Slaughter went
into precise details concerning a number of crimes, Cos-

ter ceased to argue. It was exile or death—he had his choice. He wound up his business and departed.

If an ordinary sheriff had tried to enforce such summary measures, the criminal probably would have laughed at him. But nobody laughed at Slaughter. The man he sentenced to exile or death knew Slaughter meant exactly what he said. The beauty of Slaughter's one-man-jury verdicts was that they were always carried out one way or the other. Which way, didn't make much difference to Slaughter. If the criminal preferred exile, all right. If he preferred to die, that was his business.

Agua Zarca was a huddle of mud huts on the Northern Mexico & Arizona Railroad. Dark and silent on the night of May 11, 1888, lay the tiny village twelve miles south of Nogales on the border. Far off across the Sonoran plains appeared a point of light. That was the express. A long-drawn, eerie, dreary whistle, that seemed the voice of the desert's loneliness, came faintly out of the distance. As the train roared to a stop at the Agua Zarca station, two highwaymen with drawn six-shooters climbed into the locomotive cab. The engineer kept to his seat at the throttle. The fireman seized the gun of the robber leader. This was a brave fireman. So a second bandit shot him dead. Four other robbers on the ground were firing guns. The conductor came running from a rear coach with a lantern in his hand. What was the matter? A bullet cut through his heart. He lay there in the dark for an hour or more, his lantern on the ground beside him shining on his dead face. The express messenger was closing the sliding side door of his car when he was killed. Every phase of heroism received the accolade of a bullet this wild night. Now at their leisure, the bandits rifled safe and mail sacks. Then they rode off. The hoofs of their horses in the darkness made fine, dashing music to which fifteen thousand dollars marched away.

But Jack Taylor, leader of the band, had lost his hat during the excitement. This bold fellow must have a hat. He stepped into a store in Nogales. He clapped a new hat on his head. Price? The clerk said only three dollars, and Mexican money at that. The Court fixed the cost at the rest of his life in the penitentiary. Another robber, a German, was arrested with him. His imprisonment for life also sent the price of that hat a little higher.

The other four robbers were Geronimo Miranda, Manuel Robles, Neives Deron, and one Federico, all Mexicans. They fled across the border to Tombstone. This was a dangerous refuge just then. The town's name had taken on a sinister significance for robbers under Sheriff Slaughter's régime. For three nights the sheriff and his men watched a Mexican woman's house. But the bandits got wind of the trap. They were next heard of at Willcox and Clifton. Then their trail was lost.

Guadalupe Robles, a brother of Manuel Robles, lived in Contention and was a dealer in firewood. He had a wood ranch in Frenchy's Cañon near Mescal Springs in the Whetstone Mountains. He would drive from Contention to the Whetstones one day, sleep at his camp that night, and return to town with a load of wood next day. Being a good, loyal brother, Guadalupe was kept under a surveillance which he did not suspect. One morning, when he drove off for his camp, he had a gunny sack filled with food in his wagon. Of course, Guadalupe must eat on his trips. He must have dinner, supper, and breakfast before he got back. But it struck the spies who were watching poor Guadalupe that a whole gunny sackful of food was a little too much even for the appetite of a healthy wood-hauler. So Sheriff Slaughter was informed at once of the bountiful supply of refreshments Guadalupe was taking to Frenchy's Cañon. Whereupon Sheriff Slaughter and Deputy Sheriffs Burt Alvord and Cesario Lucero mounted in hot haste and rode for the Whetstones.

Night fell moonless and dark. The Whetstones went up blackly into dim obscurity. Slaughter knew the location of Guadalupe's wood camp, but he and his men did not ride up Frenchy's Cañon. They hid their horses in thick brush, and, on foot, struck along the top of a heavily timbered ridge that parallels the cañon. They blundered through thickets, stumbled over rocks, bumped blindly into trees. Far back in the mountains, they waited for the peep of day.

Far across the San Pedro Valley, the first faint suspicion of blue dawn appeared over the Dragoons. The three men took off their boots, tied them over their shoulders with pieces of twine, and in their socks, set off on the hunt. They slipped through the dark woods as warily and silently as Indians, guarding their steps lest the upsetting of a stone or the snapping of a twig give warning of their approach. Their quarry was not far away. They examined their guns, adjusted their cartridge belts. They were beginning to close in when Alvord showed sign of hanging back. Just a little. This was the young deputy's first big adventure. Slaughter caught him by the sleeve and swung him forward.

"Stay there in front of me," whispered the sheriff. "If you run, I'll kill you."

Before them on the slope of a hill, they saw through the dim, misty light three forms rolled in blankets and stretched on the ground. Only three. They had expected five. The three sleeping men were Manuel Robles and Neives Deron, robbers, and Guadalupe Robles, wood-hauler guilty of nothing except loyalty to his scape-grace brother. Federico and Geronimo Miranda, the other two uncaptured bandits, had gone elsewhither.

"Hey! Roll out of those blankets and throw up your hands."

Slaughter's voice cut through the dewy stillness. Called back, perhaps, from pleasant dreams, the three Mexicans flung aside their blankets, seized their six-shooters which had been lying beside them, and leaped to their feet. Surely a wild awakening. No time to rub the sleep from their eyes. No time for anything but fighting. Unless it was dying. There almost upon them were three grim spectre figures with levelled guns ready to send them to blazing death. Manuel Robles and Neives Deron rose shooting. Guadalupe Robles with his cocked six-shooter in his hand straightened to his full height. Slaughter's first shot killed him, and the Mexican crumpled down on his blankets and seemed to have gone back to his pleasant dreams. Deron fled up the hill at a stumbling run and dodged behind an outcropping rock. There he turned at bay, only head and shoulders showing. Three times his revolver flamed. A neat, rounded notch in Slaughter's ear dripped blood. One of Slaughter's bullets dropped Deron, mortally wounded, behind the boulder. Manuel Robles went bounding down into the cañon. Alvord fired several shots at him, the balls knocking up spouts of dirt beyond him.

"Pull down, Burt," shouted Slaughter. "You're over-shooting."

Which might have seemed to indicate remarkably cool and keen observation on the part of the sheriff during the furious flurry of a battle. But Slaughter did not wait for his deputy to obey instructions. He gave a practical demonstration of how the shooting should be done. Turning his six-shooter on Manuel, he sent the Mexican sprawling with the first shot. But Manuel was up in an instant. He ran a short distance when Slaughter's second bullet knocked him over once more. Again the Mexican scrambled to his feet and went scurrying away. This time he plunged into a thicket and Slaughter's third bullet missed him just as he passed out of view.

After the battle was over, Slaughter and his men trailed Manuel Robles two miles by his blood. Then his trail suddenly ended and it was believed some Mexican had helped him to escape on horseback. Deron was still alive. The wounded man and the dead man were carried back to Contention in Guadalupe's wood wagon. While being taken to Nogales to be turned over to the Mexican authorities, Deron died on the train after confessing that he was the robber who had killed the locomotive engineer.

Slaughter's ruthlessness in dealing with the train robbers who had wandered into his corner of the country caused the survivors of the band to plot vengeance. Learning that Slaughter was to visit San Bernardino ranch, which he now owned but which had not yet become his place of residence, Federico and an accomplice lay in ambush. Possibly Slaughter's Guardian Angel was on watch. At any rate, the sheriff did not make the

trip he had planned. Deputy Sheriff Cesario Lucero
went in his stead and rode into the trap that had been
laid for Slaughter. The ambushed Mexicans fired upon
Lucero who, without a chance to fight for his life, was
instantly killed. Federico and his companion escaped
into Mexico, where they were captured several months
afterward. Manuel Robles, wounded in the fight in the
Whetstones, fled to Sonora, where he rejoined Geronimo
Miranda, and word came back to Tombstone that the
two outlaws finally met death in a battle with rurales
somewhere in the Sierra Madre Mountains.

Chacon, a Mexican bandit, had filled all the border
country with the fame of his bold exploits. Sallying
from his strongholds in the Sierra Madres with a troop
of desperadoes at his back, this Fra Diavolo of Sonora
sacked towns and haciendas, pillaged the stores of
merchants, tortured citizens to make them divulge the
places in which their wealth was hidden. He had killed
many men and his merciless ferocity had made him the
terror of northern Mexico. Against Slaughter, this murderous robber had conceived a violent hatred. Up and
down the frontier line he flung his boasts that, if he
ever met the sheriff, he would shoot him down like a
dog. At these threats, Slaughter smiled grimly. But
behind the smile was a purpose as deadly as Chacon's
own. Slaughter, too, bided his time. For a year or more
the long-distance feud smouldered, but the trails of the
two men did not cross. Then Slaughter received a warning direct from Chacon himself.

"I am coming to Tombstone to kill you," the message
said.

The story of Chacon's visit to Tombstone was one of
Burt Alvord's reminiscences of the sheriff.

"I was sitting in my office in the courthouse one night," said Alvord, "when Slaughter came in with two double-barrelled shotguns in his hands. His teeth were clenched and his black eyes burned like points of fire.

"'Take this gun and come with me,' he said, shoving one of the weapons in my hands.

"That was all until we reached the street. Then he stopped for a moment.

"'Chacon is in town,' he snapped savagely. 'I'm going to get him.

"I knew of the hatred between the two men, and I knew there was no man on earth Slaughter would rather kill than this Mexican bandit who so often had threatened to murder him. Slaughter led the way down into the deep gulch that runs back of the courthouse along the western edge of town. On a bluff at the side of this ravine stood a long house made of canvas stretched over a wooden frame. No light showed in the house, but we could see the white canvas dimly in the darkness.

"'Chacon is in there,' said Slaughter. 'You knock at the front door. Chacon will run out the back door.'

"I waited until Slaughter had gone to the rear of the house. Then I stepped to the front door and thumped on it with the butt of my gun. I heard no movement inside. But while I was still knocking, the roar of Slaughter's shotgun shook the hills. I ran round to the rear.

"'I say, I say, I gave him both barrels,' said Slaughter. 'He pitched off into the gulch. He must be lying down there dead.'

"We went back to the courthouse and got lanterns. Up and down the ravine we searched, as carefully as prospectors looking for ore. But no Chacon could we find, dead or alive. Near the back door we found a taut wire that was one of the supports of the tent house. It was clear that, just as Slaughter fired, Chacon had tripped over this guy and plunged headlong down the embankment. The accident had saved his life. The double charge of buckshot had gone over his head. The Mexican had mounted his pony hidden in the gulch and escaped.

"The situation struck me as funny. But I looked as solemn as an owl. A sly chuckle just then would have been dangerous. Slaughter had been waiting for a year to kill Chacon, and he was wild with anger at his failure. This was the last chance he ever had. The Mexican had had enough of Tombstone and never came back. After it was all over, I went off where no one could see me and had a big laugh all by myself."

Burt Alvord long afterward took part in the capture of this murderous Mexican outlaw. Chacon's career ended on the gallows at Solomonville.

John Slaughter was the last knight of Tombstone's Round Table. The succession of heroic men ended with him. His name is burned into the town's history as with a branding iron. He shines out as a type of competent, splendidly equipped frontiersman. Daniel Boone was not better fitted for pioneer Kentucky than he for pioneer Arizona. His mission was to clean up Tombstone, and he did a thorough job. He brought peace at the blazing end of a gun. He shot the town full of law and order. He is not classed as a bad man in the traditions of the Southwest, but no desperado was ever more feared than this inscrutable man who stood uncompromisingly for law and shot from the hip with amazing dexterity. He was a constructive force—building with a six-shooter, but building. While he was sheriff, there was law in Tombstone even if the law, in large measure, was John Slaughter himself. When after four years of hard service he retired to his San Bernardino ranch to pass the remainder of his life, he left Tombstone as quiet as it is to-day. That is pretty quiet.

CHAPTER XX

D AWN in the Sierra Madres. Purple darkness in the glens and twisting cañons. Ripples of faint daylight breaking in rose against the tallest peaks. Over the shadowy chaos of mountains, unutterable silence. Above the undulant flow of coldly gray summits, a formless, incandescent splash that was the morning star.

For ten years there had been peace between the white men and the Apaches. Geronimo and his warriors who had of old terrorized and laid waste the frontier had been deported to Florida. A handful of braves grown weary of inglorious peace had broken from San Carlos reservation in May, 1896, and left a black trail of burned homes and death along the upper waters of the Gila River and through the San Simon Valley. They had crossed into Mexico at San Bernardino ranch and found refuge in the fastnesses of the Sierra Madres, fifty miles below the international line.

For three weeks a troop of the Seventh Cavalry had been in pursuit. At San Bernardino, the command had picked up John Slaughter to act as scout and guide. At fifty-five, the eyes of the frontier man-hunter were as keen as ever and his knack at following a trail as uncanny as in old days. Working like a hound on the scent, he located the encampment of the Apaches perched on a bench high on a mountain. Day was breaking as the troopers stole through the pine forest. The Indian camp was asleep. The cracking of army carbines was reveille for the renegades. Bucks and squaws came tumbling from the little group of wickiups in the clearing. Into the woods they plunged in mad flight and scattered over the mountain like quail. The pursuit of the soldiers was useless. The Indians had vanished as by magic. The chase abandoned, the troopers returned to burn the village.

John Slaughter stepped inside a wickiup. Something that, in the shadowy light, looked a little like a sack of flour caught his eye. Curious, he reached out the muzzle of his rifle to give the thing a poke. The sack of flour gave a sudden little tossing movement. It was a baby—a tiny Apache girl perhaps a year old, fast asleep on a deerskin. Black hair was tousled on the little head; long black eyelashes lay against the cheeks of dusky rose; the breath came and went as peacefully as if the child were sheltered in its mother's arms. All the noise of the attack and flight had left the baby's slumbers undisturbed.

"I say, I say," crooned Slaughter, bending over, "wake up, little fellow."

The baby girl opened her black eyes drowsily. A shadow of a smile flickered for an instant about her mouth. She probably expected to see her mother's face hovering above her. When she saw the black-bearded white stranger, her eyes filled with sudden terror. But no cry or whimper escaped her. She rolled off her deerskin and, like a baby wild animal taken by surprise, went scurrying off on all fours across the earth floor in a blind effort to escape.

"Well, baby," soothed Slaughter, "you needn't be so scared. Nobody's going to hurt you."

He caught up the little thing in his arms, wrapped her in an old shawl lying on the ground, and took her outside.

"Hey, fellows. What do you think of this?"

Soldiers gathered round, laughing. They peered into the frightened little face, patted the bronze cheeks, shook the chubby hands, tugged playfully at the tiny bare feet.

"Well, I'll be good gosh-darned."

"Hello, baby."

"Has your muvver gone and left you? Poor little baby."

A rifle crackled behind a rock high on the mountainside. A bullet whizzed past the heads of the group and knocked up earth and stones near by. An Indian, eh? Come prowling back. Several carbines made reply. No more shots came from the lone rifle on the mountain. A stalking party discovered an Apache buck lying dead behind the rock.

"The baby's daddy, I reckon."

"Come back to see what he could do for his kid."

"You've got to give it to that Indian. He loved his baby."

Was ever a tiny daughter of Apaches in such tragic misadventure as this mite of a baby cuddling in Slaughter's arms? Abandoned by her people. Captured as prize of war by the enemies of her race. Her father—probably —killed before her eyes. Her mother far off in the mountains, doubtless weeping out her heart. Now the soldiers were applying the torch. The infant's home was going up in flames. Still not a whimper from her lips. This baby was an Apache.

"What you goin' to do with the kid, Slaughter?"

"Take her home."

On the home trail, the baby slept beside Slaughter in his blankets. He woke one night and found her gone. He heard a rustle off in the darkness. The little Apache girl was crawling away silently through the grass. The starlit mountains had whispered, "Come back." She was going home. Her wild little heart had heard the call of the wild.

So the Apache baby took her place as one of the family at the San Bernardino ranch. Mrs. Slaughter, having regard to the month, named her Apache May. But this was too big a name for such a mite. It was changed to Patchy. Civilization's first gift to Patchy was a bath. Then some pretty new dresses. But Patchy's original clothes were preserved as curiosities. And very curious they were. Her entire wardrobe was on her back and consisted of only two pieces—an under waist and a frock. But these had a history. The baby was clothed in the vestments of murder.

Riding forth on their wild foray from San Carlos, the Indians of the band to which Patchy had belonged had attacked a ranch on the Gila River and massacred a Mormon family named Merrill, consisting of father, mother, and daughter. Farther south, in the San Simon Valley, they had murdered a lone ranchman named Hand. Friends of the Merrills identified Patchy's under waist as a part of the dart-fitted, many-buttoned, embroidered basque of the Mormon girl, and the shawl in which Slaughter had wrapped the baby, as having belonged to the Mormon mother.

Patchy's tight-fitting outer waist was made of a flour sack, and the little skirt attached to it was of white cloth of equally coarse weave. Patchy's frock was very dirty but on the skirt, beneath the grime, Mrs. Slaughter noticed dark figures which she believed were elaborately wrought aboriginal ornamentation.

"These quaint markings, so dim with dirt, intrigue me," said Mrs. Slaughter. "They are probably a swastika pattern. Or some sort of intricate scroll work. Or picture writings. I imagine they must have some mysterious significance. I wish some Apache would ride this way who could interpret their meaning for me. Very probably, Patchy's mother was, in her way, an artist."

Profoundly interested in these cryptic designs, Mrs. Slaughter had Patchy's frock washed. After it had been soaked in a tub of suds, scrubbed on the washboard, and dried in the sun on the clothes-line, the figures that adorned it stood out with startling distinctness. They read as follows:

REPUBLICAN TICKET

Delegate to Congress
    Thomas F. Wilson
For Joint Councilman
    J. W. Calkins
For Representatives
    . . . Hicks
    J. O. Stanford
    J. S. Robbins
    A. Wight
    E. G. Norton
County Surveyor
    H. G. Howe

Supervisors
    J. Montgomery
    B. S. Coffman
Sheriff
    S. H. Bryant
District Attorney
    W. H. Stilwell
Treasurer
    James P. McAllister
County Recorder
    W. F. Bradley

It was laughable, of course, to think of little Patchy romping about the parental wickiup in the Sierra Madres clad in an old Cochise County election poster, identified by Arizona antiquarians as of 1888. But it was also tragic. The old poster had hung for years on the walls of Hand's cabin and had been carried off by the Apaches after the lonely rancher had been butchered.

From the wickiup in which he found Patchy, Slaughter had also brought away a war bag and two papoose-carriers. The war bag had been made from a pair of buckskin pantaloons, stitched with bright thread on a sewing machine and probably once belonging to some Mexican dandy whom the Apaches had murdered. The papoose-carriers consisted of a jacket attached to a head band. With the band across their foreheads, Apache mothers carried their babies in these jackets on their backs. Mrs. Slaughter tried carrying Patchy in one. She placed Patchy in the jacket so the child faced backward, and walked out into the sunshine. Patchy, she thought, would be delighted to be carried in the way her Indian mother used to carry her. But Patchy yelled and waved her chubby fists indignantly.

"You've got her on wrong," said Slaughter. "The child must face the same way as you. That's Apache fashion."

Mrs. Slaughter readjusted Patchy. Facing forward and steadying herself with arms and legs, the baby was as contented as a mouse in its nest.

"Patchy was just a little wild animal when she came to San Bernardino ranch," said Mrs. W. E. Hankin of Bisbee, who has preserved in manuscript much interesting history of the Slaughter family. "She ate anything, picking up scraps of food from the ground. When thirsty, she would run to a ditch and, lying face downward, drink from the stream. When drowsy, she curled up anywhere and went to sleep.

"When she became accustomed to her new home, she proved an unusually bright child. She understood much that was said to her. Sign language was natural to her; if she wanted bread and sugar, her signs were quite eloquent. She was soon lisping English. She forgot her Indian habits and in a little while was eating from a plate, drinking from a cup, and sleeping in her own little bed.

"She was a vain little creature. She used to strut like a robin in the pretty clothes Mrs. Slaughter had made for her, and she was particularly proud of her long, thick black hair. Once, when her hair was cut off, she cried as if her heart would break. 'All my pretty hair is gone,' she wailed. But when her hair grew back more luxuriantly than before, she was vainer than ever. When she was four years old, an amateur photographer took her picture. The look of pride on her flat little face was comical as she sat before the camera after having carefully spread her hair out over her shoulders.

"There were other waifs who had found a home at San Bernardino—a little Mexican girl, a pickaninny as black as tar, and a freckled-faced American youngster. With these playmates, Patchy romped all day. She had nothing to do but play, and the years for the little wild girl passed like a happy dream.

"Above everything else in the world, Patchy loved Mr. Slaughter. She would toddle about the place, holding to the strap of one of his boots to steady her wavering feet. If he took her in his lap, she would sit serenely happy for any length of time. If he rode away, she would wait at the front gate for hours, watching patiently for his return. When she saw him far off riding back, she would dance for joy. She called him Don Juan and when Don Juan took her for a little ride over the ranch, as he often did, holding her on his saddle in front of him, Patchy revelled in the greatest happiness the world had to give. Caresses were not in Patchy's line. All the affection she had was expressed by her eyes, and she used to sit on the floor at the feet of her Don Juan as he smoked his pipe or read his paper and gaze at him by the hour with the rapt expression of a pagan worshipper before an idol."

But the daughter of the wilderness in the white man's home remained an Apache. She had an instinct for ambush. She took delight in frightening feminine visitors at the ranch by slipping noiselessly through the house and suddenly appearing as if from nowhere. If, at her games, she hid from her playmates, her lithe body became as motionless as a rock on a hillside. Sometimes she had spells of silent anger when her baby face froze in hard, savage lines and her black eyes snapped impishly. Though usually obedient, she could be sullen and obstinate. Once, when Mrs. Slaughter reprimanded her, the child's face twisted with rage.

"I'll kill you when I grow up," she flared.

Pessimists shook their heads over Patchy. They warned Mrs. Slaughter. They feared that the Indian in the child some day might flame into quick and possibly tragic savagery. A leopard, they sermonized, could not change its spots, and an Apache would never be anything but an Apache—and a devil.

Four years after Patchy had come to the ranch, she was standing one February morning in 1900 beside a fire that she and her playmates had kindled in front of the

house. A gust of wind whipped her skirt into the blaze.
Flames shot up and enveloped her. In panic, she ran
down the road. Will Slaughter, John Slaughter's son,
caught her, after a chase, smothered the flames, and bore
her in his arms into the house. She was put to bed and
soothing embrocations were applied. A telephone message was sent to Bisbee for a doctor. Bisbee, the nearest
town, was fifty-five miles distant—modern Douglas was
not yet in existence—and it was eight hours before the
physician arrived. He found the case hopeless.

Patchy suffered exquisite agony. But she did not
writhe or scream or moan. She lay on her pillow silent
and motionless, the courage and stolid fortitude of her
race in her grim little face, only the look in her black
eyes giving evidence of the torture she endured. The
little Apache was approaching the end like an Apache.

"Don Juan," she said to John Slaughter with
womanly calmness, "I am going to die. You have been
good to me. Good-bye, Don Juan."

So Patchy went to join the ghosts of her fathers, leaving unsolved the riddle over which the learned of the
world have pondered and argued for years. What effect
would civilization have had in moulding the character
of this little savage of the Stone Age nurtured among the
refinements of a modern home? Would she have grown
into the gentle womanhood of the white race or into the
hard, bitter maturity of her own wild people? Would
she have been a lady or a squaw? Which would have
won in her case, heredity or environment?

San Bernardino ranch was purchased by John
Slaughter in 1884 and became his home in 1890. It was
originally a land grant awarded in 1822 to Ignacio
Perez by the government of Mexico and comprised

29,644 hectares or 73,240 acres. It lay entirely in Mexico, until the Gadsden Purchase of 1853, which added an extensive border strip to the vast territory that had fallen to the dominion of the United States as a result of the Mexican War. Then the line as established between the two countries divided it into two unequal parts, the larger in Mexico, the remainder in Arizona. Slaughter bought the property from the descendants of Perez.

In the days of Spanish dominion, a presidio garrisoned by Spanish soldiers stood at San Bernardino guarding the northern frontiers of Mexico against savage Indian tribes. The mesa near the ranch house is still called the Mesa de la Avansada or the Mesa of the Advance Guard. Near the presidio, the pioneer Spanish padres established a mission. Crumbling adobe walls of a once extensive building in Mexico a mile south of the ranch house are believed to mark the site of this ancient religious house.

Twenty years ago, two Mexicans with pack burros camped for the night at these ruined walls. No one at the ranch paid any attention to them. Next morning they were gone. But they had left exposed to view in the earth within the old cloister enclosure a deep box-like receptacle lined with cement from which had been removed a cement slab that had served as lid. The cavity was empty. What it had contained remained an enigma. The two strangers had plied pick and shovel only in this one spot, and it was evident they had worked with a chart or secret directions to guide them. The cement-lined receptacle, it was suspected, had been the treasure vault of the old padres.

The old emigrant trail to California crossed the ranch

land, and in the gold rush days of 'Forty-nine was crowded with ox teams and prairie schooners. The ruts of the heavy wagons are still deep in the earth, and at a distance, the old road shows as a distinct yellow line running for miles across the mesa east of the ranch house. Opening upon this mesa is Guadalupe Cañon leading through the Guadalupe Mountains to the Animas Valley in New Mexico. It was in Guadalupe Cañon that Old Man Clanton and his five companions were ambushed and murdered by Mexicans. Twenty miles northeast is Skeleton Cañon, scene of the massacres of Mexican smuggler trains by Curly Bill outlaws.

San Bernardino ranch, intact to-day, is a domain of baronial extent. Its boundary fences are mountain ranges, its corner posts sun-kissed peaks. Watered by Guadalupe Creek and the Rio San Bernardino, it occupies the width of San Bernardino Valley and extends from the Guadalupe Mountains on the east to the Silver Creek range on the west and from the San S mon Valley watershed on the north to six miles south of the Mexican border. The international line is within a stone's throw of the front porch. Back of the barn lies Mexico. You may see a mule cropping grass in the United States while its tail is busy switching flies in a foreign land.

John Slaughter built a home here at San Bernardino worthy of a cattle king. About his long, one-story adobe house with its deep, cool verandas, giant cottonwoods formed an oasis in the treeless valley. Like a little village were the great stables, granaries, work shops, and outhouses, with a commissary store for employees. Orchards and vineyards arose. Five hundred acres, ir-

rigated by seven artesian wells, yielded crops of corn,
wheat, oats, barley, and vegetables. Thirty thousand
cattle under Slaughter's brand pastured on the San
Bernardino ranges.

The hospitality of San Bernardino ranch grew into a
tradition. John Slaughter kept open house. Everybody
was welcome. The family hardly knew what it was to sit
down at a table without guests. Soldiers, statesmen,
diplomats, frontiersmen, American cowboys, Mexican
vaqueros, distinguished men and men undistinguished
came and went in endless procession. When Douglas had
boomed into a city eighteen miles west, with Agua
Prieta adjoining it across the border, house parties
filled the ranch with gaiety almost every week-end.

Men who were making history in Mexico rode over
the line and sat at ease on the piazza while they discussed international adventures and problems with
John Slaughter in Spanish, which he spoke as fluently
as his native language. Among them were such notable
persons as Madero of tragic memory; Huerta who rose
on the ruins of Madero's fortunes; Pancho Villa, romantic bandit of the hills, who fought his way to the capital
at the head of a victorious army and, from the ancient
palace which had been the home of viceroys and
emperors, ruled supreme in Mexico; and Alvaro Obre-
gon who broke Villa's power at Celaya and Leon and
sent him reeling back into the deserts from crushing and
final defeat at Agua Prieta.

Days of peace at San Bernardino brought out the
kindly human side of John Slaughter's character. He
loved children and children loved him. The old frontier
fighter was never happier than when sitting on the
porch watching a troop of boys and girls at play. His

grandchildren were constantly visiting at the ranch and brought their little friends. Slaughter made the little ones his companions, took them on horseback rides, bought them candy, harmonicas, and trinkets at the store, told them stories, fished with them in the creek, heaped their plates with good things at the table, and always sent them home with a silver dollar in their pockets.

"Willie Greene, four years old, Mr. Slaughter's grandchild, came to the ranch with a pocketful of marbles," said Mrs. Hankin. "But it happened that just then no little boys were there with whom to play marbles. So Master Willie, being a shrewd merchant, offered his marbles to Mr. Slaughter for five cents.

"'That strikes me as a good bargain,' said Mr. Slaughter, and he bought the entire stock.

"Then some boys arrived and Willie needed his marbles.

"'I want my marbles back,' he said to his grandfather, rather expecting to get them back for nothing.

"'All right,' said Mr. Slaughter. 'I'm always ready to trade. I'll sell them back to you for ten cents.'

"'But,' argued Willie, 'you got 'em for five.'

"'That's so,' replied Mr. Slaughter. 'But you must never go into a business deal unless you see that you can turn your money over at a profit.'

"So Willie had to pay ten cents to get his marbles back, but, with the lesson that went with them, they were doubtless cheap at the price."

Old Bat, who had come out from Texas with Slaughter, lived at San Bernardino until his death in 1921. A brave old Negro of lordly airs was Old Bat, and he looked upon himself as a member of the family. Of the ranch, cattle, and all Slaughter possessions, he used to say, "They belongs to us." In the old days, when Old Bat guarded the large sums of money carried on cattle-buying expeditions, Slaughter knew no robber would ever get the treasure without killing the Negro first. Old Bat was faithful to the last drop of his blood. Bat's courage shone out notably in an incident during one of Geronimo's raids in the San Bernardino country. Gus Hickey, Bunk Robinson, and George Bridges of Tombstone, prospecting in Guadalupe Cañon, were surprised by the Apaches. Robinson and Bridges were killed. Hickey entrenched himself behind a rock and fought for several hours. Deciding his only chance for life lay in flight, he left his hiding place and ran down the cañon in the open under the fire of the Indian guns. As by a miracle, he escaped without a scratch and reached San Bernardino ranch eighteen miles away. The ranch hands talked of organizing a party to bring in the two dead bodies.

"Pshaw, what you-all talkin' 'bout?" said Old Bat. "Ain't no need o' no party. I'll go fetch 'em in."

He hooked up a team of mules and drove alone to the scene of the fight and brought in the bodies. As it chanced, Geronimo and his band had gone.

Old Bat's last years were passed in important and busy idleness. Loyal to those who were loyal to him, Slaughter surrounded the old Negro with every comfort. Old Bat died at the ranch at the age of ninety. He had been in Slaughter's service forty-three years.

Nigger John, who with Old Bat had come from Texas on the honeymoon cattle drive, had been a slave in the Slaughter family. As a pickaninny he had been given by his mother on her deathbed to John Slaughter, and remained in his master's service for twenty-five years after slavery days had ended. He married in Tombstone and settled down in a home of his own. He still lives there, very old and in comfortable circumstances.

Old age robbed John Slaughter of some of his restless energy, slowed his brisk step, caused him to stoop a little, and turned his hair and beard white, but it did not change his eyes.

Some novelists have it [wrote Michael J. Phillips in 1921] that the man with the bright blue eye is the real article when it comes to brawls, battles, and ruckuses. Maybe so. But John Slaughter's eyes proclaimed to me without a word on his part and without an effort on his part to impress me, that he is clear strain. They are black eyes, cold and unyielding as frosted granite. They are sharp. They probe you. His low voice and rather deprecatory manner are set at naught by one glance of those fearless eyes. So long as he lives, John Slaughter will never be merely one of the crowd in an assemblage. And it is because of his eyes. I would not care to be called on even to-day to shoot it out with John Slaughter, though he is a very old man.

I asked him how much land he had here at San Bernardino.

"About one hundred thousand acres, leased and owned," he replied in his drawly voice.

He pointed to a mountain peak six miles below the international border which passed at our feet. "That's one boundary," he said. He pointed to another peak perhaps ten miles from us and six miles from the first. "That's another. The American boundaries are over yonder." He flirted his thumb over his shoulder toward an empire's expanse of plains, hills, and mountains behind us.

San Bernardino ranch was steeped in peace on the night of May 4, 1921. There was no moon, but the bonfire stars that blaze in Arizona skies gave a crystal clearness to the darkness. Mrs. Slaughter, Miss Edith Stowe, a guest, and Jess Fisher, foreman of the ranch and Mrs. Slaughter's cousin, were talking in desultory

wise in the living room. John Slaughter sat in the
dining room absorbed in a newspaper. The window beside him looked out upon the commissary store thirty
feet distant across the back yard. The window shade
was raised. A kerosene lamp of great brilliancy lighted
the room.

Suddenly, one of Slaughter's old-time, unaccountable,
mystic warnings of unseen danger flashed upon him.
He flung aside his newspaper and hurried from the
room. His bedroom across the hall was dark. He stepped
into it. He had no reason for doing this. He had neither
heard nor seen anything out of the common. He did it—
that was all. As his fingers closed on the handle of his
six-shooter lying in its place on the chimney piece, two
shots sounded loudly at the rear of the house. He rushed
for the door. Feeble with age, he was the fighter still.
But Mrs. Slaughter and Miss Stowe threw their arms
around him and bore him into a chair.

"You must not go outside," screamed Mrs. Slaughter.
"You will be killed."

Jess Fisher had heard a noise at the store. He had
stepped out to investigate. Immediately had come the
crash of two guns. Whatever was taking place, it was
quickly over. Running footsteps faded into the distance. Then silence.

Slaughter and the two women found Fisher lying dead
on the little platform in front of the door of the store.
His pockets were turned inside out and his watch was
gone. Eighty dollars was missing from the cash drawer
of the commissary. From the bunkhouse, Manuel
Garcia and Jose Perez, employed on the ranch, had
disappeared.

Four Mexicans, it developed, had been concerned in

the robbery. Garcia and Perez were caught next day at a neighbouring ranch. Garcia, nineteen years old, had lived on the Slaughter ranch since boyhood. Perez, who had been in Slaughter's employ only a few days, was said to have served with Pancho Villa's guerrillas. Arcadio Chavez, taken in Agua Prieta with Fisher's watch in his possession, made a clean breast and implicated Manuel Rubio as the fourth man. The robbers, Chavez said, had planned to murder the entire family at the ranch and loot the place. He and Rubio had shot Fisher. If Slaughter had come running out, as they expected, they would have killed him. But as the old fighter had been saved from the trap, the fear of his six-shooter, Chavez declared, prevented the carrying out of the plan for wholesale murder.

Garcia and Perez were sent to the penitentiary for life. Rubio was never apprehended. Chavez, it was reported, went through a form of trial at Hermosilla in Mexico and was acquitted. Manuel Garcia, according to Chavez, had planned the robbery. His murderous treachery was a shock to Mrs. Slaughter. He had been her personal chore boy, and she had taken a mother's interest in his bringing up.

Slaughter's life was saved that night by his mysterious warning. His murder was to have been the crux of the plot. If he had continued a minute longer to read his newspaper by the window in the brilliantly lighted dining room, he unquestionably would have been killed. His lifelong confident assertion that he could not be killed seemed to have been verified again. Now, near the close of his career, his Guardian Angel was still on watch.

Slaughter's last years were as serene as the sunlight

that bathes the San Bernardino Valley. He lived in peace and contentment. He rode occasionally; he pottered in his kitchen garden; he walked among his flower beds, bringing a fresh rose every morning to lay beside his wife's plate on the breakfast table. He sat on the pleasant veranda in the long, languorous afternoons and watched the cloud shadows drift across the vegas or let his eyes rest on the shadowy beauty of the blue mountains of Mexico. His eighty years of life, that from first to last had been one long romance of the frontier, ended from apoplexy February 15, 1922. He had done his work well and had earned his rest. No more forceful or picturesque character ever made history in pioneer Arizona than this John Slaughter who, carrying law in one hand and a six-shooter in the other, established peace and prosperity in his corner of the wilderness of the Southwest.

CHAPTER XXI

HANDS UP!

BISBEE is a city, you might say, of only one dimension—length. It lies like a piece of string along the bottom of a narrow cañon in the Mule Mountains. Its main street in the bed of the winding slit is miles long with handsome business blocks near the middle of the thread and good-looking residences out at the ends. Of course, if one wishes to be precise, there is a little width and a little height to the town, and the height up the cañon walls is about as great as the width across the cañon. The residences hang on the steeps as if glued there. A business man going home to lunch journeys straight up by a series of ladderlike steps that bear street names. If you enjoy mountain climbing, Bisbee will appeal to you as an ideal place of residence. If you happen to be fat, you will fall into a panic at mere sight of the town.

Under the main street is a giant subway to drain off the water when it rains. After a storm, the water roars through the subterranean sluice like an express train and flows out in a spreading flood on the plains at the south end of the cañon. It is surprising what a seething torrent the tiny drops of a light rain will form when they trickle down the mountain-sides and merge at the bottom of the cañon. If it were not for this subway, a light shower might wash the town away.

Right in town at the edge of the business centre is the Copper Queen mine. It seems, in a way, to merge with the stores. You pass a soda fountain and a haberdashery shop with windows full of shirts and come to one of the richest copper mines in the world. Crushed in between its mountain walls, this bizarre little city of 22,000 people is the metropolis of southeastern Arizona. Twenty-six miles north is Tombstone. An equal distance south are Douglas and the Mexican border.

Bisbee, with its schools and churches and wealth and culture, has travelled a long road since its boom days as a mining camp in the early 'eighties when copper was struck in the Mules. Then it was a rough town full of boozing kens and brothels and dance halls, and Brewery Gulch was famous as a rendezvous for hard characters from the four corners of the frontier. But it was a busy, money-making place, too, and from the first it grew steadily and solidly. It was like a piece of string in that yesterday of long ago, as it is to-day, and its one-story frame business houses and shanty saloons were strung out up and down the cañon in twin rows along its single winding street, while the mountain-sides were plastered with the precariously clinging pine shacks of miners. Among the merchandising establishments of that pioneer time, none did a more flourishing business than the general store of Goldwater & Casteñeda.

Dan Dowd and Red Sample, rough-looking customers in their cowboy paraphernalia, stood in front of Goldwater & Casteñeda's store at 7:30 o'clock on the night of December 8, 1883. The Christmas shopping season was in full swing and Bisbee's main street was bright with street lamps and the light shining from store windows.

"All set?" asked Dan Dowd out of the corner of his mouth.

"Yep," replied Red Sample.

"Then let her rip."

Whereupon these two hard-looking customers slid six-shooters from the scabbards at their sides and one shot up the street and the other shot down.

The street a moment before had been, in a manner of speaking, full. A moment afterward, the street, as you might say, was empty. Shoppers on the sidewalk ran into the stores. Shoppers in the stores, though curious, stayed there. Dan Dowd kept on firing up the street, and Red Sample kept on firing down.

As their bullets were singing Christmas carols on the sidewalk, three friends and business associates, Tex Howard, Bill Delaney, and Dan Kelly, were inside the store doing their Christmas shopping with six-shooters. While proprietors, clerks, and customers stood lined along the walls with hands in the air, the trio rifled the cash drawers, ransacked the safe, looted the show cases of watches and jewellery, and scooping everything into a sack, rejoined their companions in the street.

Meanwhile, Dan Dowd and Red Sample had been having a busy time. When their first shots had sent the street crowds scurrying, John Tapiner had been a little slow in getting inside a saloon, and a bullet knocked him over dead in the barroom door. Mrs. Anna Roberts, a restaurant keeper, was slain accidentally, it was said, with a bullet meant for a fugitive man. J. A. Nolly was wounded and lay crumpled on the sidewalk, dying later. Deputy Sheriff D. Tom Smith and James Kriegbaum, indignant that five bandits should overawe an

entire town of able-bodied citizens, stepped out in the
street and for a while turned the one-sided affair into a
battle. Smith was quickly killed. Kriegbaum wounded
Red Sample in the arm. With three citizens dead and
one dying, the five robbers swung on their horses and
went galloping down the cañon, terrorizing the lower
town with revolver shots. When they rode out of the
mountains at the south end of the cañon, they turned
east and headed across Sulphur Springs Valley for the
Chiricahuas.

This affair was known in the chronicles of the period
as the Bisbee massacre.

While the rattle of shots in the lower cañon was still in
his ears, Kriegbaum leaped on his horse and in a mad
Paul Revere ride across the mountains, reached Tombstone in an hour and a half. Automobilists who travel
the up-and-down road to-day think they are doing
pretty well if they cover the distance in fifty minutes.
Kriegbaum's news threw Tombstone into a furore.
Deputy Sheriff William Daniels and a posse were soon
riding hard for Bisbee. They found the mining town
wild with excitement, its streets swarming with armed
men. Several posses were already out scouring the
country. A number of citizens joined Daniels. Among
them John Heath.

Heath had been stirred to the depths of his soul by
the red-handed atrocity. Among all the voices lifted
against the perpetrators, his was the loudest.

"Damnable outrage," he declared. "Them fellers
deserve no mercy. Track 'em down. Hang 'em to the
nearest tree. Them's my sentiments."

Where the trail of the robbers turned east at the
south end of the cañon, Heath led the posse south.

"Here's the trail, boys," he shouted. "They're headin' for Mexico."

The posse clattered after this lynx-eyed fellow who could read a trail in the dark.

Close to the Mexican line, Heath turned west.

"This way, boys," he called out. "The trail's gittin' hot. We'll ketch them fellers before noon. You bet."

When morning came, Heath was spurring hard on a trail no one else could see. But no criticism of John Heath, mind you. This honest lad was plainly doing the best he knew how. The posse thought he was wrong—that was all—and back it rode to the mouth of the cañon. Now that it was daylight, the trail of the robbers was plain. It led east.

Somewhere around Soldier Holes in Sulphur Springs Valley, Heath announced that the trail turned north. The others saw that it still ran east. Again Heath was overruled. But merely with deprecatory smiles. He meant well. His mistake was evidently due to his over-anxiety "to ketch them robbers and string 'em up."

Before the posse reached the Chiricahuas, Heath attempted to lead it off on several other false scents. Vague suspicion gradually took form. It began to look as if a pretty crafty gambler was overplaying his hand.

In the Chiricahuas the five horses the robbers had ridden were found dead at the bottom of a chasm. When the animals had given out from hard riding, the bandits had driven them over a precipice after stealing fresh mounts from a ranch. The tragedy of the five horses was a heartless piece of deviltry. The animals could have been turned loose with no danger to the robbers. A little deeper in the mountains, the pursuit ended. The fugitives had scattered.

When Heath had returned to Bisbee, he was still vociferous in anathema.

"Them bandits didn't have no call to kill citizens the way they done," he said. "Ef I'd run on to 'em, I'd shot 'em down like dogs."

After one of these tirades, Frank Buckles measured Heath with cold eyes.

"Those five fellows," said Buckles, "stopped at my ranch in Pole Bridge Cañon two nights before the robbery. And, Mr. Heath," he added, "you were with them."

Heath was arrested and placed in jail at Tombstone. It was established later that he had planned the robbery. Just a shade too much of enthusiasm had landed Heath in the shadow of the gallows.

Deputy Sheriff Daniels traced Dan Dowd into Chihuahua. The two men met one day on the street of Corralitos, a little mining town in the Sierra Madre Mountains.

"Hello, Dan," said Daniels.

"Hello, Bill," said Dowd.

But Daniels spoke over the barrel of a forty-four and Dowd returned the greeting with his hands in the air. Extraditing a criminal from Mexico was slow work in those days. So Daniels smuggled his prisoner across the line, and Dowd was soon in a cell in Tombstone. Delaney was arrested in Minas Prietas in Sonora by a Mexican officer. Without extradition papers, Daniels brought the prisoner over the border in a box car. Kelly was arrested in Deming in a barber's chair while his face was covered with lather. The barber had identified him by a photograph.

Red Sample and Tex Howard arrived in Clifton with

plenty of money and cut a splurge in underworld resorts. Howard, in princely fashion, bestowed a gold watch upon a woman. Vain of the gift, the siren exhibited it to an admirer who examined it with eyes green with jealousy but not too green to identify the timepiece, by description sent broadcast, as having been part of the loot of the Bisbee massacre. So the enamoured Howard did not bask long in beauty's smiles. The jealous lover betrayed him, and Howard and Red Sample, shackled hand and foot, took the trail for Tombstone.

Dowd, Sample, Howard, Kelly, and Delaney were tried together before Judge D. H. Pinney in Tombstone and sentenced to hang. Their execution was set for March 28th. Heath, tried separately, was convicted of murder in the second degree, and on February 21st, sentenced to life imprisonment. Bisbee had viewed the hanging verdict for the five robbers with deep-seated satisfaction, but it burst into a storm of rage when it learned that Heath had escaped the gallows. A mass meeting was held. Citizens thundered indignation. Resolutions were passed. And next morning, while the dawn of Washington's Birthday was red over the Mule summits, a committee of fifty Bisbee men, mounted and armed, rode over the divide on the road to Tombstone.

Tombstone had hardly rubbed the sleep out of its eyes when the Bisbee horsemen rode into town. The streets were empty. Only a few stores had opened. A few housewives cooking breakfast caught a glimpse of the cavalcade. A few drowsy citizens drawing on their trousers stared out the windows wonderingly as it passed. The Bisbee men dismounted at the courthouse. A knock sounded on the iron portal of the jail. Swing-

ing open the door, Sheriff Ward looked into the barrels
of several six-shooters.

"Well," he gasped in astonishment, "I thought it was
the Chinaman bringing breakfast for the prisoners."

Sheriff Ward surrendered the keys, expecting a wholesale lynching. But Heath alone was taken from his cell.
The five robbers under sentence of death were in adjoining cells. They were relieved when the committee
paid no attention to them. They were justly doomed.
These men of Bisbee had come to do justice in the
single case in which they were convinced the Court had
erred. Heath, in their opinion, was as guilty as the others.
He, too, deserved to die.

Heath was led to a telegraph pole north of the courthouse in Tough Nut Street. He stood there in the early
morning sunlight as cool and unperturbed as if being
lynched were habitual before-breakfast routine, like
lemon in hot water or orange juice.

"Got anything to say before you go, Heath?"

"I wish," replied Heath, "you'd promise not to shoot
my body full of holes after you swing me up."

"All right. We'll promise you that."

Heath drew a red bandanna from his pocket and
bound it around his head so that it hid his face. A hanging had certain punctilios of etiquette to be observed.
It was the correct thing for men who went into the other
world at a rope's end to depart with their faces covered.
His handkerchief took the place of the official black
mask. When the noose had been slipped about his
neck, he sensed a certain ineptness. He was fastidious
in this matter of dying.

"Shove the knot around under my left ear," he said
through his handkerchief.

"Thank you," he acknowledged politely when his request had been complied with.

The Bisbee horsemen rode out of town as quietly as they had come. Perhaps not fifty people in Tombstone knew that anything unusual had taken place. Citizens going to their work saw with surprise a dead man hanging twenty feet in air against the telegraph pole in Tough Nut Street. They noticed curiously a placard fastened just below his feet. It read:

JOHN HEATH
Was hanged to this Pole
By the
Citizens of Cochise County
For Participation as a Known Accessory in the Bisbee Massacre
At 8:20 A. M. February 22, 1884
Washington's Birthday

The Heath lynching resulted in a famous coroner's verdict. The jury was confronted with a delicate problem. The usual verdict of "death at the hands of parties unknown" was impracticable. All the lynchers were known. But the jury had no intention of naming the parties at whose hands death had occurred; Tombstone heartily approved the hanging bee. Dr. George Goodfellow in his testimony hinted at a way out of the dilemma. He declared death had been caused by emphysema. The jurors had not the slightest idea what emphysema meant, but they caught at the learned word as drowning men at a straw. Dr. Goodfellow explained that emphysema was swelling caused by air in the cellular tissues and was sometimes due to strangulation and sometimes to the effects of high altitude. What more could any honest jury want? The verdict read:

We, the jury of inquest impanelled and sworn by the coroner of Cochise County, after viewing the body and hearing the testimony, find that the name of the deceased was John Heath, 32 years old, a native of Texas, and that he came to his death from emphysema of the lungs, which might have been, and probably was, caused by strangulation, self-inflicted or otherwise, as in accordance with the medical evidence.

A gallows built for five stood back of the Tombstone courthouse. The high board fence about the yard shut it off from the view of the public. A thrifty citizen erected a grand stand from which the hanging might be witnessed. There seemed prospect of his making considerable money. One morning, when he went to put the finishing touches on the structure, he found it a mass of wreckage. Tombstone did not approve of turning the tragedy into a box-office attraction.

Two miners sat on the dump of the Lucky Cuss mine on the hill back of town. Far below, they could see the courthouse yard, the yellow pine gallows, the strong cross-bar above it, the five dangling hempen nooses. The door of the jail opened. Dowd, Sample, Howard, Kelly, and Delaney walked out, herded by deputies, Sheriff Ward at their head. The little procession crossed the yard and mounted the gallows stairs. The five condemned men took their places in line on the trap.

"I've knowed all them boys well," said one of the miners on the Lucky Cuss dump. "Fine fellers as you'd want to meet."

"Hard to understan'," remarked the other. "Five husky young fellers. Full of life this minute. Dead as this chunk o' rock five minutes from now."

"Had many a drink with them boys. Been to the Bird Cage with 'em. Set in poker games with 'em. Shore wuz nice boys."

"Look like soldiers standin' up thar. Heads up. Shoulders back. Game, all right."

"Yes, sir, knowed 'em well. Set and talked with 'em many's the time jest like I'm settin' here talkin' to you. Dan Dowd played as purty a game o' bank as you ever seen. Shore knowed how to handle chips."

"What're them deputies doin'?"

"Stroppin' their hands behind their backs and stroppin' their ankles together. That's the way they do. Old pals o' mine, all them fellers. Spent their money free. Many's the——"

"That's the black caps, ain't it? They're slippin' on the nooses. The sheriff's shootin' them knots tight agin their necks. What's that deputy steppin' back to the rail fer?"

"He's goin' to cut the string. Good-night. Thar she goes."

"God!"

"Done dropped 'em through. Well, I'll be damned. And jest to think I knowed all them boys well. Yes, sir, knowed 'em well."

"Can't see 'em. Can't see nothin' but a black slit in the floor of the gallows."

"Jest a black slit. That's all. And black as hell."

Into the blackness, five men had dropped to death. The Bisbee massacre had been expiated.

Train robberies came into vogue among Arizona outlaws in the 'nineties. Lonely deserts, convenient mountains, and trains bearing fortunes in their safes made the crime attractive. Train robberies at Cañon Diablo, Maricopa, Rock Cut, Willcox, and Stein's Pass were pioneer successes for daring spirits to emulate. Black Jack Ketchum was one of the most famous of these early-day robbers. After robbing a bank at Nogales, he killed a man of Sheriff Fly's pursuing posse at Skeleton Cañon, adding one more tragedy to the many tragedies of that famous pass in the Peloncillos. Black Jack, it was supposed, buried much of his loot in a cave in Wild Cat Cañon at the south end of the Chiricahuas near William Lutley's ranch. He called this cave Room Forty-Four. Captured after a train robbery, Black Jack imparted to Leonard Alvorsen full directions as to how to lift this treasure. But, unfortunately, Alvorsen had no opportunity to go on a treasure hunt, being detained behind bars at Yuma. Falling heir to Alvorsen's information, Bert and Harry Macia of Tombstone ransacked Room Forty-Four, but no doubloons or pieces-of-eight rewarded them. Black Jack, a Falstaffian robber much given in prosperous days to fat capon and flagons of sack, was sentenced to hang at high noon in Clayton, New Mexico. On the gallows he appeared anxious. "What time is it?" he asked. He was told it lacked one minute of twelve. "Well, hurry up," urged Black Jack. "I'm due to eat dinner in hell at twelve sharp." The drop, it is said, severed the giant's head from his body.

They still laugh in Arizona at the silver-rain train robbery at Willcox in 1895. Grant Wheeler and Joe George, the bandits, found $60,000 in Mexican silver dollars stacked in sacks in the express car. This money was too bulky to carry away, and they used it to weigh down the dynamite they placed against the safe. The explosion wrecked the car. The dollars went flying through the roof and on toward the stars, and fell in a silver rain over all the landscape. Telegraph poles were shot full of coins, which later were scraped off like barnacles, and a pile of cross-ties beside the track was turned into a silver mine. Searchers worked for days picking up the money, some of the silver pieces being found a half mile from the railroad, and, strangely enough, all but $600 was recovered. The two robbers got only $1,500 from the safe and were trailed by bills with corners singed off which they spent in saloons during their flight. Joe George was caught and sent to Yuma. Billy Breakenridge, Sheriff Behan's famous deputy, who was now Detective William Breakenridge of the Southern Pacific Railroad, tracked Grant Wheeler to Mancos, Colorado. There, when the robber was cornered without hope of escape, he blew out his brains.

Burt Alvord, Sheriff Slaughter's old deputy, was living during this period at Willcox. He owned a cattle ranch, took a hand in politics, and had been elected constable. But he was the same genial roistering, devil-may-care fellow as in old Tombstone days, and everybody liked him. Living in Willcox, too, was William Downing, a cattleman reputed rich and looked upon as an honest, substantial citizen. But Downing had been a member of the notorious Sam Bass band of outlaws in Texas, had served two terms in the penitentiary, and had been run out of Texas by the Rangers. Downing and Burt Alvord became friends, and this sinister friendship marked the turning point in Alvord's career.

The Southern Pacific express, westbound, was robbed at Cochise southwest of Willcox in September, 1899. Two men flagged the train at midnight, overawed the train crew with six-shooters, dynamited the safe, and escaped with $10,000. Sheriff Scott White with a posse, of which Burt Alvord was a member, pursued the robbers into the Chiricahuas, where the trail was lost. No clew to the identity of the bandits was discovered. They had vanished into mystery, and the Cochise robbery passed into history as one of the most skilfully managed criminal enterprises that had ever occurred in Arizona. It was not until six months later that Jeff Milton turned the light of a blazing shotgun on the secret history of this interesting affair.

Jeff Milton of Fairbank, a famous fighting man of the Tombstone country, was born in Florida in 1861. He has been a part of the Southwest since his youth, as Texas Ranger, chief of police of El Paso, cattle association detective, railroad detective, and shotgun messenger, and for years immigration agent and customs inspector along the border between Arizona and Mexico. Gray of hair and moustache, the old fire-eater is still a gallant figure and, for all his years on the frontier, still retains the manners, speech, and kindly courtesy, touched with a certain courtliness, that belong to the tradition of the Old South.

The train from Nogales to Benson pulled into Fairbank at dusk on a February day in 1900. Jeff Milton, express messenger, was leaning in the doorway in the side of the express car, his shotgun in the crook of his arm. He smiled when he saw a half-dozen citizens lined up on the station platform with two cowboys behind them with drawn six-shooters. The idea of a train robbery did not occur to him. It was pretty dark, and he thought the cowboys, half-tipsy perhaps, were having fun with some tenderfeet. He chuckled aloud when one of the cowboys shouted, "Git up your hands." But when he saw a cowboy, using the row of citizens as breastworks, point a six-shooter in his direction, he woke up. That gun looked a little like business. Maybe, after all, this was the real thing.

"Come out of that car," yelled the cowboy.

"If there's anything in this car you want," Milton flung back, "come and get it."

Flame leaped from the cowboy's gun. The bullet shattered the bone in Milton's arm and knocked him over on the car floor. The cowboy rushed for the door. He was climbing in the car when Milton got to his knees, one arm dangling like a rag, and raising his shotgun with one hand, fired. The robber tumbled back on the ground with a load of buckshot in his body.

"Look out, boys," he shouted, "this fellow's shootin' to kill. He's got me."

"I slammed the door shut and locked it," said Milton. "Then, as there was no way for those fellows to get in unless they dynamited the car, I staggered over to a piece of baggage and sat down. An orchestra began to play. Thinks I, 'That's the most beautiful music I ever heard in my life.' The next thing I knew, a setter pup was licking me in the face and Baca, the engineer, was standing over me."

Milton's heroic duel saved a valuable treasure in the safe and ended the train robbery. The man he had shot was Three-fingered Jack Dunlap. The other bandits were Bravo John Yoes, Bob Brown, and Jack and Lew Owens. Three-fingered Jack was being held in the saddle when the robbers rode off in the darkness. Milton was rushed in a caboose drawn by a special engine to Tucson where surgeons removed several inches of bone from his upper arm. The wound left him a cripple for life.

Sheriff Scott's posse found Three-fingered Jack, half

dead and abandoned by his comrades, at Buckshot Springs in the Dragoons and took him to Tombstone where he was placed in the hospital. Bob Brown and the two Owens brothers were arrested a few days later. Bravo John was taken at Cananea in Mexico. Three-fingered Jack died six days after his capture. On his deathbed, he told the story of the Cochise train robbery. Burt Alvord and William Downing, he declared, had planned the crime; Billy Stiles, a constable at Pierce, and Matt Burts, a cowboy, had committed the robbery. Alvord, Downing, and Stiles were soon in jail at Tombstone, and Burts was arrested in Wyoming. For a time Willcox and Tombstone refused to believe two such respectable citizens as Alvord and Downing were implicated in a train robbery. Then Billy Stiles confessed. He and Burts, Stiles said, had turned over the $10,000 taken at the robbery to Alvord and Downing. These "master minds" of the conspiracy, according to Stiles, had made a masterful division of the spoils, giving Stiles only $480 as his share. This niggardliness had rankled with Stiles, and his confession was the outcome of the grudge he had nursed.

But having betrayed his accomplices, Stiles suffered from remorse. Permitted a certain amount of liberty as a state's witness, he held up the Tombstone jailer, whom he shot in the leg, and getting possession of the keys, released Alvord and Bravo John. Arming themselves with guns taken from the sheriff's office, the three men rushed from the jail. At the door they met Matt Burts, back from Wyoming in custody of a deputy sheriff. Burts joined them, and the four outlaws galloped out of town on stolen horses. Downing had refused to join in the jail break.

Stiles, Bravo John, and Burts were recaptured, and after two years of liberty spent in Sonora, Alvord surrendered to Sheriff Del Lewis, an old friend, at Naco. But, tiring of imprisonment, Alvord and Stiles escaped from the Tombstone jail a second time in 1903 by tunnelling through the walls. Both were recaptured, and at last all the men concerned in the Cochise and Fairbank robberies went to Yuma prison. Stiles was killed in Nevada in 1908 by outlaws whom, it is said, he was planning to betray. Downing was killed by Territorial Ranger Speed at Willcox the same year. Bravo John passed into oblivion in Mexico. After serving two years in the penitentiary, Alvord went to Honduras where, it was said, he married a wealthy coffee-planter's daughter, and where, according to word that came back to Tombstone, he died in 1912.

Jeff Milton, George Scarborough, and Eugene Thacker had trailed Bronco Bill Waters, Bill Johnson, and Jack Pitkin into the White Mountains in northeastern Arizona and were in camp at McBride's Crossing on the headwaters of Black River. The three fugitives had robbed a Santa Fe train at Belen, New Mexico, and killed three men of a sheriff's posse that had gone out from Socorro.

"I was fishing near camp," said Milton, "and had landed several nice trout when I heard firing. Bronco Bill and his two pals had given us a little surprise. I stuck my fishing pole in the bank and slid my Winchester off my shoulder. I saw Johnson churning his gun behind a juniper two hundred yards away. I clipped him in the hip. The bullet split against the bone, and we buried him next morning. Bronco Bill, who had been fighting from the ground, jumped on his horse.

'Hold on, Cap,' I called to him, 'I've got a little business I want to talk over with you.' But he didn't stop until I knocked him out of the saddle with a bullet. Pitkin got away. After serving twenty years in the penitentiary, Bronco Bill was pardoned out only a couple of years ago. I met him in Naco. He didn't look much like the bold, bad train robber I had once nearly killed. He was white-haired and stooped and feeble. Old age," added Milton philosophically, "seems to treat us all alike. I felt kind o' sorry for the old devil."

CHAPTER XXII

TOMBSTONE, that in its days of glory as the metropolis of Arizona had 15,000 people, had dwindled to a ghost town in 1900, when only 646 inhabitants stood between it and utter extinction. But the old town refused to die. It rallied in its last ditch. It added 500 to its census roll in the next quarter of a century. It now has a population of about 1,200. So, you see, Tombstone is growing.

Tombstone is a pretty live little town. You wouldn't think so to look at it, but it is. You must be careful to distinguish between the physical town and the people who inhabit it. The buildings are of the dead past; the people of the live present. There is much public spirit. The town has its Commercial Club; the business men get together at a luncheon every week; the welfare and improvement of the town are always uppermost. Tombstone is on a coast-to-coast motor highway. Cars go through by the hundred every day. The historic associations interest these travellers, whose flying trade is of great annual value. Camps have been established; tourists are made welcome. To increase interest in Tombstone, it is planned to turn the old Bird Cage Theatre into a museum to be filled with mementos of the town's early history. Which would seem an excellent idea. The town's isolation is an element deterrent to its development as a business or manufacturing centre but

378

the citizens hope in time to build it into a great health resort, for which its situation might seem ideal. Its winters are springlike and, because of its elevation, it is immune from the intense summer heat which prevails in some other sections of Arizona. It has an abundant supply of cold water piped from springs in the Huachucas; its air is pure and dry; its glorious sunshine perennial; and about it is the beauty of deserts and mountains.

The business section of Tombstone is much as it was in early days. The one-story buildings with wooden awnings shading the sidewalk are the same that Wyatt Earp and Johnny Behan knew. The old Oriental, where Doc Holliday dealt faro and Buckskin Frank tended bar, is a drug store, and dainty young women gossip over ice-cream sodas where hard-eyed gamblers once bucked the tiger. The Crystal Palace is empty; dust covers the windows through which in old days could be seen the monte tables piled with gold and silver money, the roulette and faro games surrounded by eager throngs, and the long mahogany bar lined with the men of the frontier. The place only recently closed as a moving-picture theatre, but one may be sure none of the dramas flashed on its screen equalled in thrilling interest the dramas of real life that once unfolded within these four walls. Bob Hatch's old billiard hall is still a billiard hall, and ivory balls click a daily requiem where Morgan Earp was killed. In the old Alhambra, a grocer fills the market baskets of housewives and suavely explains a rise in the price of onions. The post office occupies the site where once stood Martin Costello's saloon, where St. Louis beer was first sold in Tombstone. Mice play in the empty darkness of the Maison Dorée where Julius Cæsar served his delectable dishes. The Can Can, run by a Chinaman, still flourishes as a popular eating house, where ham and eggs are seasoned with history. Johnny Montgomery's O. K. corral is a garage.

The Bird Cage Theatre is like a building that has died and been embalmed. It looks natural, as they say when they turn down the sheet, but its songs, its dancing, its merry doings, and its tipsy revelry, which were its life, have vanished. The famous old honkytonk has become in these days of evil fortune a storehouse for odds and ends of old furniture. The stage is deep with dust, and the dingy boxes where queens of song boosted beer sales between arias look down on piles of rusty beds and broken tables. On one of the walls off-stage, you may read these names scribbled in black paint by actors and actresses who in the long ago appeared in the glare of the Bird Cage footlights: Amy Brandon, Ella Davis, Charles Keene, Manning Barthylarr, Nick Williams, William Walker, Ada Grayson, Jessie Field, Jules Garrison, Eddie Moore, Irry Conley, Jennie Melville, Lillie Melbourne, Tony Hewitt, Ollie Bingleford, Ida Grayson, Stella Elton, William Baker, Joe Fuette, Ella Gardner, Soldern & Dixon. These names may mean something to somebody somewhere.

Where the red lights used to twinkle is now a district of homes in pretty yards filled with trees and flowers, and in the midst of the residences rises the high school, Tombstone's most imposing building. Fremont Street is empty and silent. Near the City Hall, built in 1882, is the vacant lot where the Earps and Clantons met in battle, a pile of tin cans and rubbish the only monument marking the historic spot. Tough Nut is a residence street; where the telegraph pole stood to which John Heath was hanged by the men of Bisbee is a cottage embowered in shrubbery and blooming plants. The old courthouse gives a touch of bustling animation to Tough Nut Street when crowds of lawyers, clients, and witnesses gather in the county seat during sessions of court. Near the south end of the thoroughfare stands the one remaining lamppost of Tombstone's early days, looking as if it had risen from the dead. Its rays once dimly illumined Nellie Cashman's boarding house, and around it formed the mob from whose fury Wyatt Earp saved Johnny Behind-the-Deuce.

Near the old lamppost is the cavelike aperture of the Million Dollar stope, so called because in this tunnel beneath the town the Grand Central mine "glory-holed," taking out $840,000. The shaft caved in at this point in 1908, carrying down a horse and ice wagon; the wagon was demolished, but the horse was uninjured and was led out through an underground passage to the old mouth of the mine a quarter of a mile away. Most of the business part of town, it is said, is undermined and criss-crossed with old tunnels.

The hill above the town is desolate. The last attempt to work the mines was made in 1901, when E. B. Gage merged all the properties in the Tombstone Consolidated Mines and installed pumps with a capacity of eight million gallons a day. The company went into bankruptcy in 1911, having lost $5,000,000. At a receiver's sale in 1914, the Phelps-Dodge interests, which own the Copper Queen in Bisbee, purchased the properties for $500,000. A little mining is still done by leasers.

Forty of the mines are under lease to thirty-five in-;
dividuals and 110 men work in the shafts daily. Fifteen
hundred tons of ore a month are shipped to the Douglas
smelters. The ore averages $8 or $9 in silver to the ton.
The company furnishes power; the leasers pay the
company 20 per cent. of the value of their ore. Their 80
per cent., it is said, amounts to a little better than day
wages. Ed Massey and Bill Williams, leasers, struck a
pay streak in 1924 and took out $50,000 apiece. This
is the only strike made on the hill since early days. The
company, after paying taxes, perhaps breaks even.
The Tombstone mines, experts declare, probably will
never be worked again.

You will find many people in Tombstone who have
lived there twenty-five, thirty, and thirty-five years.
Not a few were there during John Slaughter's terms as
sheriff. But not more than eight or ten date back to the
days of the Earps. C. L. Cummings is one of the oldest
inhabitants. Also the wealthiest. He owns many of the
old landmarks, including the Bird Cage Theatre. Mrs.
Martin Costello, now of Los Angeles, probably owns
more Tombstone property than Mr. Cummings. What
Mrs. Costello doesn't own, Mr. Cummings does, is the
way the town folks put it.

The famous figures in Tombstone's early history are,
for the most part, dead. Sheriff Behan became superin-
tendent of Yuma prison and later special agent of the
Department of the Treasury with headquarters at El
Paso. He served in the quartermaster's department of
the army in Cuba during the Spanish War, then in the
Philippines, and in China during the Boxer Rebellion.
He died in Tucson in 1912.

If you drop into the Old Pueblo Club in Tucson, a

liveried servitor will take your card and fade across soft
carpets through portières. When he ushers you into the
luxurious lounge of the establishment, you will find a
distinguished-looking gentleman, white of hair and
moustache, fingering your card. This is Col. William M.
Breakenridge, known as Billy Breakenridge in days of
happy-go-lucky adventuring among Curly Bill's outlaws. The Colonel is in his eighties, hale, vigorous, and
full of interesting talk of old times. If you should happen
to miss him at his club, you will doubtless find him at the
pleasant quarters of the Arizona Pioneers Historical
Society, where the old-timers of the frontier foregather,
and where strangers within the city's gates are made
welcome by E. L. Vail, president, and Mrs. Edith Kitt,
custodian, with the courtesy and kindliness that are the
essence of the old frontier's spirit of hospitality.

Ike Clanton, who, with boastful tongue, swaggered
among Tombstone's bars and whose running feet left
indelible prints across Tombstone's early history, was
killed in 1887 on Bonita Creek twenty miles west of
Montmorenci. Deputy Sheriffs J. V. Brighton and
George Powell, who held a warrant for his arrest, waited
in hiding for him at his cabin. "Hands up!" was the
last articulate sound the outlaw heard on earth. Yuma
yawned for him; liberty was sweet. He put spurs to his
horse and fell dead with two bullets between his shoulder
blades before he had gone twenty yards. Finn Clanton,
last of the famous family, died in bed at his ranch near
Miami after serving ten years in prison for cattle stealing.

Tales of the old, wild days in Tombstone were heard
in Boston at the recent trial of the Crabtree will case
in the Suffolk Probate Court, and caused the prim, blue-

stocking city of the Puritan Fathers to gasp in scandalized bewilderment. Lotta Crabtree, famous stage beauty, died in Boston without known heirs and left something like $4,000,000 to charity. Mrs. Carlotta Crabtree Cockburn of San Gabriel, California, claiming to be a niece, sued for a share in the estate. According to the plaintiff's story, Jack Crabtree, only brother of Lotta, married Anne Leopold in San Francisco and lived with her in Tombstone in 1880-81. After the birth of a daughter, he deserted his wife and baby and joined his sister, in the management of whose theatrical affairs he had a hand until his death five years later. Soon after he disappeared, his wife levanted, it is said, with Jack Rabb, a gambler. Within a few years, she also died. Deserted by both parents, the little girl was adopted by Ed Bullock, a Tombstone liveryman and Jack Crabtree's most intimate friend. The girl grew up in Bullock's home in California, and at her marriage became Mrs. Cockburn. In seeking to invalidate Mrs. Cockburn's claims, lawyers for the Crabtree estate contended that Jack Crabtree and Anne Leopold were never married and that Bullock was the child's father.

Nothing in recent years had given Tombstone such a delicious morsel of scandal to roll over its tongue as this interesting case. Citizens divided into two factions. Whether Jack Crabtree and Anne Leopold were married and whether the baby was their child were questions which threatened to precipitate a vendetta in Tombstone society comparable in flaming intensity to the Earp-Clanton feud. Tombstone pioneers in many parts of the country gave depositions on one side or the other. Among these witnesses were Wyatt Earp, William Breakenridge, and Mrs. Alec Derwood, once the wife

of Buckskin Frank Leslie. John B. Wright, lawyer of
Tucson, who has fought Mrs. Cockburn's battle from
the first, went to court in Boston armed with sixty
depositions from old Tombstone citizens in support of
his client's claim.

Mr. Wright, Arizona lawyer for thirty-four years,
enlivened the Boston court proceedings with a frontier
anecdote.

"I was on a train bound for Tombstone," said Mr.
Wright, "when it was boarded by two masked robbers. I was travelling with a deputy sheriff who wore
two six-shooters. 'Are you a good shot?' I asked him
in a whisper out of the corner of my mouth as we stood
in the aisle with our hands above our heads. 'No,' he
replied emphatically. 'Then,' said I, 'for God's sake,
don't shoot.' The robbers took our money and watches
and the deputy sheriff's guns, but politely returned my
office keys."

The Boston court, in its decision, denied Mrs. Cockburn's claim. It held that Jack Crabtree and Anne Leopold had never been married, that their relations did not
even constitute common-law marriage, and that Mrs.
Cockburn was not an heir and had no legal claim of any
kind upon the Lotta Crabtree estate.

Life goes pleasantly in Tombstone, if quietly. It is
a sociable, hospitable little community. The women
are forever entertaining. There are church affairs and
Woman's Club affairs and Literary Society affairs and
amateur theatricals by the Drama League and con-
certs by the high school band. Roads about town are
excellent; it is an easy, pleasant drive to Tucson, Benson, Bisbee, Douglas. Motor parties go frequently to
Agua Prieta, Naco, and Nogales across the Mexican

line, where they dine on encheladas, tamales, and frijoles, and, if the truth must be known, drink a few
bottles of ice-cold beer. One drives in an hour to Naco.
pleasant oasis of wetness.

The *Epitaph*, as in old days, keeps Tombstone abreast
of the times. It is a weekly now, published in a plant
equipped with linotype machines and modern presses,
and with its scareheads and typographical technique,
it looks much like a big city newspaper. William H.
Kelly, who edits it and manages its business affairs, is
the grandson of George H. Kelly, state historian. He is
a college-bred man and a trained journalist, and he gets
out a lively and interesting paper. Tombstone has already elected Billy Kelly an alderman and promises
to send him to Congress some day.

The gossip and happenings of Tombstone as recorded
in the *Epitaph* are widely different from those of an
earlier time. . . . Mrs. William Lutley entertained at
bridge last evening. . . . Mrs. C. L. Cummings gave a
delightful dinner. . . . Mrs. Porter McDonald's card
party was an enjoyable affair. . . . Mrs. A. H. Gardner
read a paper before the Literary Society. . . . Mrs.
Ethel Macia was hostess at a dinner dance. . . . Mr.
and Mrs. J. D. Taylor returned from a visit to Warren.
. . . Judge and Mrs. Albert M. Sames are back from
Douglas. . . . C. J. Sheldon presided at the luncheon of
the Business Men's Club. . . . Porter McDonald spent
yesterday in Naco, driving over in his new car. . . .
Bud Marr is making good in his new position as chief
of police. . . . Jeff Milton was in from Fairbank. . . .
A. M. Morris, superintendent of the Bunker Hill Mining Company. has been transferred to Montmorenci.

, . . Greenway Albert has returned from California. . . .
J. T. Kingsbury and wife spent Sunday in Nogales.
. . . R. B. Krebs, and J. A. Ivey, and wife are visiting
in Bisbee. . . . Sheriff George Henshaw and Mayor
Charles Schneider are back from Tucson. . . . This sort
of thing constitutes news in Tombstone nowadays.

Allen Street, with its dilapidated old stores, looks a
little forlorn in daylight, despite its asphalt and its automobiles. But when a coyote lifts a weird song in the mesquite and the moon hangs over the Dragoons, it is
easy to imagine it the frontier boulevard it used to be.
Then the disfiguring scars left by the years disappear,
and the ancient buildings, bathed in the soft light as
in a fountain of youth, seem clothed in the strength
and freshness of old days. The present fades; the past
rises like a picture. There in the street are the lumber
trains coming in from the Chiricahuas; the sixteen-mule
ore teams with their clanking trace chains, the yells
of mule-skinners, the cracking of whips. The arcaded
sidewalks are crowded. Swing doors of saloons flail back
and forth. Laughter of roistering throngs comes from
the brightly lighted bars. You hear the click of faro
chips, the rattle of roulette wheels. The scent of spiced
drinks and orange peel is in the air. That tall man there
with the six-shooters buckled around him is Wyatt
Earp. Doc Holliday is lounging in a doorway. Yonder
are Virgil and Morgan Earp. Johnny Behan bustles
along. And the Clantons and McLowerys and Buckskin
Frank and John Ringo in his great buffalo coat, his
hands rammed in his pockets on his guns. And Curly
Bill and his bold buccaneers, riding in from the San
Simon, go clattering past . . . when a coyote lifts a weird

song in the mesquite and the moon hangs over the Dragoons.

Tombstone flames no more. Its wild days are a tale that is told. It lives with its memories and its ghosts. Sunshine and peace are its portion. Once it was romance. Now it's a town.

THE END